RELIGION AND WELFARE IN EUROPE

IN EUROPE

Gendered and minority perspectives

Edited by Lina Molokotos-Liederman
with Anders Bäckström and Grace Davie

THE IMPACT OF RELIGION

Challenges for Society, Law and Democracy

First published in Great Britain in 2017 by

Policy Press
University of Bristol
1-9 Old Park Hill
Bristol
BS2 8BB
UK
t: +44 (0)117 954 5940
pp-info@bristol.ac.uk
www.policypress.co.uk

North America office:
Policy Press
c/o The University of Chicago Press
1427 East 60th Street
Chicago, IL 60637, USA
t: +1 773 702 7700
f: +1 773-702-9756
sales@press.uchicago.edu
www.press.uchicago.edu

© Policy Press 2017

British Library Cataloguing in Publication Data
A catalogue record for this book is available from the British Library

Library of Congress Cataloging-in-Publication Data
A catalog record for this book has been requested

ISBN 978-1-4473-1897-2 hardcover
ISBN 978-1-4473-3478-1 ePub
ISBN 978-1-4473-3479-8 Mobi
ISBN 978-1-4473-2899-5 ePdf

The right of Lina Molokotos-Liederman to be identified as editor of this work has been asserted by her in accordance with the Copyright, Designs and Patents Act 1988.

This research project was funded by the European Commission 6th Framework Programme. The project was also supported by the Foundation Samariterhemmet, the Faculty of Theology at Uppsala University, and the Bank of Sweden Tercentenary Foundation.

SIXTH FRAMEWORK PROGRAMME

Cover design by Hayes Design
Front cover image: Teamwork © Relif/iStock.com
Printed and bound in Great Britain by Clays Ltd, St Ives plc
Policy Press uses environmentally responsible print partners

MIX
Paper from
responsible sources
FSC
www.fsc.org
FSC® C013604

Contents

List of tables, figures and maps

Acknowledgements

As editor of this volume, it is a privilege to extend my thanks to Anders Bäckström and Grace Davie (the coordinators of the Welfare and Values in Europe: Transitions Related to Religion, Minorities and Gender project, or WaVE) for asking me to edit this book. Since the very beginning, their support has been invaluable in bringing the book to a successful conclusion; it is an honour to have worked with them.

The book would have never materialised without the contributions of each and every member of the WaVE project team (see Appendix). Among them Effie Fokas deserves special mention for her careful management of the project as a whole, and in that capacity for her authorship of Chapter Eleven, which draws the threads of this work together. I must also thank the 'new' scholars who wrote a chapter or contributed other material to the book, including Pia Karlsson Minganti, Margarita Markoviti and Johan Gärde. Finally, I would like to thank the Impact of Religion programme and the Uppsala Religion and Society Research Centre for 'housing' the WaVE project and in that capacity for their support, both material and financial, of this book.

Notes on contributors

Olav Helge Angell is Professor Emeritus of Diakonia and Professional Practice at VID Specialized University in Norway. He has a PhD in sociology which focused on the religious foundation and secular professionalism of faith-related welfare organisations. His interests include the role of faith-related welfare services in a multi-religious society in relation to the secular welfare state; the organisation and management of social welfare provision; and how faith-related organisations contribute to community cohesion. He has been involved in several international research projects and has published numerous articles in peer-reviewed journals and books.

Anders Bäckström is Professor Emeritus of Sociology of Religion at Uppsala University. He has directed several major research projects including the Diaconal Studies Project; From State Church to Free Folk Church; Welfare and Religion in a European Perspective (WREP); and, together with Effie Fokas and Grace Davie, Welfare and Values in Europe: Transitions Related to Religion, Minorities and Gender (WaVE). In 2008, he established the Uppsala Religion and Society Research Centre of Excellence and its 10-year research programme The Impact of Religion: Challenges for Society, Law and Democracy.

Grace Davie is Professor Emeritus of Sociology at the University of Exeter. Together with Anders Bäckström, she co-directed the WREP and WaVE projects. She is a senior advisor to The Impact of Religion: Challenges for Society, Law and Democracy programme, based at the Uppsala Religion and Society Research Centre (CRS). She continues to publish widely, her latest book being *Religion in Britain: A Persistent Paradox* (Wiley-Blackwell, 2015), and is currently involved in the International Panel on Social Progress (www.ipsp.org).

Effie Fokas is Principal Investigator of the European Research Council-funded project examining Grassroots Mobilisations in the Shadow of European Court of Human Rights Religious Freedoms Jurisprudence (Grassrootsmobilise), based at the Hellenic Foundation for European and Foreign Policy (ELIAMEP), and Research Associate of the LSE Hellenic Observatory. She was a member of the Greek case study team in the WREP research programme (2003-04), as well as Scientific Programme Manager and Greek case study researcher for the European Commisssion FP6-funded project on WaVE. Her publications include

Islam in Europe: Diversity, Identity and Influence (Cambridge University Press, 2008), co-edited with Aziz Al-Azmeh, and *Religious America, Secular Europe? A Theme and Variations* (Ashgate, 2008), co-authored with Peter Berger and Grace Davie.

Annalisa Frisina has a PhD in sociology and is an Associate Professor at the University of Padua, where she teaches sociology, qualitative research and visual methods. She worked as a researcher for the Italian case studies in the WREP and WaVE projects with Professor Chantal Saint-Blancat. Her publications include *Giovani Musulmani d'Italia* (*Young Muslims of Italy*) (Carocci, 2007), and three books on qualitative/visual research: *Focus Groups* (Il Mulino, 2010), *Ricerca Visuale e trasformazioni socio-culturali* (*Visual Research and Socio-Cultural Transformations*) (UTET Università, 2013) and *Metodi visuali di ricerca sociale* (*Visual Methods for Social Research*) (Il Mulino, 2016).

Marjukka Laiho holds an MSc in political science from the University of Tampere, and an MTh in sociology of religion from the University of Helsinki. She has worked on topics ranging from the European Union and post-socialist transition, to multiculturalism and welfare, and contemporary theology of religions. She has a passion for unconventional empirical research combining social sciences and theological studies, crossing the traditional methodological boundaries. She has worked as a consultant on European Union affairs and a research assistant at the Faculty of Theology, Helsinki. She has also held various posts on large-scale research and development projects for the National Council of the Evangelical-Lutheran Church of Finland. She is currently working on a doctoral thesis focusing on the theological views of cosmopolitan young adults.

Annette Leis-Peters is Vice-Dean of the Faculty of Theology, Diakonia and Leadership at VID Specialized University in Norway and Associate Professor in Sociology of Religion at Uppsala University. Her research interests are in the field of welfare, civil society and religion. She is part of the Linneaus research programme The Impact of Religion: Challenges for Society, Law and Democracy at Uppsala University and the South African/Nordic research project Youth at the Margins, a comparative study of the contribution of faith-based organisations to social cohesion in South Africa and Nordic Europe.

Martha Middlemiss Lé Mon is Director of CRS and a researcher at the same centre based at Uppsala University. Her current research interests include the relationship between religion and welfare in the European Union, particularly the role of faith-based organisations as part of civil society and the relationship between religion and values in contemporary society. She holds a PhD in the sociology of religion from Uppsala University, the fieldwork for which was conducted as part of the WREP project. She is currently conducting research on issues of welfare, religion and values within the Linneaus research programme The Impact of Religion: Challenges for Society, Law and Democracy.

Margarita Markoviti is a post-doctoral researcher at the European Research Council project Grassrootsmobilise, based at ELIAMEP. She completed a PhD entitled 'Education and the Europeanization of religious freedoms: France and Greece in comparative perspective' at the London School of Economics and Political Science (LSE). She holds a BA in history from King's College, London, a Master's in European affairs from the Paris Institute of Political Studies (Sciences Po), and an MSc in European studies, ideas and identities from the LSE. Her research focuses on religion and national identity, education and European integration, religious freedoms and social cohesion in light of religious pluralism.

Pia Karlsson Minganti is a researcher and Associate Professor of Ethnology at Stockholm University. She was a guest researcher at the University of Bologna (2009-11) and at CRS, where she is currently a member of The Impact of Religion: Challenges for Society, Law and Democracy research programme. Her research fields include young Muslims in Europe, transnational migration, religious pluralism and cultural transformations of identity and gender relations. Her recent publications include *Muslima. Islamisk väckelse och unga kvinnors förhandlingar om genus i det samtida Sverige* (*Muslima: Islamic Revival and Young Women's Negotiations of Gender in Contemporary Sweden*) (Carlssons, 2014 [2007]) and 'Challenging from within: youth associations and female leadership in Swedish mosques' in *Women, Leadership and Mosques: Changes in Contemporary Islamic Authority*, edited by Masooda Bano and Hilary Kalmbach (Brill, 2011).

Lina Molokotos-Liederman holds a PhD in sociology of religion from the Ecole Pratique des Hautes Etudes (2001). As a Visiting Fellow at CRS, she was invited to edit a thematic book based on the findings of the WaVE project. She worked in both the WREP and WaVE projects, initially as a researcher and subsequently as an editor for the national and case study reports. Since January 2016, she has been the editorial manager of *Religion, State and Society*. She is also a postdoctoral research associate of the Groupe Sociétés, Religions, Laïcités at the Centre national de la recherche scientifique (GSRL/CNRS) in Paris. Since 2015 she has worked on the Faith and Fashion research project at the London College of Fashion. She has also worked as a researcher for the Open Society Foundation, the Centre for European Studies at the University of Exeter, the International Organization for Migration and the International Orthodox Christian Charities. Her research interests include religion, social welfare and international humanitarian action; and religion, migration and identity in Europe. She has published numerous peer-reviewed journal articles and book chapters on these areas. She also co-edited with Trine Stauning-Willert *Innovation in the Christian Orthodox Tradition? The Question of Change in Greek Orthodox Thought and Practice* (Ashgate, 2012).

Anne Birgitta Pessi is Professor of Church and Social Studies at the Faculty of Theology, University of Helsinki. She is also docent in Welfare Sociology at the University of Eastern Finland. Between 2005 and 2013, she was a Fellow at the Collegium for Advanced Studies, University of Helsinki. Her research interests include volunteering, altruism, civil society, togetherness, compassion, sense of meaning and experiences of good life, as well as individualised religiosity. She has worked on various international and national research projects, including WaVE. She has also directed Academy of Finland-funded research projects, including Religion in Transforming Solidarity and Cooperation in Care – Meaning Systems, Chances, and Conflicts. She is currently directing CoPassion, an interdisciplinary project of 15 researchers, focusing on the power of compassion in workplaces. She is the author of numerous publications.

Pål Repstad is Professor Emeritus in Sociology of Religion at the University of Agder, Norway. From 2005 to 2015, he was editor of the *Nordic Journal of Religion and Society*. He has written and edited a large number of books and journal articles, mainly about changes in mainstream religious life in Norway. Publications in English include *An Introduction to the Sociology of Religion* (Ashgate, 2006) with Inger Furseth. He was a contributing author to *Christianity in the Modern World. Changes and Controversies*, edited by Giselle Vincett and Elijah Obinna (Ashgate, 2014), and *Sociological Theory and the Question of Religion*, edited by Andrew McKinnon and Marta Trzebiatowska (Ashgate, 2014). He holds an honorary doctorate from Uppsala University.

Siniša Zrinščak is Professor of Sociology and Social Policy at the University of Zagreb. His main interests include religious and social policy changes in post-communism, church–state relations, European and comparative social policy, gender, and civil society development. He served as President (2006-14) and Vice-President (2001-06) of the International Study of Religion in Central and Eastern Europe Association and Vice-President of the International Sociological Association RC 22 (2006-14). He has been General Secretary of the International Society for the Sociology of Religion since 2013. He has also been involved in several, mainly international, research projects, and his work has been widely published in numerous peer-reviewed journals and books.

ONE

Introduction

Anders Bäckström

The question of how welfare is to be organised, and how large groups of migrants are to be integrated into the receiving countries, are major challenges for contemporary European societies. Equally important is the trust of citizens in the state's ability to address these issues. Such questions have two clear connections to religion: the ways in which the welfare state coexists with varying religious traditions, and the fact that growing religious pluralism has made religion increasingly visible as a legal, social and political force. How is social cohesion to be understood in a Europe that is being pulled apart, economically, socially and religiously?

The relationship between welfare and religion, as it developed during the 20th century, was shaped during the formative 'golden years' following 1945. Welfare became part of a modernity in which the relationship between religion and societal institutions, such as school, health and social care, was weakening rapidly or in some cases had ceased to exist. Studies of different welfare regimes have revealed, however, that their roots lie in contrasting political, social and religious circumstances. These circumstances function as a historically based 'glue' that helps to explain the subtle values that connect religion and welfare within these different systems – a point developed further in Chapter Five. As David Martin (2010) notes, the continuous relationship between religion and politics has resulted in different pathways to modernity and it is the character of this interaction that is important in European societies. This forms the basis for different types of trust in the individual and the state, both of which are necessary for the cohesion of society. Danièle Hervieu-Léger (2015) calls this trust or understanding a 'grammar of collective memory', based on values that are connected to deep cultural mentalities, which are slow to change.

Religion itself has different meanings. It can be both 'hot' or strong (manifested through strong family ties, or strong religious affiliations), but also 'cool' or broad (based on citizenship, human rights and the rule of law); it also unfolds in diverse ways and in different contexts. At one and the same time, moreover, religion is diminishing as a

1

result of secularisation, evolving into something more spiritual, and reasserting itself through migration and growing diversity (Furseth, 2015). Unsurprisingly, states have difficulties managing this situation. On the one hand, diversity is understood as an asset that enriches culture and contributes to the prosperity of a market economy; on the other hand, it is perceived as a problem that creates religious and social divisions (Giddens, 2007). Are these divisions handled better by a hot or cool understanding of culture (see also Chapter Five)? The answer to this question is not straightforward.

Another set of questions lies parallel. Is the European social model still a unifying and identity-shaping factor (Hettne, 1997, p 149; The Social Dimension of Europe 2020 Strategy)? Or is there an ever greater cleavage between what Lipset and Rokkan (1967) call the centre and the periphery, which today is manifested in the divide between Brussels (the so-called elite) and the citizens in the member states where national and even nationalist sentiments have emerged (leading at times to support for populist parties)? The President of the European Commission Jean-Claude Juncker claims that the social dimension as a unifying factor is now a critical point for Europe.[1] Historically, the 'unity in diversity' of the European project has its legacy in the formation of European states after the Treaty of Westphalia in 1648, through which religion became the unifying factor within the nation, as Casanova (2013) puts it. But this unity is now challenged by growing diversity, a shift in which the presence of Islam is perceived as a politically worrying element. This renders the cohesion of Europe an important but highly problematic enterprise.

At the same time, the neoliberal global market has freed religion from its institutional moorings, making it a new and more visible partner in civil society (Martikainen and Gautier, 2013). These developments – the pressures of the neoliberal market and growing diversity – are closely linked to each other and require greater commitment from policymakers, faith-based communities and civil society networks. Such developments highlight the need for bottom-up, local conversations on religion and new forms of collaboration: what I call a new ecology of conversation and cooperation that goes beyond established areas of (inter-confessional) collaboration (Bäckström, 2014). As Grace Davie argues in Chapter Thirteen, the need for religious literacy is a vital prerequisite in the quality of these debates.

It is equally clear that questions relating to the ability of the welfare state to deal with a growing religious and social diversity challenge very basic identities: who are we and who do we want to be in the future? Unsurprisingly, these questions have triggered extensive research in Europe.[2] Much of this is concerned with the relationship between religious values and social diversity, and how such values are regarded by political parties and social institutions in the second decade of the 21st century. The project on which this book is based exemplifies this trend. Its essence will now be outlined.

The European Commission's call

The project Welfare and Values in Europe: Transitions Related to Religion, Minorities and Gender (WaVE) responded to a call by the European Commission's 6th Framework Programme for research on 'values and religions in Europe'. The call invited projects aiming 'to better understand the significance and impact of values and religions in societies across Europe and their roles in relation to changes in society and to the emergence of European identities'. The Commission sought in-depth explorations of the social impact of religion as a bearer of solidarity, social cohesion, tolerance and inclusion, or as a source of discrimination, intolerance, exclusion or xenophobia. Through a comparison of policies and practices in European countries, and a consideration of their relative degrees of success, the Commission was looking for further insights on what might ensure the peaceful coexistence of different religions, ethnic groups and value systems. It was the positive response by the European Commission to a proposal submitted in 2005 by the Uppsala Religion and Society Research Centre (CRS) that enabled a European research group, made up of researchers from 12 different countries, to carry out the project between 2006 and 2009. The WaVE project partners and researchers are listed in the Appendix (p 299).

The WaVE project had three main objectives:

- First, to assess the impact of religion in societies across Europe as a bearer of values of solidarity and social cohesion, or as source of tension and exclusion. WaVE pursued this aim through an in-depth examination of the values expressed by majority religions in their interaction with minority communities in the domain of social welfare needs and provision.
- Second, to study the values expressed by minority groups (religious minorities in particular), both in their use of welfare services and their search for alternatives (welfare networks created by minority groups). Here WaVE offered insights into the extent to which minorities are perceived to challenge or strengthen the values and cultural identities of the local majorities.

3

- Third, to highlight elements of tension or cohesion embedded in values relating to gender, and to the rights and needs of women and men. In this case, WaVE sought to bring to light the gender-related values underpinning conceptions and practices of welfare in the localities under review, and to examine the critical relationship between religious values, minorities and gender.

Background to the WaVE study

The WaVE project was part of a wider research programme in religion and society developed at Uppsala University in the 1990s. This began with a project on church and state that examined the social/diaconal function of the Church of Sweden.[3] The separation of church and state in Sweden that took place in 2000 was analysed as part of the gradual separation between religion and society, but the study also looked at the deregulation of the welfare state and the increase of relative poverty as a result of the financial and refugee crises in Europe at the beginning of the 1990s (including the collapse of Yugoslavia). These developments sparked a new interest in the role of civil society organisations, including churches and religious associations. The study formed the background for the inauguration of the Uppsala Religion and Society Research Centre at Uppsala University, developed in conjunction with the Foundation Samariterhemmet.[4]

As part of the work of the church and state project, an international reference group was formed. This group evolved into an international network of researchers focusing on the place of religion in the welfare regimes of Europe. In 2003, the Bank of Sweden Tercentenary Foundation funded the Welfare and Religion in a European Perspective: A Comparative Study of the Role of the Churches as Agents of Welfare within the Social Economy (2003-09) project, or WREP for short. The aim of this project was to analyse the function of majority churches as agents of welfare in a comparative European perspective. It paid attention to ageing populations, a new poverty among the elderly, greater demands for wellbeing, growing equality between women and men, and an increase in the numbers of single women and of migrants. An awareness of an ever greater strain on the economy, resulting in austerity programmes, underpinned this work.

The study focused on four welfare models and four church traditions: the social democratic model of the European north that developed within the context of Lutheran state churches (Sweden, Finland and Norway); the liberal model typical of Anglo-Saxon countries (England with its established Anglican Church and its blend of Catholic and

Reformed theologies); the conservative or Christian Democratic model, found mainly in continental Europe where the Catholic Church is dominant (France, Italy and, to some extent, Germany); and countries of southern Europe where the state plays a weaker role compared with that of the family (in Orthodox Greece but also in Catholic Italy). In total, eight countries were included in the project, which focused on one medium-sized town in each country. Mapping and in-depth interviews with representatives of local government, churches and the wider population shed light on church–state relationships within different welfare regimes.

WREP brought together different areas of society (a new idea at the time), namely religion, welfare, gender and civil society. The project revealed the interconnectedness between the welfare regimes of Europe and their roots in social, political and religious circumstances. The study also showed that social care by religious organisations and by state welfare systems is disproportionately carried out by women. Finally, it was clear that representatives of the local majority churches, local governmental organisations and the population as a whole expected churches and voluntary organisations to function as complementary organisations to the state, but that these institutions (and indeed the population as such) wished to retain a critical voice on these matters. The fact that church membership and the role of churches overall are contracting, while demands for their involvement in social care are growing, represents a mounting dilemma. Two edited volumes brought the findings of this project together (Bäckström et al, 2010, 2011).

The Welfare and Values in Europe (WaVE) project

The WREP project formed the background to the project featured in this volume. That said, WaVE expanded the work in two ways. First, it extended the remit to selected post-communist countries in central and eastern Europe, where the majority churches had experienced a very different history – recognizing, however, that the role of religion is very different depending on the country in question (see Part Two). Second, the WaVE team appreciated that the growing diversity of Europe cannot be adequately investigated without serious attention to religious minorities. At the same time, the focus shifted from the interaction between majority churches and welfare regimes embodied in WREP, to the study of welfare as a 'prism' through which core values are perceived, for example, those of inclusion and exclusion. The methodological approach and the comparative nature of the project were also expanded in the sense that the religious minorities found all over Europe were considered primarily in relation to the values of the majority cultures.

The underlying assumption of the project was that values are best understood through the ways in which they are expressed and developed in practice. Thus the study of values as they appear through the prism of welfare formed the core of the research. By adopting this approach, the project filled a gap in the study of religion, minorities and gender. At the time of the European Commission's call, new insights in this area were of special importance in order to find ways of strengthening both tolerance and social cohesion in European societies.

WaVE also raised important questions regarding the relationship between the religious and the secular. The social involvement of religious organisations has implications for the role and identity of the secular state and the presence of religion in the public sphere. This challenged the prevailing understanding that religion is a private matter, a fact very often assumed by theorists of secularisation, especially in Europe. Thus the interconnections between the privatisation of welfare in a mixed economy and the pluralisation of religion through migration questioned very directly existing understandings of European identity. At the same time, the intersections of these issues with questions about gender, on the one hand, and minorities, on the other, are central; hence the overall focus of this book on religion and welfare from gendered and minority perspectives.

To expand: women, as carriers of both religious and social values, are part of the social care fabric, either through the family (in southern Europe), or as social workers (employed by the municipalities further north). Women and men, however, are increasingly viewed as equal partners in most of Europe – an equality that extends to leadership roles, not only in social authorities but also in (some if not all) faith-based organisations. Chapter Eleven is illuminating in this respect. It illustrates different views on women's rights from different theological perspectives, but at the same time, it demonstrates clearly the drawing together of women from both majority and minority communities.

More problematic are the expectations of family-based care in some minority communities, which affect the lives of women more than men. It is the former who are criticised for a failure to uphold traditional religious values and/or to integrate into the majority culture of the receiving society. This tension between the freedom of and the freedom from religion is very often focused on women's bodies, dress and rights, for example the right to wear the *hijab* or veil. Such issues raise more general questions about how religious minorities are to be integrated in a majority culture without losing their cultural and religious specificities. Minority communities are simultaneously part of the majority culture through the citizenship of their members, and part of a religious tradition through ritual practice. A key question in this respect is whether the care networks of minority communities result in an increased isolation that hinders integration, or – more positively – in effective bridge building, not only within minority groups themselves, but in relation to the majority culture.

Central to these issues are the challenges in defining the term 'minority': who should do this, how and in relation to whom? Even numerical definitions are tricky. Determining whether a group is smaller than the majority is not always a straightforward matter. For example, a group that is a minority at the national level may be a majority in a particular region or locality. Keeping this in mind, a broad definition of minorities was adopted in WaVE, referring to minorities arising from migration into or within Europe on the one hand, and to autochthonous ethnic/religious groups and national minorities on the other. Attention was also paid to the self-definitions of the 'minorities' themselves. Religious minorities are 'created' in many different ways: they can be the outcome of 19th-century revivals in northern Europe, the consequence of shifting borders (in 1918, 1945 and 1989), or the upshot of migration into and within Europe. Some national minorities are recognised by the state (for example, the Sami people in Finland, Norway and Sweden), but the term could equally well refer to 'origins' (for example, the Greek Orthodox and Turkish Muslim communities in the diaspora). In this volume, the main focus is on religious minorities resulting from migration into or within Europe and their relationships to the majority culture of the societies in which they have settled.

Methodological considerations

The WaVE project was an empirical study concerned with the relationship between majority cultures and minority religions across Europe and their relationship to welfare and values as they appear in a local context. From the start, it was a comparative exercise looking for similarities and differences along the north–south and east–west dimensions of Europe. It covered a considerable geographical breadth as well as religious and social complexity.

The complexity of the religious and social developments taking place in Europe, and the substantial differences concerning both welfare organisations and religious majority/minority relations in each country, prompted the WaVE research team to opt for qualitative research methods (see Chapters Two and Three). Quantitative data, which are useful in framing values across countries and religious communities in Europe, tracking changes over time, and offering a comprehensive understanding of the religious and social situation in each country, were readily available as background material through the World Values Survey and the International Social Survey Programme, which covered most of the countries involved in the project.[5]

The qualitative research model used in the WREP project was also adopted in WaVE and applied to a medium-sized town in each country (see Table 1.1 below).

Table 1.1: Selected towns and their population at the time of research

Country	Town and location	Population (circa 2006)*
Croatia	Sisak (central Croatia)	53,000
England	Darlington (south of Newcastle)	98,000
Finland	Lahti (north of Helsinki)	98,000
France	Evreux (north-west of Paris)	54,000
Germany 1	Reutlingen (south of Stuttgart – dominated by Protestant Christianity)	110,000
Germany 2	Schweinfurt (northern Bavaria – predominantly Catholic)	55,000
Greece	Thiva and Livadeia (north of Athens)	43,000 (combined population)
Italy	Padua (west of Venice)	200,000
Latvia	Ogre (east of Riga)	29,000
Poland	Przemyśl (in south-east Poland, near Ukrainian border)	68,000
Romania	Medgidia (near the Black Sea)	44,000
Sweden	Gävle (north of Stockholm)	90,000
Norway	Drammen (south-west of Oslo)	57,000

* More information about each town can be obtained from the WaVE project description and from the working papers published by the Uppsala Religion and Society Research Centre: www.crs.uu.se/Research/former-research-projects/WaVE (Bäckström 2011, 2012a, 2012b).

The towns in question had to be 'medium-sized' relative to the population of the respective country and to exhibit values connected to post-industrial change with growing employment within the service economy. Most important, they had to reveal a majority religious tradition alongside minority communities, either as autochthonous ethnic/religious groups, or as religious minorities as a result of migration into Europe (for more details see Chapters Two and Three, and Repstad and Ziebertz, 2011). Equally important, however, were practical issues, such as accessibility and appropriate contacts with the locality in question. The location of each town can be seen in Map 1.1.

Map 1.1: Map of case study locations

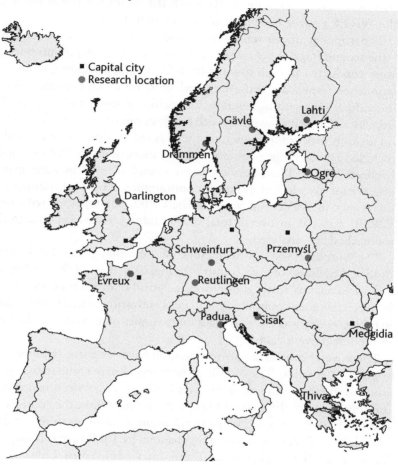

The data collection was carried out from late 2006 to early 2008 and took place in two stages.

The first stage was a mapping exercise to gather the following information: the types of groups present in the locality with a description of 'majority' and 'minority' communities; whether these groups provided welfare services, either internally to the group or externally to other communities; and the interactions between these various entities. The researchers obtained this information by approaching local authorities (for statistical data); central offices of majority churches (for welfare-related activities); selected representatives of minority groups (for information about themselves); and the local media. Online material and information published by churches, religious communities and voluntary organisations, including quantitative data and national statistics, were also obtained. Research data from the interviews for the WREP project were used whenever appropriate.

The mapping process was also used to select respondents for interview – the second stage of the research. On average 30 in-depth interviews were conducted in each town with individuals representing religious majorities (especially those engaged with minority communities), individuals representing religious minorities as such, and individuals from local authorities working with religious minorities. The focus was on the minority groups present in the selected localities. The schedule included a broad range of questions on a variety of topics (Repstad and Ziebertz, 2011). The interviews were complemented by participant observation in selected minority communities. The total number of interviews in WaVE was approximately 400, but together with the WREP material an overall total of 800 interviews were conducted, transcribed and analysed.

The outcome was a broad range of examples grounded in the historical tradition of each country. To make the most of the fieldwork and to extract as many illustrations as possible of local cooperation between religious communities and local authorities, the research team in each country was asked to focus on examples of tension or cohesion in the respective locality.

There was, however, an obvious tension between comparability and contextual realities. The WaVE project was clearly comparative: the aim was to capture the similarities and differences between majority–minority relations throughout Europe. At the same time, the contextual nature of the data needed very careful attention in order to reflect the complexity of each situation. The chapters by Pål Repstad (Chapter Two), and Olav Helge Angell and Lina Molokotos-Liederman (Chapter Three), both of which focus on the use of comparative and qualitative case studies, offer an in-depth examination of qualitative methodological approaches, considering both their advantages and disadvantages in the area of religion and welfare. Particular attention is paid to the tension outlined previously. These questions are also addressed in Chapter Four in connection with the circle of cohesion that emerged from the analysis.

The renewed relevance of the WaVE project and the rationale of this book

Both during and after the project, the question of multiculturalism became an ever more central issue, compounded by an increase in terrorist attacks and the need to integrate an unprecedented number of migrants and refugees into western Europe. Debates on multiculturalism per se reached a peak in 2010-11 when the political leaders of Germany, England and France declared the failure of multiculturalist policy.[6] As Andreas Johansson Heinö (2011) argues, the integration of newcomers in western societies has been transformed into 'a slow-paced assimilation', viewing immigrants as a collective whole, rather than widely diverse individuals.[7] Anthony Giddens (2007, p 27) is more constructive, suggesting that the issue of cultural diversity lies at the centre of welfare debates given that it is a basic element in the reform of the social model in Europe. The idea of multiculturalism, he continues, is not about setting immigrants or minority communities apart, but about looking for ways to link diversity with mainstream values.

Quite apart from this, the following issues have added new social relevance to the WaVE project: the prolonged weakness of the European economies and the contraction of welfare states; the growing gap between the relatively prosperous north and the high levels of unemployment in the south of Europe; the growth of (secular and faith-based) voluntary groups/networks outside established organisations and churches, especially during the peak of the refugee crisis in 2015; growing nationalist and populist tendencies seeking some form of security against global uncertainty and uncontrolled immigration; increasing questions about the governance of the European Union (EU); and the progressive weakening of the EU as an integrating project. Every one of these trends is symbolised by 'Brexit' (the shorthand term for the UK's withdrawal from the EU following a referendum in June 2016), which has become a defining moment. Several explanations have emerged to account for this situation, all of which reflect a major shift in the world order as a result of globalisation, ever-increasing mobility, changing forms of technology and new media. Twentieth-century Europe lived in the shadow of the industrial revolution. Today, people feel increasingly anxious as the world around them changes alarmingly.

Against this background, this volume brings together the key themes from the WaVE project and new insights regarding the intersections of religion and welfare from gendered and minority perspectives. It is structured as follows: methodological considerations in the use of comparative case studies (Part One); key regional case studies in welfare and religion (Part Two); and gendered and minority perspectives (Part Three). The aim of the book is to expand the comparative perspectives of the WaVE case studies keeping in mind recent changes and an abundance of new material pertaining to the European reality – most significantly the impact of the ongoing economic crisis, prolonged violence in the Middle East and the subsequent influx of refugees.

Part One illustrates the project's focus on a multidisciplinary, qualitative and case study approach. These chapters reveal the complexity of a European project such as WaVE. This is especially apparent in so far as the project is based on a social problem identified by the European Commission, but which can be approached in a multiplicity of ways (by different research traditions and employing different definitions of the topic under review). This point is discussed by Pål Repstad in a chapter that illustrates the challenge of obtaining notably rich data from the respective localities (illustrating as many examples of welfare–religion relationships as possible), while at the same time being able to draw effective and insightful comparisons.

In order to obtain common knowledge within the project, every researcher was asked to use the same interview questions, including: 'In your opinion what is welfare?' and 'In your opinion does the [respective church] have a role to play in the welfare and well-being of people?' This model of research, examined by Olav Helge Angell and Lina Molokotos-Liederman, is characterised as a mixed-methods approach deploying interviews, observation, surveys and document analysis, but with an emphasis on qualitative interviews. The authors discuss the implications of this type of work for policy debates and for a variety of end users (including politicians and religious leaders). In addition, they raise questions about policy debates as such, asking whether these affect the reliability and validity of such studies. These questions are even more relevant today as the Horizon 2020 call stresses not only the scientific quality of the research but the importance of impact and the implementation of results.[8]

The need to put research results into practice through policy recommendations is highlighted by Olav Helge Angell, Marjukka Laiho, Anne Birgitta Pessi and Siniša Zrinščak, who write on the question of social cohesion. This was a key concept in the WaVE project; it is a multi-layered idea, characterised by at least four dimensions: people's trust, help and cooperation with each other; people's tolerance towards each other; people's sense of belonging in the social system; and people's manifestation of these values through behaviour. The authors argue that most majority–minority interactions in the domain of welfare lie somewhere between conflict and cohesion in a large grey area that needs very careful attention, a point developed further by Effie Fokas in Chapter Twelve. They summarise the relevance of the WaVE project through the idea of a 'circle of social cohesion' in welfare where knowing and doing is the relationship between a better understanding of diversity and the transformation of this understanding into crucial skills in everyday practices. In order to convert the ideal of cohesion into everyday practice, the 'circle of social cohesion' is, however, dependent on political values and financial resources. This is one of the major themes addressed in the WaVE project.

Part Two considers the relationship between welfare, religion and gender in three key regions: northern, southern and eastern Europe. At the same time these chapters consider different theoretical perspectives within the WaVE project as they pertain to regional case studies in welfare and religion. These are: the relationship between the religious and the secular in different modernities; the notion of familism in social care, notably the role of women; and the growth of neoliberal economies, as they have developed within post-communist countries.

Chapter Five, by Anders Bäckström, examines the idea of secularisation or religious change and the increasing visibility of religion in northern Europe. In the 20th century, the links between welfare and religion were thought to be fading. Today, however, it is clear that this assumption was based on a definition of religion as something for 'others', for those deviating from a dominant secular culture. In the Nordic countries, culture is understood as broad, 'cool' or inclusive. It is based on the rule of law and is linked to modernisation and the emancipation of the individual rather than close family ties. This is also true of religion, which is similarly perceived (understanding the church as a public utility). This provides the basis for a broad culture of trust to which minority as well as majority religions can adhere. From this follow two important questions: is religion itself becoming part of an ongoing renegotiation of the social contract that is already in progress; and will the religious communities themselves become partners in a global economy which is increasingly driven by contracts set up and negotiated by the state?

Chapter Six, by Margarita Markoviti and Lina Molokotos-Liederman, examines the fragile organisation of welfare in southern Europe, with Italy and Greece as examples. In the Mediterranean countries, the situation is the reverse of the Nordic countries. It is the idea of 'familism' that best captures a system where the family – more especially women – is the basic unit of care for dependent family members (children and elderly), migrants and refugees. Although a state welfare system does exist, it is essentially a stopgap when the family is no longer able to cope with the demands of a particular situation. Trust in public institutions is low and the relationship between church and state is blurred. The precise nature of this relationship (political and financial) varies from country to country. The religious majorities, in this case the Catholic Church in Italy and the Greek Orthodox Church in Greece, have different approaches to social care. In both cases, church organisations (such as the Orthodox diaconal institutions and Catholic Caritas), together with a range of voluntary groups, participate locally in order to reduce poverty and exclusion. The Greek tradition has, however, resulted in a much weaker civil society in terms of 'voice'. In Italy, conversely, Caritas is involved both in local activities (food banks and so on) and in social advocacy work, alongside other social movements in support of migrants.

Chapter Seven, by Siniša Zrinščak, examines the complex situation in post-communist Europe, where the transition from a command economy to a neoliberal system has created new forms of exclusion, with rudimentary (Romania and Poland) or conservative (Croatia and Latvia) welfare regimes that have great difficulty in providing social coverage for every citizen. In the same way as Italy and Greece, post-communist countries have different degrees of familism and different degrees of civil society activism, depending on the religious and social legacy and the degree of change. Both Croatia and Poland, with their dominant Catholic churches and welfare charities, are somewhat similar to Italy, while Romania with its dominant Orthodox Church shares some similarities with the Greek situation, but with a weaker social and religious organisation. In Latvia, there are Lutheran, Catholic and Orthodox churches that are related to different ethnic and language groups. In all our post-communist cases, religious minorities are more or less welcomed, but their welfare activities are mostly directed towards their own members. This is exemplified by the neo-Protestant minorities in Poland and Romania that have developed extensive social assistance networks.

Part Three focuses directly on gender and religious minorities, especially on women who belong to such groups, through four in-depth case studies in Germany, England, Sweden (with some reference to Italy) and Italy.

In Chapter Eight, Annette Leis-Peters argues that research in the field of religious minorities needs to move away from the perspective of the majority society in favour of a civil society approach in which the interests of the religious minorities are built into the research design. Through her study of generational shifts among religious minorities in Reutlingen, Germany, Leis-Peters shows that the younger generation is under pressure not only to assimilate the values of the majority culture when it comes to professional development, but also to maintain the family's traditional (that is, religious) values. She concludes that integrating the perspectives of the religious minority communities into the research design itself permits markedly more nuanced findings, offering a more in-depth and accurate picture of the new ecology of religion.

Similarly, in Chapter Nine, Martha Middlemiss Lé Mon argues that migrant women in Darlington, England, who strive both for self-fulfilment and to maintain family responsibilities, face a values clash. This clash, however, is not specific to women from religious minorities, but is inherent in more general tensions between individual freedoms and family responsibilities. In practice, this very often means that the same individual holds contradictory values simultaneously. This mirrors the findings of the German study mentioned above. In both cases, therefore, the women from minority communities are reflecting a broader value conflict typical of late modernity in which the content and meaning of a good life is constantly renegotiated.

In Chapter Ten, through a case study on women's shelters in Sweden (with some references to Italy), Pia Karlsson Minganti shows that it is not only the north–south divide that stands out in Europe, but also the conflictual notions of religion (and especially Islam) and secularity. She points to an assimilationist discourse that is widespread in Europe, which results in Muslim women being treated as victims of an oppressive religion. Such a normative secularism is dissolving religion as a resource and turning it into a source of exclusion. The shelter known as Somaya in Stockholm has been obliged to 'tone down' its Muslim profile by emphasising the idea of intersectionality as its political goal. The chapter raises interesting questions about two frequently competing human rights, namely the freedom of religion and the rights of women – including those from minority religions.

In Chapter Eleven, Annalisa Frisina focuses on reproductive health among migrant women in Italy. She argues that the welfare crisis in Italy and southern Europe has not only had negative effects on women, but is also a sign of the siege mentality of the European social model. Populist political movements are using religion, especially Islam and Muslim women, as a scapegoat to avoid dealing with the underlying issues of social and economic solidarity in Europe and indeed beyond. Despite the fact that this study is based on reproductive health among Muslim women, it reveals broader tensions: between conservative and progressive Catholics in Italy, and between religious and secular values in the gendered and moral crisis of the Italian welfare system. The chapter also illustrates a novel form of research dissemination – that is, the production of a video in order to raise awareness of the social rights of migrant women.

In **Part Four**, Chapter Twelve, by Effie Fokas, applies a comparative lens both to the material emanating from the WaVE case studies and to the chapters gathered in this book. It highlights the transversal patterns found in the case study material, offering thereby further insights on the practices, tendencies and mechanisms leading to conflict or cohesion, or to the large 'grey' area in between. Finally, Grace Davie's Afterword highlights the overall significance of the WaVE project: first, within the rapidly changing – indeed volatile – situation currently discovered in Europe; and second, within the development of a new field in European research, that is, the interconnectedness of religion and welfare, and the need to examine, both historically and sociologically, the effect of each on the other.

A new ecology of conversation and cooperation

The WaVE project was developed at a time of major transition in the welfare state, which included the growth of religious organisations in the domain of social welfare (frequently offering services for those on the margins of society, including migrants). It unfolded in a period that witnessed both the deregulation of the welfare (nation) state and the growth of civil society organisations in social care. Exactly how this happened, however, varies considerably, depending on the historical traditions and political settlement of the country in question.

Such developments reflect wider changes in the religious field: from obligation to free choice and from established faith to new forms of practice. That said, it is important to note the hesitation on the part of the voluntary sector, including faith-based organisations, to take on greater responsibility in the area of welfare – a field in which different logics of care are competing for attention: the logic of the market, based on efficiency and profitability, on the one hand, and the logic of high quality social relationships and wellbeing on the other. It is equally clear that welfare services operating through contracts and competitive bidding reinforce a professionalism that presents real challenges for voluntary organisations that do not have the financial resources to compete. Moreover, the tendency to work contractually allows – indeed encourages – governments to regulate the growing religious and social diversity in the field (Beckford, 2010; Middlemiss Lé Mon,

2015). This noticeably neoliberal agenda is, however, being increasingly called into question (Berggren and Trägårdh, 2015), resulting in the following paradox. At one and the same time, religion has become both a provider of welfare and a powerful critic of unregulated global economic forces.[9]

A further finding of the WaVE project is that trust in the household and in family values is still important, not only in the south and east of Europe, but also (and more unexpectedly) in the north. Neither the state nor the market has the ability to maintain and improve the wellbeing of the individual without the support of a family. For example, migrants in every part of Europe trust and turn to their relatives for support, rather than the state, especially within the first generation. For the same reason, religious minorities prefer to take care of their own, deploying their informal, but effective, networks. Regrettably, however, this form of care is all too often misunderstood by the majority media as an example of self-isolation, or even extremism. This is unhelpful in that local communities are often better at handling issues of inclusion, integration and cohesion than the state, or indeed the media, noting that the latter consistently under-report the often very positive features of religious minorities. This is particularly the case with regard to women who have regular contact with schools, hospitals and special interest groups, such as sewing circles – a point revealed in the Swedish case. Such links – and the feelings of inclusion that derive from them – are clearly facilitated by access to appropriate language groups and by the encouragement of religious and social literacy, both for the staff in local authorities and the religious minorities themselves.

A final challenge is to accept that migrants very often want to become full members of the receiving country without relinquishing their religious affiliation. This double aspiration is indicative of the cohesive as well as divisive aspects of religion. In order to achieve the former (better cohesion), it is important to create what Zygmunt Bauman (2017) calls 'a culture of dialogue', capable of healing the wounds of a multicultural and multi-conflictual world. Contradicting Samuel Huntington's (1996) argument that conflicting identities will be key in shaping a future world order, Bauman insists that every individual should play an active role in the creation of an integrated and reconciled society. It is for this reason that a new ecology of conversation and cooperation that goes beyond established areas of collaboration should be high on the agenda of European societies.

Conclusion

Deploying sophisticated and diverse methodologies, the WaVE project has displayed the complex interactions between welfare, gender and religious minorities in different parts of Europe. It also raises important theoretical questions about the religious and the secular, and the private and the public, both of which have become ever more porous or 'de-differentiated'. Religion is becoming multidimensional and appears in different spheres of society (welfare, law, health, media and science). At the same time there is an ongoing tension between the freedom of religion and the freedom from religion, illustrated through ongoing and difficult debates about gender.

This is the context in which this volume should be read. Its strengths lie in the fact that it is anchored both in the social transformations of the 1980s and 1990s and in the research data collected in the early 21st century. The following chapters have also taken account of more recent developments – notably the global economic collapse in 2008, the subsequent political and social upheavals (both in Europe and the Middle East) and the consequent refugee or migration crisis, especially in south–eastern Europe. These developments raise basic questions about how social welfare should be organised: who should provide what, to whom and under what conditions? These are all the more pertinent in a context of growing diversity and lead to a further, crucially important question: to what extent do citizens trust the ability of the state to address these issues?

One final point is worth noting: the WaVE project has been one element in the development of a major European research programme at Uppsala University entitled The Impact of Religion: Challenges for Society, Law and Democracy.[10] This programme runs from 2008 to 2018 and incorporates six different themes.[11] Among other things it symbolises a widespread and growing need for multidisciplinary approaches to research that pay attention to the transitions and interactions between majority cultures and minority religions both in Europe and across the globe. The chapters that follow should be read in this light.

Notes

[1] Jean-Claude Juncker gave his State of the European Union address to the European Parliament on 14 September 2016 in light of the UK referendum on whether to remain in or leave the European Union on 23 June 2016: www.independent. co.uk/news/world/europe/jean-claude-juncker-european-parliament-speech-in-full-a7298016.html

[2] Examples of ongoing and completed research programmes include: Tolerance, Pluralism and Social Cohesion: Responding to the Challenges of the 21st Century in Europe – ACCEPT PLURALISM (EU-funded); Religion and Society Research Programme (United Kingdom); The Future of the Religious Past: Elements and Forms for the 21st Century (the Netherlands); Impact of Religion. Challenges for Society, Law and Democracy (Sweden); Religion and Diversity Project, Ottawa (Canada); Religion, the State and Society: National Research Programme, NRP 58 (Switzerland). The forthcoming Horizon 2020 call within the work programme Europe in a Changing World – Inclusive, Innovative and Reflective Societies includes a call on 'religious diversity in Europe – past, present and future'.

[3] The project was part of a broader initiative by the Swedish Research Council entitled The State and the Individual: Swedish Society in the Process of Change. The results were summarised in Bäckström et al (2004).

[4] The initial agreement was signed in 1999. The centre moved to new premises at Uppsala University in 2007. See www.crs.uu.se for further information.

[5] For the World Values Survey, see www.wvs.org, and for the International Social Survey Programme, see www.issp.org. Pål Repstad and Hans Georg Ziebertz were methodology advisers to the WaVE project. Their observations were compiled in the project's Work Package 2: Development of Methodology (Repstad and Ziebertz, 2011, p 289). See also the comments in Chapters Four and Twelve of this volume.

[6] In October 2010, Angela Merkel declared the failure of multiculturalism in Germany, followed by David Cameron in the UK and Nicolas Sarkozy in France in early 2011. See www.telegraph.co.uk/news/worldnews/europe/france/8317497/Nicolas-Sarkozy-declares-multiculturalism-had-failed.html

[7] http://andreasjohanssonheino.blogspot.se/2011/01/integration-eller-assimilation.html

[8] Horizon 2020 is the European Commission Framework Programme for Research and Innovation. See especially Work Programme 13: Europe in a Changing World – Inclusive, Innovative and Reflective Societies, page 91: Religious Diversity in Europe – Past, Present and Future: http://ec.europa.eu/research/participants/data/ref/h2020/wp/2016_2017/main/h2020-wp1617-societies_en.pdf.

[9] The candidacy of Bernie Sanders, a 'social Democrat', in the 2016 election campaign in the US and the election of Jeremy Corbyn as leader of the Labour Party in the UK in 2015 are examples of this trend, which remains less visible in the Nordic states.

[10] www.impactofreligion.uu.se

[11] The principal themes are: religious and social change; integration, democracy and political culture; families, law and society; wellbeing and health; welfare models – organisation and values; and science and religion.

References

Bäckström, A. (ed) (2011) *Welfare and Values in Europe: Transitions Related to Religion, Minorities and Gender. National Overviews and Case Study Reports, Volume 1. Northern Europe: Sweden, Norway, Finland, England*, Studies in Religion and Society 4, Uppsala: Acta Universitatis Upsaliensis.

Bäckström, A. (ed) (2012a) *Welfare and Values in Europe: Transitions Related to Religion, Minorities and Gender. National Overviews and Case Study Reports, Volume 2. Continental Europe: Germany, France, Italy, Greece*, Studies in Religion and Society 5, Uppsala: Acta Universitatis Upsaliensis.

Bäckström, A. (ed) (2012b) *Welfare and Values in Europe: Transitions Related to Religion, Minorities and Gender. National Overviews and Case Study Reports, Volume 3. Eastern Europe: Latvia, Poland, Croatia, Romania*, Studies in Religion and Society 6, Uppsala: Acta Universitatis Upsaliensis.

Bäckström, A. (2014) 'Religion in the Nordic countries: between private and public', *Journal of Contemporary Religion*, 29(1): 61-74.

Bäckström, A. and Davie, G., with Edgardh, N. and Pettersson, P. (eds) (2010) *Welfare and Religion in 21st Century Europe: Volume 1. Configuring the Connections*, Farnham: Ashgate.

Bäckström, A., Davie, G., Edgardh, N. and Pettersson, P. (eds) (2011) *Welfare and Religion in 21st Century Europe: Volume 2, Gendered, Religious and Social Change*, Farnham: Ashgate.

Bäckström, A., Edgardh Beckman, N. and Pettersson, P. (2004) *Religious Change in Northern Europe. The Case of Sweden*, Stockholm: Verbum.

Bauman, Z. (2017) *Retrotopia*, Cambridge: Polity Press.

Beckford, J.A. (2010) 'The return of religion? A critical assessment of a popular claim', *Nordic Journal of Religion and Society*, 23(2): 121-36.

Berggren, H. and Trägårdh, L. (2015) *Är svensken människa? Gemenskap och oberoende i det moderna Sverige* (*Are Swedes Human? Community and Independence in Modern Sweden*), Stockholm: Norstedts.

Casanova, J. (2013) 'Exploring the postsecular. Three meanings of "the secular" and their possible transcendence', in C. Calhoun, E. Mendieta and J. van Antwerpen (eds) *Habermas and Religion*, Cambridge: Polity Press, pp 27-48.

Furseth, I. (2015) (ed) *Religionens tilbakekomst i offentligheten? Religion, politikk, medier, stat og sivilsamfunn i Norge siden 1980-tallet* (*The Return of Religion in the Public Square? Religion, Politics, Media and Civil Society in Norway since the 1980s*), Oslo: Universitetsforlaget.

Giddens, A. (2007) *Europe in the Global Age*, Cambridge: Polity Press.

Hervieu-Léger, D. (2015) 'Religion as a grammar of memory: reflections on a comparison between Britain and France', in A. Day and M. Lövheim (eds) *Modernities, Memory and Mutations. Grace Davie and the Study of Religion*, Farnham: Ashgate, pp 13-29.

Hettne, B. (1997*) Den europeiska paradoxen. Om integration och desintegration i Europa* (*The European Paradox. On Integration and Disintegration in Europe*), Nerenius and Santerus Förlag: Stockholm.

Huntington, S. P. (1996) *The Clash of Civilizations and the Remaking of World Order*, New York, NY: Simon & Schuster.

Johansson Heinö, A. (2011) 'Integration eller assimilation' (Integration or Assimilation) http://andreasjohanssonheino.blogspot.se/2011/01/integration-eller-assimilation.html.

Lipset, S.M. and Rokkan, S. (eds) (1967) *Party Systems and Voter Alingments: Cross-National Perspectives*, New York, NY: Free Press.

Martikainen, T. and Gauthier, F. (eds) (2013) *Religion in a Neoliberal Age. Political Economy and Modes of Governance*, Farnham: Ashgate.

Martin, D. (2010) 'The settled secularity of happy Denmark', in L. Christoffersen, H.R. Iversen, H. Petersen and M. Marburg (eds) *Religion in the 21st Century. Challenges and Transformations*, Farnham: Ashgate, pp 183-9.

Middlemiss Lé Mon, M. (2015) *Frivilligarbete inom och för kyrkan. En lösning på de problem som kyrka och samhälle står inför?* (*Voluntary Work in and for the Church. A Solution to the Problems faced by the Church and Society?*), Stockholm: Forum-idéburna organisationer med social inriktning.

Repstad, P. and Ziebertz, H.G. (2011) 'Development of methodology (Work Package 2)', in A. Bäckström (ed) *Welfare and Values in Europe: Transitions Related to Religion, Minorities and Gender. National Overviews and Case Study Report, Volume 1. Northern Europe: Sweden, Norway, Finland and England*, Studies in Religion and Society 4, Uppsala: Acta Universitatis Upsaliensis, pp 289-310.

The Social Dimension of Europe 2020 Strategy, http://ec.europa.eu/progress.

Uppsala Religion and Society Research Centre, Uppsala University, www.crs.uu.se.

Part One:
Thinking methodologically:
approaches to research and practice

TWO

Between contextuality and comparability: a dilemma in qualitative comparative case studies

Pål Repstad

As a young assistant professor teaching public administration, I sometimes took my students with me to a municipality in northern Jutland, Denmark. There was (and still is) a regular ferry service over the Skagerrak between the towns of Kristiansand in Norway, where I lived and worked (and still do), and Hirtshals in Denmark. My contacts in the Danish municipality presented some boxes and arrows on paper to the students. Through these simple presentation techniques (this was long before PowerPoint), the students gained some valuable insights into the different ways that public services might be organised, each with its advantages and disadvantages. In other words, they encountered the intellectual blessings of comparative analysis.

The main topic of this chapter is to discuss the tensions inherent in the strategy of comparing case studies, especially those that use mainly qualitative methods. I was a methodological adviser for the Welfare and Values in Europe: Transitions Related to Religion, Minorities and Gender (WaVE) project from start to finish, so there is an implicit element of self-criticism in my text. It is true that my reflections are partly inspired by several years of contact with the WaVE project and its research team. However, my aim is to provoke a more general discussion, which is not primarily intended to be an overall evaluation of WaVE. Furthermore, I do not only point to dilemmas that the individual researcher may face. Social science consists increasingly of collective ventures, and I try to trace some institutional factors that may influence the researcher's journey between rigid standardisation and isolated case studies.

Tracing social mechanisms

The French philosopher Auguste Comte is often identified in textbooks as the father of sociology, because in 1830 he coined the term 'sociology'. The fact that he first suggested the term 'social physics' for the new discipline was a sign of his optimism on behalf of science. Just as the natural sciences of his time were successfully uncovering laws of nature and using insights to make technological innovations, Comte envisaged a future where sociology's grasp of universal social laws could be used to create a society closer to perfection. Some of the other classical figures in sociology's formative years had similarly ambitious thoughts on the scientific potential of detecting the universal laws of society. This came to an end in the 1960s with the critique of positivism. No longer was it possible to think about society as a complicated and advanced clockwork. To simplify, two dimensions were criticised.

First, society is not a mechanical device. People are intentional: they can act in different directions and sometimes succeed in transcending the frames and constraints set by social frameworks, such as technology, power, traditions and other structures. It follows that the question of how wide an actor's frame of action can be is empirical rather than dogmatic. Second, even researchers have human traits. They carry with them intellectual and emotional baggage and this can – often in subtle ways – influence what they look for as well as the interpretations that they make. Most social scientists today, including researchers of religion, muddle through a landscape in which they believe there is a reality outside language and imagery, but also that this reality is not accessible without interpretation. There is still a demand for empirical evidence in studies of society, but conclusions in social science tend to be humbler and more contextually limited than in Comte's social physics. We may add that there is still an interest – perhaps one that is increasing – in tracing social mechanisms. Looking for social and causal mechanisms is a way of trying to open the black box between a possible cause and a possible effect, and follow the dynamics between them. The modesty of such attempts stems from the fact that such dynamics are not deterministic; they are probabilistic.

The most common method of looking for causal mechanisms is to look for statistical co-variations between variables. In quantitative studies one tries to test causal hypotheses on the relation between two or more variables, keeping constant all potentially disturbing elements. But we can never be sure that we have relevant information on all such elements.

There are other methods as well: we can follow a process over time and try to identify what follows what, for the time sequence is important. The cause must precede the effect. There are practical problems following such a process and there are difficulties in generalising from single case studies. A case study usually provides a rich and detailed description. A classical definition of a case study can be taken from Robert K. Yin: A case study is an empirical study: '(1) Investigating a contemporary phenomenon; (2) within its real life context; (3) when the boundaries between phenomenon and context are not clearly evident; and (4) in which multiple sources of evidence are used' (1989, p 23). Single case studies can be very interesting. They can deal with cases that are important in themselves and offer good ideas for developing or revising general theories. However, we need broader sets of empirical material in order to make more general claims. Herein lies the value of comparative work. Comparative case studies can put researchers on the track of more persuasive claims of causal mechanisms – not of a deterministic kind, but showing regular patterns that can be presented for critical scrutiny to peers in the scientific field as well as to the general public.

The logic of comparison is simple in principle. If X and Y are found in the north and Y, but not X, is found in the south, there is a case for a stronger argument to look for other causes than those of X behind Y. If X and Y are found in several countries and none of them are found in other countries, we may be on the trail of a connection between X and Y. We can also identify contrasting cases, dominated respectively by X or Y, and look for other traits that may differentiate the two units we study. Then we may attempt to explain the occurrence of X and Y.

These and other comparative strategies are described here in a very abstract way. In the empirical world the situation may be much more complicated. Usually we will find neither X nor Y as well-defined entities that are ready to be compared. We will have to conceptualise the units to be compared from pieces of information that are often messy and intertwined with irrelevant stuff. We will also have to engage in a great deal of interpretive work. And we will encounter many of the dilemmas presented in this chapter.

Exploring unique qualities or giving priority to comparability?

Religion is in many ways going through a process of globalisation. At the same time, there are many examples of reactions against globalisation. Both tendencies increase the need for comparative and transnational studies. The latter are growing in number. Here, however, I will focus on qualitative comparative studies, not studies of transnational processes. Researchers conducting comparative case studies face a dilemma that may be especially acute in qualitative studies where a lot of information is gathered in less standardised ways than in quantitative surveys. We shall, however, return briefly to the fact that there are also challenges in international quantitative studies, for example, in surveys.

What is the main dilemma? It is this: whether to give priority to 'thick' descriptions or to comparability. On the one hand, it is important for collaborative studies across country borders to obtain a minimum of standardisation in the empirical material collected. If not, researchers risk being left with a number of isolated case studies going in very different directions and with few possibilities to compare in a fruitful way. On the other hand, an exaggerated standardisation may do violence to the real situation in the diverse empirical world and important local or national contextual factors may be ignored. Let us have a closer look at the two alternatives.

The value of in-depth studies: looking for unique qualities and holistic descriptions

Representative surveys and other quantitative strategies seem to yield precise and standardised data, while information from qualitative strategies, such as fieldwork, informal interviews or hermeneutical studies of texts, are far from uniform. We should, of course, add that the data gathered from surveys or existing statistical overviews are sometimes only apparently precise and offer comparable items only on the surface. For example, people may assign rather different meanings to the questions and the predetermined responses, but that is another story. In qualitative studies, however, neither the process of gathering information nor the information gathered is standardised. Nevertheless, qualitative methods may yield very solid information. When informants trust the researcher and they are allowed to speak using their own words about issues that matter to them, this enhances the quality of the data in comparison with the often fragmented and a-contextual pieces of information from a survey or a statistical table.

Flexibility is another advantage of qualitative interviews. Pre-constructed questionnaires are often of limited value, especially when the same questions and response options are used in different countries or contexts. People may not understand the questions, or find them unimportant in comparison with other topics that the researcher may not have thought about beforehand and therefore not included in the interview. In qualitative studies, the researcher has the opportunity to gain more knowledge during the project and consequently to adjust questions and the analytical framework. In qualitative interviews or fieldwork, there is also room for unexpected findings that can be taken into account in the research process. This flexibility is very different from a quantitative study where the phases of the research process are more detached and allow for little room for manoeuvre. Once a questionnaire is distributed, it cannot be changed.

Furthermore, the value of a qualitative study and mixed-method case study can be improved because there is room to consider the context, which can provide a more complete picture of the overall situation, especially when describing the structural framework. Yin's advice to gather information 'from multiple sources' constitutes an opportunity to grasp something of the structural framework, such as supra-individual structures, including traditions, power structures, dominant discourses and knowledge regimes. Even if a study is not longitudinal, some of the history may still be of interest and researchers can understand more of this if they are personally present in the field. Of course a qualitative study may also suffer from structural blindness, for instance, in a phenomenological interview focusing one-sidedly on the agent's subjective thoughts. However, it may be easier to correct structural blindness in a qualitative case study than in quantitative studies, especially if a researcher spends some time in the field.

Being in the field and spending time with informants may also direct the researcher's attention to the fact that context matters in the process of data collecting. For example, during interviews teachers talk differently about their school when they are physically in the school and when they are outside (Kuntz and Presnall, 2012). People are more positive towards the display of religious symbols on buildings in public spaces when they actually look at such symbols than when they are asked in the abstract, as they would in a survey (Løvland and Repstad, 2015). Such considerations of validity may go unnoticed when gathering research data from a sheet of paper or computer screen without having spent any time with the informants.

The value of comparability and the limitations of isolated case studies

So far, we have pointed to the many positive qualities of qualitative case studies. However, there are also well-known limitations. The main problem is the question of generalisation. Although we may approach promising and interesting social mechanisms in a single case study, it may be problematic to make a convincing argument that a single case can prove something more general. There are multitudes of single case studies, including those in the field of religious life. The findings often go in very different directions. For example, some case studies of new religious movements warn against sectarian and authoritarian traits, while others see new religious movements as a liberating phenomenon. As single case studies they both may have their merits, but the problem arises when researchers generalise on such thin empirical evidence. Having a broader empirical basis opens up possibilities for gathering more general knowledge and for greater success in drawing convincing conclusions about causal mechanisms.

To ensure comparability, it helps to start with a precise problem formulation and with research questions common to the cases under review. Agreeing on the working hypotheses guiding the empirical research in the different cases facilitates the comparison. But working hypotheses can be dangerous: they can blind researchers to the unexpected and prompt them to look only for what they expect. The ideal is to have working hypotheses that help focus the research while remaining open to other findings, or to the fact that other issues may turn out to be interesting and relevant for the original problem formulation.

The WaVE study and another example

As already mentioned, this chapter is not meant as a comprehensive evaluation of the WaVE project. My focus is more specific: namely, the dilemma between contextualising and comparing. I will use examples from WaVE, but also from another comparative case study on the Catholic Church and political processes in five European countries (Dobbelaere and Pérez-Agote, 2015). However, most of the illustrations come from the WaVE project. How did the latter succeed in balancing the need for studying each case *sui generis* with the need for a somewhat standardised design in order to obtain comparability?

In my view, the autonomy of each local research team to pursue its own special interests was given priority over comparability. I am less certain, however, whether this was a conscious decision, or whether it was something that emerged unintentionally from a complicated research process. Whatever the case, each team of researchers in the 12 European countries was given a considerable amount of freedom in choosing both the medium-sized town (that is, the research site) and the minorities for the case studies, the type of welfare activities to be reviewed, as well as the definitions of important concepts, such as majority, minority and welfare. As a result of taking contextuality as our guide (see Chapter Twelve), the research offers a more complete and realistic perspective of the range of arenas of minority–majority interaction and thus a better grasp of the types of problems that might be encountered and types of solutions found, in the efforts towards social cohesion in diverse societies across Europe.

The complete list of the countries, the minorities and the types of welfare provisions that were studied need not be repeated here. To show the breadth and variety of WaVE, it suffices to mention some examples. Muslim groups of different ethnic backgrounds were chosen, but also other ethnic and religious minorities, such as Jews, Germans from the former Soviet Union, Pentecostals, Roma, Poles (in England), Ukrainians (in Poland), and so on. Different majority organisations were studied, such as churches, welfare organisations and professionals in the majority population. Furthermore, many different types of welfare services were examined, ranging from reproductive health, care for the elderly, the school system, the reception of asylum seekers, care for children and other care services.

Similar principles were employed in the study on the ways in which the Catholic Church has acted in political matters concerning legislation of abortion, divorce, euthanasia, medically assisted procreation and same-sex marriage (Dobbelaere and Pérez-Agote, 2015). As in WaVE, the researchers in this study were allowed to focus on the issues within so-called life politics that they found most topical and interesting. The operational criterion seems to have been to choose the issue most discussed in each country at the time of the study. Thus euthanasia was studied in Belgium, same-sex marriages in France and Portugal, abortion in Spain and assisted procreation in Italy. The project was not very ambitious in terms of comparison and sociological theorising; it was, however, for the most part, a detailed and very informative research study in the field of contemporary history.

The question that faces us now is the following: could a more active and determined project oversight in both the WaVE project and the Catholic Church study have improved the possibilities for comparison? As it stands, the publications emanating from both projects are mainly descriptive presentations of case studies, with one key difference. In the project on Catholicism the contextualisation of the topic varied from country to country. In *The Intimate,* the main publication emanating from this study (Dobbelaere and Pérez-Agote, 2015), some authors give a broad presentation of religion in the national context, while others go more directly to their main topic.

The approach in WaVE was more systematic and consistent. The research teams in all of the countries began by writing a national overview of the role of religion, its welfare system, minorities, majority–minority relations and gender issues. This part of the work was conducted mainly through existing research and statistical overviews. Although these national overviews took some time to write, they have proved to be valuable tools in the contextualisation and comparability of the project. They provide both qualitative and quantitative data. Such overviews may illuminate the significance of the local data. They may also be useful in comparative work as they discourage researchers from treating local peculiarities as national characteristics. Nevertheless, up until now, publications from the WaVE study have been overwhelmingly descriptive – hence the need for this thematic volume. That said, it is important to mention an article published in 2011 by the senior researcher in Croatia, Siniša Zrinščak. This makes connections between the different types of welfare systems in Europe and the degree of integration of religious and ethnic minorities. Zrinščak does not identify any clear co-variations. Rather, the goal of his article is to nuance stereotypes rather than to establish strong connections between variables. For instance, the social democratic welfare regime in the Nordic countries, with its seemingly limited space for non-governmental social work activities, seems nonetheless to encourage voluntary work, although more as an added source of welfare provision than as a replacement of state welfare:

> [D]espite limited involvement in service provision, local case studies in all Nordic countries showed more intensive contacts with minority organisations than in other European countries as well as public discussion about how to take into account the specific needs of immigrants. (Zrinščak, 2011, p 205)

The old stereotype of social democratic welfare regimes of universal services provided in an impersonal, unempathetic way is called into question.

It is probably easier to compare and theorise on the basis of subgroups and contrasting pairs of cases. Even with a very standardised design, it would be difficult to include all 13 case studies in a comparative study looking for social mechanisms. So far, most of the studies I have seen from WaVE and similar large international comparative studies have focused on a few of the cases, or they have used the material as a reservoir of illustrations and examples rather than as a point of departure for tracing social mechanisms. Just to hint at one possibility for systematic comparisons and causal analyses in the WaVE material: even though the cities in the project are all defined as medium-sized, the number of inhabitants varies quite a lot. Is it possible to trace differences in client satisfaction from social welfare services? Is small beautiful? A comparison of all the cities may be too ambitious and precarious here. The 13 cities are different in so many respects other than size. However, a comparison between subgroups such as the Nordic countries, with more similar welfare systems, might offer the opportunity for a more realistic analysis. Of course, one would even then have to be very cautious about drawing conclusions, but the point here is the pursuit of ideas about tracing probabilistic causality through comparison.

Organisational centrifugal forces

Many textbooks in sociological methods have a rather unrealistic understanding of the individual researcher, struggling with his or her methodological choices in an institutional vacuum. It is abundantly clear, however, that comparative cases as a method of study in social sciences are not the work of 'lone riders' but part of a complex set of organisational dynamics. With this in mind, let us now look at a number of factors that come into play in these circumstances, such as open and, at times, rather vague research calls, individual career plans, a fragmented world of social science, and, finally, the tendency towards more interdisciplinary research.

For many reasons, applied science is becoming an increasingly important part of science, including sociology. A substantial number of studies are, moreover, commissioned research. This most certainly opens up possibilities, but at the same time it imposes limitations on comparative case studies. International projects require extensive coordination and financial backing. In Europe, EU programmes have been very important in this respect and have initiated and facilitated a great deal of comparative research. On the other hand, many of the calls for research have been open rather than specific. There are many good reasons for this. Such calls are often formulated as a compromise between many divergent interests. Furthermore, a very precise and very narrow call might be criticised as a form of political control. In combination with tight deadlines, the result may be rather vague applications and project descriptions, full of good intentions, but lacking a crystal-clear design. The WaVE application is a typical example. The European Commission funded the 6th Framework Programme (FP6) which invited researchers to strive for a better understanding of 'the significance and impact of values and religions in societies across Europe and their roles in relation to changes in society'. The WaVE team responded to this. Core concepts in the application included welfare provision, minority–majority relationships, values, conflicts, cohesion, change, religion and gender. Moreover, the approach was innovative: changes in religion, minorities and gender were to be studied through the prism of welfare. It was this metaphorical idea of a prism rather than explicit hypotheses indicating causal chains between all the phenomena that provided the guiding thread of the project description.

For this reason, many questions regarding research design were left unanswered at the outset. This became more and more apparent during the first project meetings: the researchers became increasingly aware of the challenges they faced, at the same time noting that their individual interests went in rather different directions. Quite apart from this, access to different areas of research varied from country to country, as did the amount of existing research in various fields, a situation by no means specific to WaVE.

Another centrifugal drive was the institutional frameworks in which the WaVE researchers found themselves. Each institution encouraged a different type of focus. For instance, some were very much focused on gender, others much less so. The junior researchers, moreover, were in a situation where they had to take their professional aspirations and research profiles into consideration, balancing these against the rather broad field of study that developed in the course of the project. Unsurprisingly, different research teams went in different directions to maximise advantage for specific, rather than general, motivations. The outcome is very clear: for better or worse, the WaVE project gave priority to individual case studies rather than to the project overall. The data that emerged were correspondingly rich; the opportunities for comparison less so.

A final consideration that may be relevant here is the evolution in contemporary academic life from discipline-based to problem-based multidisciplinary research. Different disciplines seem to converge in thematic studies, and at present there is some blurring of the boundaries between the disciplines that developed in the humanistic and social sciences in the late 19th and early 20th centuries. We have seen this in religious studies. Furthermore, partly because of the immense volume of scientific work, thematically organised fields tend to be divided into subfields such as ritual studies, pastoral studies, and so on.

There is no compelling reason to respect the strict and established boundaries between disciplines. They are the historically contingent results of institutional interests, power structures, cultural ideas and sheer coincidence. In the ongoing process of academic restructuration there are both gains and losses. It may make more sense to organise academic work thematically to deal more directly with solving real problems in the contemporary world. Very few problems follow the borders of academic disciplines, so there are good reasons why many large research programmes (such as those funded by the EU) encourage multidisciplinary efforts.

On the other hand, precision in methods and concepts, and the intellectual rigour that has developed in academic disciplines over the years, is likely to become weaker in thematic and multidisciplinary studies. There is also a risk that researchers in such projects become too narrow in focus. In the case of the WaVE project, this might mean focusing too much on religion and too little on how religion is intertwined with other factors. We may become prisoners of the field in the sense that we adopt too uncritically the concepts and perspectives used by the actors in question. As researchers, we have an obligation to present the actors' points of view correctly, but we should not abstain from introducing the researchers' theoretically informed perspectives on what is happening in the field, even if such perspectives may differ from the internal, emic understandings of the actors.

Conclusion

Comparative case studies contain an inherent tension between offering a useful and problem-oriented opportunity for conducting research keeping the local situation in mind and seeking more general patterns, which may turn out to be fruitful and rewarding for social science in the long run. I hope that it is clear that I am not advocating the development of universal and deterministic social laws in research, but causal mechanisms with a wider potential for application beyond the single case study.

The inherent tension in the case study method illustrates that there is no perfect research design for study in social science; we lose something and gain something all the time. However, when an international group of researchers has been given the means to conduct a large international study and has succeeded in the painstaking job of establishing an international framework, there are some good arguments to develop a design for the study with a minimum level of standardisation, to increase the possibilities of identifying causal mechanisms.

Some may think that an obsession with finding causal mechanisms in social science may be a remnant of naïve positivist days. It would be as if we returned to Comte's belief in the world as well-functioning and predictable clockwork. Our ambitions as contemporary social scientists are rather more humble. We can never avoid the necessity of interpretations and there should always be an element of doubt when we present our analyses. My main point here is that researchers should be more explicit when they discuss possible causal explanations. Such explanations should always be qualified, preliminary and contextualised, but they are interesting and they may have practical value. And it is not as if social scientists are uninterested in explanations. Reading a sociological article, one is often struck by the fact that the text is surprisingly full of statements about causality, many of which are implicit, and abundant in metaphorical language. In my view, it is better to present one's causal hypotheses and conclusions explicitly and transparently, so that other members of the academic community as well as interested, more general readers can relate to what is presented – and support, criticise or nuance the findings.

References

Dobbelaere, K. and Pérez-Agote, A. (eds) (2015) *The Intimate. Polity and the Catholic Church*, Leuven: Leuven University Press.

Kuntz, A. and Presnall, M. (2012) 'Wandering the tactical: from interview to intraview', *Qualitative Inquiry*, 18(9): 732–44.

Løvland, A. and Repstad, P. (2015) 'Religious symbols in public spaces: asking people in and out of context', *Nordic Journal of Religion and Society*, 28(2): 155–70.

Yin, R.K. (1989) *Case Study Research. Designs and Methods*, London: Sage.

Zrinscak, S. (2011) 'Local immigrant communities, welfare and culture: an integration/segregation dilemma', in E. Carmel, A. Cerami and T. Papadopoulos (eds) *Migration and Welfare in the New Europe*, Bristol: Policy Press, pp 197–212.

THREE

Using case studies in religion, values and welfare research

Olav Helge Angell and Lina Molokotos-Liederman

Introduction

This chapter both continues and deepens the conversation initiated in Chapter Two. Its purpose is to address a series of methodological and ethical issues that emerge from the study of religion, values and welfare using a case study approach. A selection of methodological choices will be considered, drawing particularly on data from the Norwegian case studies in the Welfare and Values in Europe: Transitions Related to Religion, Minorities and Gender (WaVE) project and its predecessor, the Welfare and Religion in a European Perspective: A Comparative Study of the Role of the Churches as Agents of Welfare within the Social Economy (WREP) project. Particular attention is paid to the challenges and implications of this type of research for policy debates and for a variety of end users (such as politicians and religious leaders). The chapter will discuss how public policy debates may affect the reliability and validity of such studies.

Methods and data

The chapter draws on the objectives, methods, data and experiences from the two European research projects mentioned earlier: WREP and WaVE. The basic aim of WREP was to analyse the function of majority churches as agents of social welfare. WaVE continued the work of WREP by setting out to study the impact of 'religion [...] as a bearer of solidarity and social cohesion, or as a source of tension and exclusion' (Bäckström, 2011, p 4) and minority values, as expressed in the search for, and use of, welfare services, paying particular attention to the extent to which views and practices challenge majority values and identities. Both projects were constructed with a comparative perspective in mind. In this chapter we use the distinction made by

Ragin and Amoroso (2011) between what we may call qualitative and comparative research strategies, but restrict ourselves to the former, considering each case study as a way of 'using qualitative methods to study commonalities' (Ragin and Amoroso, 2011, chapter 5).

In both projects, the data collection was based on a qualitative research strategy, primarily qualitative interviews (Yeung, 2006; Bäckström, 2011). Both WREP and WaVE sought to address a significant weakness in research on welfare, values and religion (Bäckström, 2003; Fokas, 2005). Local-level research should yield findings that allow a fruitful comparison between generalised expectations, based on perceptions of the relevant issues at the national level, and practices at the local level. More generally, as an example, the methodological challenge in WREP was how to bring together research on challenges to the welfare state, the place of religion in modern European societies and the role of the voluntary sector within the social economy (Bäckström, 2003). In the WaVE project, the model of investigation established in WREP was continued to enable the researchers to obtain a 'profound understanding of the complex relationships in the locality between majority and minority relations' (Bäckström, 2011, p 5). Studying welfare and values through the prism of welfare, that is, in a setting of welfare service provision (see Bäckström, 2011; Fokas, 2011) is a methodically challenging task.

The case study method and its challenges

In both projects, the research strategy chosen was the case study method. In WREP, the case studies documented, analysed and interpreted the interaction between the majority church(es) and public authorities. The project was based on mixing qualitative and quantitative methods in the form of triangulation with the use of interviews, observation, surveys and document analyses, with the main emphasis on qualitative interviews. In WaVE, more or less the same methods were used to study majority–minority relations and social cohesion and tension, again with an emphasis on in–depth interviews.

What characterises a *case*? John Walton provides the following elements to an answer:

> [C]ases are situationally grounded, limited views of social life.... When researchers speak of a 'case' ... they invest the study of a particular social setting with some sense of generality.... A 'case' implies a family; it alleges that the

particular is a case of something else. Implicit in the idea of the case is a claim. (Walton, 1992, p 121)

Taking this way of thinking one step further, the next question would be: the case, '[a] case of what?' (Walton, 1992, p 135). Walton argues that any case may offer a variety of answers to that question. But 'any answer presumes a theory based on causal analogies' (Walton, 1992, p 135).

What characterises a *case study*? One of the most widely read introductions to case study methods is Robert K. Yin's book *Case Study Research* (Yin, 2014). Yin defines a case study in the following way:

> A case study is an inquiry that investigates a contemporary phenomenon in depth and within its real-life context, especially when the boundaries between phenomenon and context are not clearly evident. The case study inquiry relies on multiple sources of evidence, with data needing to converge in a triangulating fashion, and as another result benefits from the prior development of theoretical propositions to guide data collection and analysis. (Yin, 2014, p 18)

In both WREP and WaVE, the case study strategy was (more or less) in line with Yin's definition. Also, in both projects the locality in each country was a 'medium-sized' town or city. The main challenge was choosing a case study locality that was big enough to contain the relevant social phenomena, but also small enough for the researchers to establish (intimate) familiarity with the locality and the case (Ragin and Amoroso, 2011; Thomas, 2011). In addition, the selection of each national case study location was based on practical reasons, rather than being solely a systematically selected 'typical' or 'average' case with the aim of being representative of medium-sized towns or cities in each country. One of the consequences of this methodological choice was that both WREP and WaVE were projects with a multiple case study design. Each case was analysed in its own right by investigating society at large, with a view to explaining its impact on the specific case under study (Burawoy, 1998) and uncovering mechanisms and tracing processes in the case material (Mitchell, 1983; Lamont and White, 2009). This approach distinguishes the case study logic from the sampling logic that characterises quantitative research strategies (Ragin and Becker, 1992).

In the following section, we introduce three important challenges connected with using a case study to study religion, welfare, values, gender and minorities, as we did in both the WREP and WaVE projects. These challenges, which are presented here in the aftermath of the projects, are discussed more or less as they evolved in the course of the research process. They are also representative of some of the challenges that we struggled with in the research process. It is important to note, however, that other researchers in the projects might have emphasised other challenges. The challenges highlighted here concern the subject matter of the research; how to define and operationalise key concepts; and the implications of using a specific method extensively (qualitative interviews) in the data collection process.

Challenge 1: studying the intersections of religion and welfare

Studying the role of majority churches in welfare at the local level required an understanding of the role of religion both historically and in the current societal context, for example, the impact of religion on the welfare system at large and the historical role of third sector faith-based actors (and the specialised welfare services that they offer). Likewise, understanding public and political attitudes towards religious diversity and its visible manifestations in everyday life helped to contextualise the local cases better – including, for example, religiosity as a private (in most Christian traditions) and/or public matter (in Islam), political goals, such as integration versus assimilation (and the limits of diversity), and education (the school) and the welfare system, as institutions for socialisation into majority society. Such extra-local conditions may have an impact on how relations between the majority and minorities, especially religious minorities, are played out and perceived in the research.

Certain key issues connected with religion, values and welfare can be illustrated through some relevant aspects from the WaVE Norwegian case study. Here the relevant welfare area was the local school. The focus was on the encounter between the majority population (and the values that are institutionalised in educational structures and processes) and religious minorities and their values. One way we approached the issue of religion, values and welfare was to ask if minority parents with schoolchildren had objections to what their children did and/or were taught in school. If so, how did the parents react? The issues that parents reacted to negatively included mixed (both sexes) swimming lessons (reactions based on religious belief in the case of Muslims) and mixed class excursions involving an overnight stay away from home (reactions based on similar grounds). Other responses from the parents included withdrawing girls from short excursions outside the school, based on the parents' view that teaching and learning takes place only in school, and that there are other domestic tasks for girls to learn (partly and indirectly connected with religious belief and tradition).

Some parents withdrew their children from the state school system altogether, based on the argument that classes were too big and that there was too little discipline in state schools, but also because Muslim parents were sceptical about the quality of religious teaching in the secular state school system. In studying these exceptional cases of minority (Muslim) parents more closely, that is, those who opted out of the state school system to send their children to private (in fact Christian) schools, it was found that this offered a more nuanced image of the relationship between religion and values in the context of welfare. As the parents saw it, both Christians and Muslims have much in common in terms of religious tenets and moral values. Also, parents were not concerned with whatever religious 'preaching' their children were exposed to in the Christian schools. In these matters, Christian schools were seen as more 'trustworthy' than the state secular schools.

In addition to interviews with the parents, other sources and methods, such as observation of interactions between parents and teachers in parent–teacher meetings, focus groups with parents, teachers and public health nurses, and analysis of local newspapers, were used to obtain the data mentioned earlier. Thus it was through the use of triangulation that we were able to collect rich data and material in order to validate the information provided and understand the case as a whole, including the interactions of welfare, religion, minorities and gender.

Challenge 2: the study of values

Effie Fokas has described the WaVE project as grounded on 'the intangible concept of "values" in the ways in which values are *expressed and developed in practice*' (Fokas, 2011, p 14, emphasis in original). In this way, WaVE aimed to understand what may be called 'lived values', that is, how values, as they are transformed into practice, action or behaviour, influence relations between the majority and the minorities, and support or undermine social cohesion and/or tensions (Repstad and Ziebertz, 2011).

The concept of value is central in many scientific disciplines. In a review of the use of 'value' in anthropology, David Graeber distinguishes three 'large streams of thought that converge' in the term 'value' in the anthropological tradition (Graeber, 2001, p 1). These 'streams' are: value in the sociological sense, where the term refers to something that is ultimately good or desirable, who we want to be and what we want to do; value in the economic sense, as measured in the willingness to pay for a certain good or service; and value in the linguistic sense, referring to the French linguist Saussure (Graeber, 2001, pp 1–2). We take the first 'stream' as our main starting point. One of the challenges in values research is to study and understand the (possible) link between values and actions: how values facilitate action(s) towards ends that enhance certain outcomes, or are perceived to do so by members of a society, and how values may be deduced from action patterns. Logically, the latter is particularly difficult, especially since observed practices may be the outcome of the interaction of several values in a given situation – values that may even be contradictory.

One way to try to come to terms with the problem is to see the relationship between values and actions as dialectical, in line with the Danish philosopher Søren Kierkegaard's statement that life must be understood backwards, but must be lived forwards (see, for example, Thielst, 1994). Along such lines we may approach the issue of values through the following question: how do we make our findings meaningful, engaging moral considerations? (See, for example, Aadland, 2010.) One way of so doing is to ascribe values to actions and attitudes, where values are perceived as heuristic devices introduced by the researcher to make sense of patterns of observations, such as 'consistency generators' (Sniderman et al, 1991, p 269; Van Deth and Scarbrough, 1995). The study of values on such premises involves considerations about what people say they do, through interviews, observations of what they do in fact, and how they explain their behaviour, including possible changes in the patterns of behaviour (Repstad and Ziebertz, 2011), again through interviews. All in all, this requires a reflective methodical approach.

The following example from the Norwegian case study approaches values indirectly as 'consistency generators'. The project's methodical design did not provide situations where a direct comparison could be made between what the interviewees said about what they did and observations of their actions. To make up for this, other interviewees in other positions in the community were interviewed about the same patterns of action, that is, about what *they* said they had observed. The trigger for this example is the issue of whether or not a Muslim-based primary school should be established in Drammen (for further details, see Angell and Briseid, 2011). Most of the parents we interviewed had been sceptical about the opening of such a school because they were afraid that it would develop into a closed social system, preventing children from learning Norwegian and from integrating into Norwegian society.

Two of the challenges mentioned by public school leaders and teachers were, first, that minority parents were less involved in the running of the school than the public authorities had expected, and second, that minority children were absent more often than majority children from extracurricular activities (such as visiting museums, exhibitions, institutions and other local excursions) and social events (such as birthday parties). In the Norwegian school philosophy, as expressed in school plans and other official documents, schooling is not limited to what is taking place within the school. For the teachers representing the school, absence from extracurricular activities has negative consequences in the long run and is a source of worry for the school representatives: the more absent the children, the less familiar they become with Norwegian society. At the same time, according to our interviews with the various Muslim communities and parents in Drammen, a high level of education for the children is considered very important.

How can we integrate these findings to ensure that they form a coherent and consistent set of values guiding the parents' behaviour? The fact that minority children took less part in extracurricular activities and social events that were directly or indirectly related to what went on at the school, which was the basis for the school's concern, may be understood as a reflection of how much the parents value education. The Norwegian professor of education, Thor Ola Engen, put forward the following hypothesis, namely, that there is a division of labour between school and home in educational matters, which is essentially the parents' functional adaptation to the Norwegian school system (Engen et al, 1997; Engen, 2006). According to Engen, minority parents may interpret the 10-year compulsory school system in Norway as the way in which the school takes the main responsibility for preparing the children as active citizens in the majority society, but leaves the main responsibility of preparing the children to be part of the minority culture to the parents (Engen, 2006, p 156). In this way there is a common interest for the school and parents to provide the children with an all-round education, with a knowledge not only of the Norwegian language, but also of how society works. This tacit agreement of a division of labour between the school and the home means that parents have to take care of an important part of 'identity work' through separate structures in the community, but parents may do and perceive this in different ways. Thus, at least in theory, there seems to be a consistent pattern of behaviour in terms of two basic values: success in school (thus education as a value) and passing on the religious and cultural identity of the parents to the children. On a similar point see Chapter Eight.

Challenge 3: qualitative interviews

Epistemologically, the qualitative research interview method draws on ideas from the phenomenological and hermeneutical philosophical traditions (Brinkmann and Kvale, 2015). An interview aims to elucidate how the interviewee perceives and understands his/her life world. The strength of the method is its flexibility. Its weakness is that some of the perspectives, issues and questions to be discussed in the interviews may not be of particular interest or concern to the interviewees nor central to their life world. In such cases, the value of the information collected may be difficult to assess. Two examples from the WREP case study may help illustrate this point: the issue of 'welfare pluralism' (namely the provision of services by more welfare actors than those in the public sector, including voluntary and faith-based actors); and the issue of gender roles and relations.

In the Norwegian town of Drammen, especially among public employees, it seemed as if the issue of 'welfare pluralism', which was the focus at the central government level, had little impact on ways of thinking. In this respect, public employees seemed to take it for granted that welfare services are provided by public sector actors.

A parallel situation seemed to exist in the local church concerning the issue of gender, which was not easy to approach through the interviews. Introducing a gender perspective failed to elicit any form of discussion on the practices and experiences in the local church where the interviewees worked, at least not in the way it was suggested in the project's common guidelines. Answers to explicit questions about gender revealed nothing other than the interviewee's level of consciousness and some reflections on matters of gender at the time of the interview. Underlying structures of thinking about gender were more difficult to probe. More generally, therefore, it may be easier to investigate structural aspects of gender using other or additional methodological approaches.

In the case of WaVE, researching religion and values in people's personal lives were sensitive topics, with a high chance of recruiting a biased sample of interviewees. This is a real possibility in recruiting interviewees from minority groups when religious affiliation is a selection criterion. The bias may be caused by selection mechanisms operating in a way that the people volunteering to be interviewed may be too similar or may form a self-selected sample. In a project such as WaVE, the bias was difficult to detect, and it may have been a methodical shortcoming in the study (Small, 2009). There were two ways to overcome this flaw and validate the interview data: first, by taking the interview context into due consideration (see the next section), and, second, through triangulation, that is, using other data sources in the data collection process. In the Norwegian WaVE case study, such alternative sources of data included – as mentioned earlier – local media, interviewing school teachers (majority and minority), head teachers and school nurses, in addition to the minority parents themselves.

Research implications of interviews with regard to reliability and validity

As a data collection method, qualitative interviews require strategic thinking. The interviewer's strategic interest is to provide relevant information pertaining to the research question(s), while also taking into account the interviewee's personal situation and social context or conditions so as to conduct the interview under the best possible circumstances. This is a delicate balancing act that the interviewer has to maintain.

Just as interviewers have their own strategies for asking questions, interviewees may also have their own response strategies during an interview. An interviewee's strategic interests are to respond to the questions and interests of the interviewer, but also to put forth his/her own interests. The interviewee has to weigh these interests against each other, which also involves a balancing act. The interviewee may see that her/his interests are best served by providing information about relevant aspects of his/her life that may have a positive effect and help improve the situation (for example, if this information is made publicly available in a newspaper article). But, after such information is published – for example, anonymised and summarised in the form of a research report – key actors in the local community may react adversely to what is being revealed in the research, thus having a negative overall social impact. It is the responsibility of the researcher to take such possible consequences into consideration (see Dixon et al, 2015, p 63 onwards.)

Using an example from the WaVE case study, we will discuss some of the implications of using the interview method to study minority values and attitudes in the context of public debates on minorities, religion, gender and welfare. Both at the national and local level, the extent of immigrant integration in Norwegian society and the will or intention of immigrants to become integrated have been topics of discussion in the media. Several questions emerged during the research in Drammen, including whether the minority representatives who were interviewed in the project were a self-selected, and thus not a representative, sample since they may have already been better adapted to, and integrated in, the local society than the average person and family in the relevant category of people. For example, in the context of an interview, when meeting the interviewers, who with regard to WaVE did not come from a minority background and thus represented the majority population, some respondents may have chosen to filter how they answered the interviewer's questions. They may have been more careful in what they said about their values, experiences and perceptions of the Norwegian welfare system and school system than in a more 'natural' situation. Equally, this is not to exclude the opposite, namely the possibility that the interviewees may have chosen to be much more explicit or direct in order to make a point. How forthcoming the interviewees were during the interviews probably depended on how significant they felt the issue in question was, and the degree of risk involved for any possible social repercussions in their local community. These observations on how researchers read and interpret the information they obtain from the respondents are important considerations when using qualitative interviews as a research method.

Social implications of research with regard to public debates and public policy

Relations between majorities and minorities, as well as the religious traditions and values of each, are key topics of concern and public debate for politicians, the media, and the population at large. Research on minorities, religion and welfare may thus potentially have an impact on society, public debates and public policies. In the following section, we discuss the dilemmas that may arise in such cases.

Qualitative research findings, including those of the WaVE project, may, or perhaps should, have an impact on public opinion, public debates and public policy; after all, research is part of society and may affect how its members define or perceive themselves. For example, on an individual level an interview is a form of conversation, which can – if it is well prepared by the interviewer – deepen the understanding and level of reflection of both the interviewer and the interviewee (conversation as elucidation).

Qualitative research findings may also challenge conventional and commonly accepted public opinions, knowledge or perceptions, or strong ideological positions. In principle, it is difficult to predict what consequences such findings will have on public opinion, public debates and public policy. In practice, 'conventional wisdom' may try to undermine the validity of the findings, as the following example illustrates. It took place at the end of the Norwegian WaVE case study in response to an invitation to address the town council during one of its meetings. In brief, findings in the Norwegian case study showed that minority and majority parents by and large shared similar values related to the local school system in Drammen. That said, one of the political parties represented in the town council displayed a rather sceptical attitude towards the town's minority population, its values and behaviour. The representative of the political party, who was present during the presentation, did not utter a word during the talk and the discussion that followed. However, he commented afterwards, and in private, that the findings were of no interest because the study was based on the use of qualitative methods and such methods lack scientific validity, so its findings would have no consequences for public policy and political debates.

One way that qualitative research projects may influence public opinion, public debates and public policy is through the media. News media, however, make choices: the way that they cover a particular social issue may be conflict-oriented (focusing on social conflict) and/ or cohesion-oriented (focusing on social cohesion). Both the WREP and the WaVE Norwegian case studies revealed how such functions may be exerted by the local media: in one instance, a newspaper took on the role of 'community booster', acting in an attempt to increase social cohesion by reaffirming the values that make up the moral foundation of the local community and of society at large, and trying to prevent the marginalisation of substance-dependent users in the public square (Angell, 2008). In another situation, however, the same newspaper adopted less of a 'community boosting' role by conveying somewhat contradictory views – that is, critical and negative views of the Turkish Muslim minority but also a positive image of cultural diversity in Drammen (Angell and Briseid, 2011).

The example above is a small illustration of how media have the ability not only to act as an important source of information on minorities but also to influence public attitudes, especially when media users do not have any previous or real experiences with minority communities.

Conclusion

The WREP and WaVE research projects that were the starting point for the methodological reflections in this chapter used the qualitative case study and interview methods as their preferred research strategy. We have presented both the opportunities and challenges linked with this methodological choice, and have suggested possible ways of overcoming some of the shortcomings associated with these methods.

The case study method involves studying a case as a whole, explaining the phenomena under study not only through internal structures, interactions and processes, but also through the impact of external factors and contexts. This is particularly useful in the study of religion and values in the context of welfare needs and the provision of welfare benefits. It is at this fundamental level that different forms of diversity, religion, cultures and values may be studied (Fokas, 2011). In this respect, despite its shortcomings, the case study research strategy is well suited for studying such interconnected and complex social phenomena.

In this chapter, we have focused on the use of interviews in case studies. The interview is one way of providing relevant information about people's life worlds in a wide variety of situations. In comparison with a survey, the qualitative interview provides rich information and a basis for 'thick' descriptions. But the qualitative interview has its limitations. Usually, if we are interested as much in what people do as what they think or say they do, interviews should be accompanied by observation and other research methods. In this chapter, we have offered some examples where triangulation was used by collecting additional research data from different sources to validate the interview data.

A project that studies the interactions between religion, values, minorities and gender, touches on personal or politically sensitive issues. These factors may influence the validity of the research data and findings, not only with regard to individuals, but also entire groups. Thinking about the reliability and validity of data on such complex topics and social phenomena requires knowledge of, and further reflection on, the social contexts in which the research takes place, something that emphasises the clear advantages of a case study strategy.

References

Aadland, E. (2010) 'Values in professional practice: towards a critical reflective methodology', *Journal of Business Ethics*, 97(3): 461-72.

Angell, O.H. (2008) 'Religion and the media: the cultural role of a church-based welfare agent in a Norwegian local community', *Journal of Contemporary Religion*, 23(2): 133-45.

Angell, O.H. and Briseid, K. (2011) 'Drammen case study report', in A. Bäckström (ed) *Welfare and Values in Europe: Transitions Related to Religion, Minorities and Gender. National Overviews and Case Study Reports, Volume 1. Northern Europe: Sweden, Norway, Finland, England*, Studies in Religion and Society 4, Uppsala: Acta Universitatis Upsaliensis, pp 128-57.

Bäckström, A. (ed) (2003) *Welfare and Religion in a European Perspective: A Comparative Study of the Role of the Churches as Agents of Welfare within the Social Economy*, Uppsala: Diakonivetenskapliga institutetets skriftserie, 4.

Bäckström, A. (ed) (2011) *Welfare and Values in Europe: Transitions Related to Religion, Minorities and Gender. National Overviews and Case Study Report, Volume 1. Northern Europe: Sweden, Norway, Finland, England*, Studies in Religion and Society 4, Uppsala: Acta Universitatis Upsaliensis.

Brinkmann, S. and Kvale, S. (2015) *Interviews: Learning the Craft of Qualitative Research Interviewing* (3d edn), Thousand Oaks, CA: Sage.

Burawoy, M. (1998) 'The extended case method', *Sociological Theory*, 16(1): 4-33.

Dixon, J.C., Singleton, R.A. and Straits, B.C. (2015) *The Process of Social Research*, Oxford: Oxford University Press.

Engen, T.O. (2006) 'Om minoritetsfamiliers utdanningsstrategier' ('The education strategies of minority families') in C. Horst (ed) *Interkulturel Pædagogik* (*Intercultural Education*), Vejle: Kroghs Forlag, pp 145-78).

Engen, T.O., Sand, S. and Kulbrandstad, L.A. (1997) *Til keiseren hva keiserens er? Om minoritetselevenes utdanningsstrategier og skoleprestasjoner: sluttrapport fra prosjektet 'Minoritetselevers skoleprestasjoner'* (*To Caesar what Belongs to Caesar? The Education Strategies and Academic Achievement of Minority Pupils. Final Report of the Project: Academic Achievement of Minority Pupils*), Vallset: Oplandske bokforlag.

Fokas, E. (2005) *Welfare and Values in Europe (WaVE): Transitions Related to Religion, Minorities and Gender. Proposal to the European Commission for a Specific Targeted Research Project (STREP) 13/4/2005*. Retrieved from the University of Uppsala, Faculty of Theology.

Fokas, E. (2011) 'State of the art report', in A. Bäckström (ed) *Welfare and Values in Europe: Transitions Related to Religion, Minorities and Gender. National Overviews and Case Study Reports, Volume 1. Northern Europe: Sweden, Norway, Finland, England*, Studies in Religion and Society 4, Uppsala: Acta Universitatis Upsaliensis, pp 13-37.

Graeber, D. (2001) *Toward an Anthropological Theory of Value: The False Coin of our Own Dreams*, New York, NY: Palgrave.

Lamont, M. and White, P. (2009) *Workshop on Interdisciplinary Standards for Systematic Qualitative Research*, Washington, DC: National Science Foundation.

Mitchell, J.C. (1983) 'Case and situation analysis', *Sociological Review*, 31(2): 187-211.

Ragin, C.C. and Amoroso, L.M. (2011) *Constructing Social Research: The Unity and Diversity of Method* (2nd edn), Thousand Oaks, CA: Pine Forge Press.

Ragin, C.C. and Becker, H.S. (eds) (1992) *What is A Case? Exploring the Foundations of Social Inquiry*, Cambridge: Cambridge University Press.

Repstad, P. and Ziebertz, H.-G. (2011) 'Development of methodology (Work Package 2)', in A. Bäckström (ed) *Welfare and Values in Europe: Transitions Related to Religion, Minorities and Gender. National Overviews and Case Study Reports, Volume 1. Northern Europe: Sweden, Norway, Finland, England*, Studies in Religion and Society 4, Uppsala: Acta Universitatis Upsaliensis, pp 289-310.

Small, M.L. (2009) 'How many cases do I need? On science and the logic of case selection in field-based research', *Ethnography*, 10: 5-38.

Sniderman, P.M., Brody, R.A. and Tetlock, P.E. (1991) *Reasoning and Choice: Explorations in Political Psychology*, Cambridge: Cambridge University Press.

Thielst, P. (1994) *Livet forstås baglæns, men må leves forlæns: historien om Søren Kierkegaard* (*Life is Understood Backwards, But Has to be Lived Forwards: The Story of Søren Kierkegaard*), Copenhagen: Gyldendal.

Thomas, G. (2011) *How to Do Your Case Study: A Guide for Students and Researchers*, Los Angeles, CA: Sage.

Van Deth, J.W. and Scarbrough, E. (1995) 'The concept of values', in J.W. Van Deth and E. Scarbrough (eds) *The Impact of Values*, Oxford: Oxford University Press, pp 21-47.

Walton, J. (1992) 'Making the theoretical case', in C.C. Ragin and H.S. Becker (eds) *What Is a Case? Exploring the Foundations of Social Inquiry*, Cambridge: Cambridge University Press, pp 121-37.

Yeung, A.B. (ed) (2006) *Churches in Europe as Agents of Welfare – Sweden, Norway and Finland, Volume 1*, Uppsala: Diakonvetenskapliga institutet.

Yin, R.K. (2014) *Case Study Research: Design and Methods* (5th edn), Los Angeles, CA: Sage.

FOUR

Social cohesion: from research to practice

Olav Helge Angell, Marjukka Laiho, Anne Birgitta Pessi and Siniša Zrinščak

Introduction

In this chapter, we explore the theory and practice of social cohesion in relation to the policy recommendations that were drawn from the findings of the Welfare and Values in Europe: Transitions Related to Religion, Minorities and Gender (WaVE) project. We also discuss how the concept of social cohesion is used in politics and social science more generally, noting the discursive contexts in which it appears. Finally, we use this concept as an analytical tool in our discussion of the policy recommendations that came out of WaVE. We develop our analysis in the context of the circle of cohesion in European localities.

The WaVE project was developed in response to a European Commission call for research to explore how religion is at one and the same time a bearer of solidarity, cohesion and tolerance on the one hand, and of tension, discrimination and xenophobia on the other. It also aimed to gain insight into how societies can ensure the peaceful coexistence of different value systems. How in other words do different European countries address these issues through policies and practices and what is their relative success in so doing?

It is important to note that the concept of social cohesion was not explicitly defined in the WaVE project, thus enabling researchers and participants to approach the values of solidarity, tolerance and cohesion implicitly and in a non-specific, or intuitive way. The outcome was a wide variety of interpretations of the relationships in question. In this chapter, we take a step forward, getting to grips with the meaning or rather meanings of social cohesion, especially its uses in politics and social science. We also reflect on the ways in which the concept so defined can be used to illuminate the findings from the WaVE project.

The concept of social cohesion

Social cohesion in social science and political discourse

The term 'social cohesion' has become widely used over the past decade or so, referring to various types of phenomena, both economic and social. It is associated with different forms of capital, values and ethics. Nevertheless, in many cases its meaning appears rather vague, even in social science publications.

Social science discourse on social cohesion draws its inspiration from sociologists such as Émile Durkheim and Ferdinand Tönnies and their analysis of the transition from a traditional to a modern society – or differences between small-scale communities and large-scale, complex, urban forms (Durkheim, 1984 [1893]; Tönnies, 2001 [1887]). Social cohesion is often analysed in terms of social integration, stability and disintegration (for instance, Berger, 1998). The problem for research is that the approach to social cohesion is rather abstract, with few attempts made to define and operationalise the concept. This renders empirical investigations difficult, thus making it a challenge to establish possible correlations between the level of social cohesion and other socioeconomic aspects of a society (Chan et al, 2006).

Jozef Ritzan and colleagues are more focused, defining social cohesion as a situation in which people collaborate in a way that produces a climate for change (Ritzan et al, 2000, p 6). Social cohesion leaves 'room for manoeuvre', which may produce better institutions and economic development to benefit the poor (p 9).

Political discourse on social cohesion is largely problem-driven. The penchant for policy-oriented recommendations has made the issue of measurement more topical. Within the European Union (EU) population, mobility, ethnic and religious diversity have created new social problems and political challenges that have made participation, both political and civic, an important political theme within a social cohesion perspective (Chan et al, 2006). The concept has become widely used in EU documents, indicating a social phenomenon of great political importance in the union (see, for example, CDCS, 2004). Though its broad use contributes even more to its blurred meaning, it is usually understood to be the opposite of marginalisation, inequality, discrimination and exclusion.

The European Commission defines social cohesion as follows:

> The promotion of social cohesion requires the reduction
> of the disparities which arise from unequal access to

employment opportunities and rewards in the form of income. Such inequality tends to have serious social consequences through the marginalisation of sections of society. (European Commission, 1996, p 14)

From an urban governance perspective, Ade Kearns and Ray Forrest summarise this unclear use of the concept as:

Typically, it [social cohesion] is used in such a way that its meaning is nebulous but at the same time the impression is given that everyone knows what is being referred to. The usual premise is that social cohesion is a good thing, so it is conveniently assumed that further elaboration is unnecessary. (Kearns and Forrest, 2000, p 996)

Some scholars have criticised the use of the concept in political discourse, claiming that social cohesion is a euphemism for social coercion or social control. For example, Suzanne Fitzpatrick and Anwen Jones argue that the government in the United Kingdom prioritises social cohesion over social justice, using 'forceful measures ... for enforcing social cohesion instead of measures that would facilitate higher degrees of social justice' (Fitzpatrick and Jones, 2005, p 389). In their analysis, social cohesion is part of a discourse used to whitewash deep societal fractures rather than addressing the real causes of a socially fractured society, which are often structural injustices or exclusions.

Paul Bernard (1999, p 2) is even more critical, viewing the concept as a 'quasi-concept' or a 'hybrid mental construction' of political correctness. One reason why the situation is described as such may be that the term 'cohesion' is part of ordinary language and therefore ordinary usage by ordinary people. The *Oxford Dictionary of English* defines cohesion as 'the action or fact of forming a united whole' (Soanes and Stevenson, 2005, p 335). Social cohesion thus refers to the social that forms 'a united whole'. This corresponds closely to Kearns and Forrest's idea of social cohesion (Kearns and Forrest, 2000). They provide no explicit definition, but state that 'the kernel of the concept is that a cohesive society "'hangs together'"' (p 996).

Three approaches to social cohesion

In their review of the policy literature on social cohesion, Chan and colleagues identify three main approaches (Chan et al, 2006, p 281 onwards):

- **Means–end approaches** define social cohesion primarily in terms of the means through which a desired end state of society is reached. Regina Berger-Schmitt's way of conceptualising social cohesion offers an example (Berger-Schmitt, 2000). She draws on political documents (both national and EU-level documents) and on social science research literature in her analytical approach. Summarising, she distinguishes two societal goal dimensions that the various uses of the concept incorporate: reducing social inequalities and social exclusion, and strengthening social relations. This distinction correlates with the broad distinction made earlier between goals of equity and justice, and goals of diversity and participation. One problem with this approach is that the two societal goal dimensions specified are perceived as conditions to promote social cohesion; thus the concept is defined in terms of its conditions or causes.

- **Pluralistic approaches** include multiple ways of defining the concept. One example is Jane Jenson's analysis (Jenson, 1998). Her conception of social cohesion, widely cited, is based on a policy literature review. It is therefore more an outcome of an analysis of the existing literature than an attempt to come up with a single definition. Jenson identifies 'five dimensions' of the concept (Jenson, 1998, pp 15-17):
  - belonging versus isolation (which refers to shared values and a sense of identity);
  - inclusion versus exclusion (which refers to opportunities in economic institutions, especially the market);
  - participation versus non-involvement (which refers to political participation at various levels of government, especially the local level);
  - recognition versus rejection (which refers to tolerance of diversity in society);
  - legitimacy versus illegitimacy (which refers to attitudes to political and social institutions).

  On each dimension, the first situation (for example, belonging) contributes to social cohesion, while the second (its reverse, for example, isolation) represents a threat to cohesion. Jenson and others, in pursuing a pluralistic approach on the basis of policy-oriented analyses, demonstrate that in this context the term social cohesion is, by and large, 'a catchword' for incorporating the most pressing social issues of the day (Chan et al, 2006, p 288).

- **Approaches based on the identification of constituent elements** tend to have two types of components in common – objective (associated with behaviour) and subjective (associated with feelings, such as trust and sense of belonging) – and two main dimensions – horizontal (cohesion in civil society) and vertical (state–citizen cohesion) (Chan et al, 2006, pp 293-4). This is the approach that Joseph Chan and colleagues adopt in their definition of social cohesion:

> Social cohesion is a state of affairs concerning both the vertical and the horizontal interactions among members of society as characterized by a set of attitudes and norms that includes trust, a sense of belonging and the willingness to participate and help, as well as their behavioural manifestations. (Chan et al, 2006, p 290)

The components and dimensions of the definition by Chan and colleagues may be put together in the Table 4.1.

Table 4.1: Aspects of social cohesion in Chan et al (2006), by constituent dimensions and components

	Subjective component	Objective component
Horizontal dimension	General trust among fellow citizens Willingness to cooperate and help fellow citizens, including those from 'other' social groups	Social participation and vibrancy of civil society Voluntarism and donations
	Sense of belonging and identity	Presence or absence of major inter-group alliances or cleavages
Vertical dimension	Trust in public figures	Political participation
	Confidence in political and other major social institutions	

Source: Chan et al., 2006: 294.

The subjective elements comprise perceptions, feelings and attitudes, such as trust and confidence, solidarity and belonging. The objective elements relate to how people behave in their relationships with other people and to various types or patterns of actions and interactions. The two dimensions refer to relationships in civil society (horizontal dimension) on the one hand, and attitudes to, and participation in, the political system and other societal institutions on the other (vertical dimension).

Kearns and Forrest's conception of social cohesion mentioned earlier represents the same type of approach. Their explicit interest is in how recent debates on 'urban dynamics and urban governance fit into [the] debates about social cohesion' (Kearns and Forrest, 2000, p 996).

Towards a combined approach: identifying the links between a means- and an end-oriented approach

Against this background, we define social cohesion in this chapter by modifying the definition by Chan and colleagues, and adding normative and subjective components related to tolerance and diversity, as per Isabelle Dimeglio and colleagues (2013, p 759). The two main reasons for this are, first, that the proposed definition identifies components, and second, that empirical research, including a large sample of countries with different types of welfare systems, reveals that the selected elements are statistically interlinked (Janmaat, 2011). The operationalisation of social cohesion as defined above enables us to use indicators of social cohesion, in conjunction with empirically established conditions or means, and the social mechanisms connecting the two. Policy recommendations, therefore, should identify policy-relevant conditions and social mechanisms mediating between conditions and outcome, that is, the level of social cohesion.

Chan et al (2006) and others claim that shared values should not be included in the definition of social cohesion, but should rather be seen as a possible empirical correlation. In the real world, the correlation between level of social cohesion and the degree to which values are shared in a given population or social system may vary, according to cultural context, for example. The presumption is that social systems may have a high level of social cohesion without a shared values system.

However, for the European countries included in the WaVE project – given their increasing ethnic, cultural and religious diversity – it is difficult to think of high levels of social cohesion without people sharing values of tolerance and respect for diversity. For our purposes, then, these values should be added to the subjective component in Table 4.1. Thus, according to our definition, a high level of social cohesion is characterised by the following conditions fulfilled by persons or individuals in the population or social systems we examine:

- people trust, help and cooperate with each other at different levels and in different ways;
- people tolerate and respect others who are different from themselves;

- people share a sense of belonging to, or identification with, the social system in question;
- people manifest these values, attitudes and feelings in the way they behave.

As mentioned in the introduction to this chapter, the WaVE project did not aim to measure degrees or levels of social cohesion in the local communities included in the project. The overall goal was rather to study how the values, attitudes and social interactions of the majority population and minorities contributed to shaping, maintaining, strengthening or undermining both the subjective and objective components of the horizontal and vertical dimensions of social cohesion (as outlined in the previous section) at the local level.

Social tensions and conflicts are not necessarily a threat to the integration of a society; conflict and cohesion are not antonyms. As Lewis Coser suggests, conflict tends to be dysfunctional in social structures only where there is insufficient tolerance or institutionalisation of conflict. Social structures are not threatened by conflict as such; it is rather their rigid character that may threaten them (Coser, 1998 [1956]). Ronald Labonte (2004, p 116) cautions against 'concepts that direct us towards a wishful desire for social harmony', often using suppression, subtly or more overtly, as a tool to achieve such harmony. A greater threat for social cohesion, if one takes Labonte's point, is not protest or disharmony, but the economic and social structures of exclusion and injustice that evoke disharmony or protest. Thus, to the extent that relevant conflicts are identified, it is of interest to study how a local community faces and handles conflicts, and, if relevant, how social structures are modified and changed in order to 'fit' the new situation. If we relate this to the means–end approach to social cohesion, and more specifically to the conditions formulated by Berger-Schmitt (2000), it is likely that a process of systematic social exclusion may in the long run increase chances of tensions or conflicts by causing increased social differences and accompanying frustrations.

We shall combine the means–end and end-oriented approaches outlined here to develop a richer foundation on which to analyse the WaVE findings and policy recommendations. The former focuses on the means or conditions for social cohesion to be achieved or improved, while the latter specifies what is to be achieved or improved. By so doing, what remains is to identify the links between the means and the end, that is, to justify theoretically, or on the basis of empirical research, the mechanisms through which means can be transformed into ends. For policy recommendations to be relevant, they should relate to the links between the means and the ends. Using Berger-Schmitt's approach as an example, the key question that emerges is how an increased level of social integration or inclusion (as a result of policy implementation) may contribute to increased levels of tolerance and respect, trust and cooperation, and a greater sense of belonging.

Policy recommendations: from the researchers' voices to the cycle of social cohesion

Social cohesion – however defined – is not easy to achieve. While the main responsibility for building a socially cohesive society in Europe is at the national level, an awareness of varying situations at the local level is also needed. One of the key findings in the WaVE comparative cross-country analysis was that most majority–minority interactions in the domain of welfare lie somewhere in between conflict and cohesion, in a large grey area. In addition, conflict and cohesion appear along complex – rather than dichotomous – lines; for example, sometimes a conflict in the short term is seen as a prerequisite for achieving long-term cohesion. In addition, resources (such as time, space and money) and communication (such as the role of the media or language) reveal conflicts of interests rather than conflicts of values. According to the WaVE case studies, these types of everyday factors play a remarkable role in creating mutually constructive or destructive interactions between majorities and minorities (Fokas, 2009, pp 2-3).

One of the requirements of the European Commission, which funded the project, was to formulate the research results into 'research-based, concrete, and practical suggestions to policy-makers, aiming to give support to political planning, guidance and decision-making'.[1] With multifaceted perceptions of social cohesion and social inclusion, the WaVE researchers were faced with the challenge of drafting policy recommendations at the end of their research. To do this, the researchers translated their research findings from each and every WaVE case study into policy recommendations and political visions, thus using 'data from data'. In a way, these recommendations communicated the very practical and even normative voices of the 'researchers'.

While drawing up the policy recommendations, the WaVE researchers relied mostly on their background analysis of the national situations in each country (the 'state of the art' reports) and the case study reports from each local context. The national and local dissemination reports for each country also provided essential information for the formulation of the policy recommendations. They were drawn from all of the 13 case studies from the 12 countries that were studied and included local, national and European-level policy recommendations.[2] They were drafted along three distinct, but intertwined, themes:

- mechanisms and practices leading to cooperation or cohesion;
- mechanisms and practices leading to tensions or conflict;
- recommendations applicable at the local, national and EU level on how to enhance cooperation/cohesion and resolve tensions/conflict.

The local and national policy recommendations reflected the specific context of each country, so they were not formulated as being applicable to other contexts. The European-level policy recommendations were drafted using a comparative and synthetic analysis of the local and national policy recommendations, thus revealing the cross-cutting issues emerging from the WaVE case studies;[3] they also often referred to implicit (rather than explicit) values and to the idea of social cohesion as a means of promoting an open conversation by creating guidelines, or sensitising European politics to certain social issues. In this chapter, our focus and further analysis is on the concrete and comparable national policy recommendations that articulated the main mechanisms and practices that contribute towards social cohesion and support local level actions. This emphasis on the local is strongly in line with the principle of subsidiarity, which has been crucial in the functioning of the European Community right from the start.[4]

Drafting the policy recommendations in each local case study was not carried out in light of any theoretical framework but was solely data-driven by a qualitative content analysis of each case study (for example, Schreier, 2014). Thus the findings pertaining to policy from the perspective of social cohesion from each case study was, and still is, an inductive result of analysis, rather than a guiding framework established at the beginning of the project. The process of putting together the policy recommendations aspired to treat the data as a whole, but to code it in a way that enabled comparison while keeping track of the specificities of the case study in question. In drafting the policy recommendations, the respective WaVE researchers were particularly careful to acknowledge that the case- or country-specific findings could not always be generalised to other cases. At the end of the project, the policy recommendations were reported to the European Commission and published online (Laiho et al, 2011).

Policy recommendations along 11 key themes

In line with the above-mentioned guidelines, the cross-cutting themes that run through the policy recommendations concerned religion and minorities and, to a lesser extent, gender, very much in line with the scope of the WaVE research as a whole. They were formulated using the following 11 themes, each one examined in a variety of local and national contexts (Laiho et al, 2011). The themes were grouped into two main categories according to resource factors (action) and communicative factors (information), thus putting the focus on mechanisms, practices and interests, rather than on values. The end result was the development of policy recommendations aiming to improve information and improve action.

The themes can also be analysed in terms of Berger-Schmitt's two goal dimensions: the *means* to achieve the *end* of social cohesion (Berger-Schmitt, 2000). In that perspective, they can be subsumed under the goal category of reducing social inequalities and social exclusion, while some of them concern the strengthening of social relations – they are not mutually exclusive.

• Improve the information

Religion: opportunities and risks
Religious communities or organisations can be a remarkable asset in providing welfare services and promoting communality. This is particularly important when services are provided as a result of the spiritual and religious orientation of the community offering them. Yet the help and assistance does not depend on the ethnicity, faith or religiosity of the users. However, a faith community that is too dominant or whose self-definition is too narrow was at times perceived to be a risk and one that might lead to the marginalisation and discrimination of minority groups.

Diversity in society: the need for more and better information
There is a need for multilingual and culturally sensitive information to reach minorities and to educate the majority about minorities. Both the information offered on welfare services and its dissemination channels need to be improved in culturally, religiously and gender-sensitive ways in order to reach the target groups.

Minority involvement in decision making
The WaVE case studies offered practical suggestions on how to improve the involvement of minorities in the planning and decision-making processes related to welfare. An active involvement of minorities may have many positive effects, including empowerment of the minorities themselves, enhancement of mutual understanding between majorities and minorities, and better capacity to build welfare services suited to a pluralist society.

Networking: efficiency through coordination
Developing better methods of sharing information between different organisations at all levels of society (local, national, EU) was seen as crucially important to establish networks in order to enhance and share best practice to help achieve similar goals.

Availability of statistical information
Demands for better indicators, statistics, research and evaluation were seen as universal throughout Europe. In this context, approaches that are both internationally comparative and locally sensitive were needed. Sharing adequate and reliable information is a basis for improving a welfare provision that is both culture- and gender-sensitive.

• Improve the action

The importance of proximity: distance matters
The importance of proximity emerged as a cross-cutting issue in almost all the WaVE case studies. Respecting the local situation and taking local knowledge into account were crucial in fostering social cohesion, thus applying the principle of subsidiarity. All European and national policies succeed or fail at the local level, which underlines the need for respecting the local situation and involving local groups and communities.

The importance of language skills
The need for majority and minority groups to be able to communicate through a common language was a key practical factor in building social cohesion. This is evident in the many requests made by minorities to have access to language training. Language was often connected with general social skills and a successful schooling and working life. The importance of language skills was thus connected with fostering social inclusion.

Challenges for the education systems
The new and growing reality of diverse student bodies in European education systems requires an effective response. This is of concern to both majorities and minorities. Equal opportunities, access to schooling, and ongoing support were flagged as priority areas.

The importance of work
Regardless of religion, culture or gender, work has an important role for individuals and for society as a whole. Equal opportunities in the workplace, a good work and family life balance and support of equal working opportunities for migrants are strong contributing factors to social cohesion. The WaVE case studies pointed to the crucial issue of promoting work opportunities for as many people as possible. Equal employment opportunity was thus recognised as a key factor of social cohesion.

Cultural and gender sensitivity to welfare services
Several WaVE case studies raised very directly the need for greater cultural and gender sensitivity in welfare provision. Cultural sensitivity is becoming a precondition in planning and offering services to different groups. The policy recommendations consisted mainly of educating welfare providers on issues of cultural diversity and effective communication.

Challenges to the political systems
Political and legal systems, resources, administration and policies require constant review and improvement in order to protect the value of religious and gender equality, especially for minorities, that is so crucial for social cohesion. The WaVE case studies indicated that in eastern and southern European countries these are significant challenges to the political systems at both local and national levels.

The cycle of social cohesion

The themes of information/communication and resources/actions can be further summarised under the categories of 'know' and 'how'. This is the key idea behind the cycle of cohesion model presented in this chapter (see Figure 4.1). It includes both context and process. The political systems involved in the WaVE study make up the background, consisting of that which creates the context of the whole cycle: political systems referring to the power structures that enable the cycle to work (or not). In the proposed model, this also applies to the crucial role of values 'enabling' social cohesion: the values of tolerance and respect for diversity. For the cycle of social cohesion to work, there needs to be political support for a society 'that hangs together' (Kearns and Forrest, 2000). The political system must help create the necessary societal conditions for this to happen (see Ritzan et al, 2000).

Religion was considered to be a key factor among others. It was also viewed as an emblematic characteristic of the majority and/or minorities having a practical effect on social and political issues. While religion was definitely included in the study of welfare in both the majority and minority communities of the WaVE case studies, it was considered more of a practical than an ideological issue. For example, the key questions related to religion concerned knowledge of religious traditions rather than a clash of conflicting values. The same approach was applied to gender in the sense that gender was taken into account in the study as a practical issue.

In the cycle of cohesion, 'knowing/knowledge' refers in most instances to a better understanding of diversity, of 'the other' – whether majority or minority. Understanding is crystallised in the idea of involvement, that is, incorporating the user perspective in the planning and providing of social welfare services (for example, Beresford, 2000). 'How' refers to the crucial skills and everyday practices of becoming aware of new forms of 'knowing/knowledge'. This means, for example, ensuring that minorities have access to education and work and improving the language skills of both minorities and majorities, not only with the minorities learning the majority language but also encouraging and supporting multilingualism in the majority society in order to find a shared language of communication.[5]

In short, it is the 'know' and the 'how' (that is, the 'know-how') that constitutes the key mechanism of a means–end approach to social cohesion, moving from the means to the desired outcome. At the same time, we must note the essential conditions within which the know-how approach can work. The subjective and objective components of social cohesion (Chan et al, 2006) are linked to each other in a dynamic relationship. Both the subjective components (such as feelings of trust, a sense of belonging and cooperation) and the context (social and political conditions) contribute to the objective components (behaviour, such as social and political participation and volunteerism) and vice versa. This emphasises not only the importance of political systems, but also the values of tolerance and respect for diversity as preconditions for the mechanism of the cycle of social cohesion to work.

Figure 4.1: The cycle of social cohesion

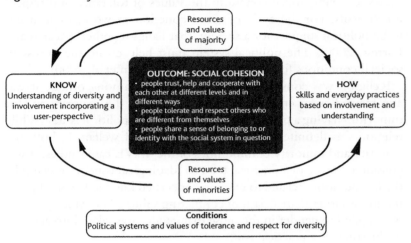

A crucial finding in the cycle of cohesion is the notion that any differences in values between the majority and minorities are not key features in promoting or challenging a high level of social cohesion. It is rather the success in 'know' (understanding)–'how' (practices) that is the crucial mechanism in strengthening or weakening social cohesion. Even if tolerance and respect for diversity are central values in social cohesion, it is the practices of everyday life (see de Certeau, 1984) in seeking understanding and involvement that give life to these values. Welfare and values are not just ideal, abstract notions, but concrete, everyday practices.

Religion, social cohesion and citizenship

The question of religion in the context of 'positive social cohesion'[6] in relation to minorities may be a specifically challenging issue in Europe, in compaison, for instance, with the United States. A crucial difference between the European and American way of integrating immigrants relates to a costly welfare state in Europe versus private welfare solutions in the US. Because of the primarily collective welfare arrangements, the integration of immigrants in Europe is both more difficult and more (much more) costly.[7] More importantly, if diversity has increasingly become part of the European integration process (de Schoutheete, 2000, p 63; Prügl and Thiel, 2009), the idea of homogeneity remains implicit even today on account of Europe's religious history (particularly the historical presence of dominant national Christian churches). For this reason it is much harder for

Europe to embrace cultural diversity and multiple religions than it is for the United States (Casanova, 2005, 2009). Thus, for instance, as José Casanova (2009) has noted, 'the manifest difficulty which all European societies have in the integration of Muslim immigrants can be viewed as an indication of the problems which the model of the European nation-state has ... in regulating deep religious pluralism.... Islam is indeed the elephant in the room in any discussion of religion and secular modernity' (p 25).[8]

These observations raise a crucial question: is a truly secular state (the definition of which may be an elusive idea in itself) a precondition for a truly multi-faith, multi-religious — and (it is to be hoped) socially cohesive — community? This is a highly complex issue. The case of France and its regime of separation between church and state (*laïcité*) is particularly instructive here, as it highlights some of the challenges of a rigorously secular state in managing ethnic and religious diversity. Peggy Levitt's analysis of the way immigrants are changing the face of religious diversity in the US offers a contrasting example. According to Levitt, new realities of religion and migration (particularly immigrants who often keep one foot in their country of origin through their religious participation in the US) are transforming, and indeed challenging, the very definition of what it means to be American (Levitt, 2007). Levitt's analysis underscores the fundamental differences between the US and Europe in this respect.

That said, recent debates in Europe reveal the growing and increasingly public role of religion, particularly in the field of social welfare.[9] The idea of post-secularity, referring to a renewed interest in spiritual life and new public roles for churches, is a topic of discussion and debate among social science researchers.[10] Religion is also gaining influence within national and local spaces, particularly with regard to the role of 'communities of interpretation' in the public arena of secular societies (Habermas, 2008). This chapter has illustrated the role not only of religion as such in this respect, but of strong links between local communities and local forms of religion. Strengthening both community and religious pluralism requires the participation of immigrants as citizens at the local level. It is this essentially civic participation that can promote, in the long run, the cycle of social cohesion. In this respect, congregations can serve as melting pots that attract a diverse membership and act as catalysts for interactions between members from different ethnic and religious communities. For example, members in multiracial congregations in the United States are far more likely than in Europe to have a multiracial circle of friends (Emerson and Woo, 2006). So perhaps it will be possible for members of majorities and minorities in Europe to participate in shared forms of social life, both religious and non-religious, at the local level.

Conversely, policies that support the distinct characteristics and traditions of minorities may prove to be problematic for integration and the cohesion of a society as a whole. Thus Albert Musschenga concluded that, although all cultures have intrinsic values, cultural majority groups should only preserve deviant 'minority cultures that are in some sense alien to them' because they have considerable intrinsic value (Musschenga, 1998, p 223). As part of his theory of the intrinsic value of culture, he makes his case using the example of Islamic minorities, such as Moroccans, in Dutch society. He argues that the culture of (Muslim) Moroccans in contemporary Dutch society is unique and alien and that therefore its assimilation into Dutch majority culture should be resisted in favour of integration.[11] The best scenario may in fact be a multi-ethnic and cohesive approach that promotes active citizenship and civic participation. This is in line with an argument based on the recognition of cultural collective rights (Parekh, 2006). Also, as the philosopher Amartya Sen (2007) has concluded, against (what he calls) 'singular identities', all majorities and minorities are in the end equally heterogeneous. Thus, true, free and will-based social cohesion has to rise from a multi-humanity viewpoint, not from any particular group(s), or even minorities. This approach would make the transition towards participation and citizenship of multiple identities.

Conclusion

This chapter has approached social cohesion in relation to the policy recommendations that came out of the findings of the WaVE project. The strongest message that came from the case studies is the wish of minorities to be part of the majority society while preserving their ethnic, religious, linguistic, and lifestyle traditions, differences and needs. In other words, minorities view integration as peaceful coexistence, not as becoming similar or identical to the majority. This message is consistent with the way the majority of Europeans wish their future to be. 'Europeans want a free society in which solidarity and social equality are of primary importance', and 'the chief element of a European identity is to have democratic values, and the strongest factor in terms of being European is to "feel European"' (European Commission, 2010a, p 162). Indeed, promoting open-minded attitudes and behaviours and encouraging experiences and interactions between majorities and minorities are factors that have the strongest positive influence on discrimination and people's views of minorities (European Commission, 2009).

Concerning policy recommendations, our analysis has indicated that social cohesion can be achieved only through concrete practices, as summarised in Figure 4.1. Since EU 2020 (the EU's growth strategy for the coming decade)[12] leaves the application of the goals of social inclusion and reduction of poverty up to national authorities, our findings suggest that this entails both threats and opportunities: threats because – for many different reasons – countries can make social cohesion a low priority in national policy agendas; opportunities because any effective policy can theoretically be adapted to the diverse needs of different social groups, depending on both the national and local contexts.

Given the increasingly challenging economic situation in Europe, the revisited cycle of social cohesion and policy recommendations has cost implications. Policy recommendations are dependent on material and human resources, both of which may be severely limited, especially in southern and eastern Europe. That said, owing precisely to the fact that money is short, the findings of the WaVE project are more apposite than ever. As the chapters in Part Three of this book illustrate, new spaces are opening up for welfare providers – from local minority networks to majority churches – all taking an active role in welfare.

The data reveal that the negative factors tearing down the possibilities for greater social cohesion range from practical to ideological issues. These include the lack of cultural competence of welfare providers and social carers, including the cultural awareness of user perspectives; the external labelling and stereotyping of minority groups, often promoted by the media; the spatial segregation of different groups, including language barriers; and poorly formulated immigration policies. Such factors are all the more relevant given the escalation in immigration in 2015-16. Faced with a humanitarian crisis of this nature, it becomes clearer almost by the day that the political efforts required to address the social, economic and political inclusion of (religious) minorities in Europe have barely begun. A great deal more work needs to be done in this area.

Notes

[1] The chosen terminology follows the guidelines of the WaVE Researchers' Handbook and the recommendations from the Finnish National Contact Point for the European Commission's 6th Framework Programme. The policy recommendations were initially part of an obligatory interim report included in the project.

2 Noting as before that there were two case studies in Germany to reflect the country's equally important Catholic and Protestant populations.

3 Three WaVE researchers representing the Finnish team drafted the original policy recommendations document to the European Commission; see Laiho et al (2009).

4 According to the subsidiarity principle, defined in the treaty establishing the European Community, decisions should be taken as close as possible to citizens. This limits the decisions and actions taken at European level only to those that are in its exclusive competence, or are justified by the principles of proportionality and necessity. For more information, see Zrinščak (2006).

5 It seems that the cycle of social cohesion still reflects, even if partially, the newest political discourse of the European Council, which puts particular emphasis on employment; see European Commission (2010b).

6 We use the notion of 'positive social cohesion' to refer to minority-respecting policies towards networks, cohesion, and integration – policies in which plurality is considered a positive value in itself.

7 On the role of religion in relation to social justice for immigrants, see, for example, Hondagneu-Sotelo (2007).

8 See also Davie (2012).

9 For example, Bäckström et al (2010); Pessi (2008).

10 See Knauss and Ornella (2007); Habermas (2008); Ziebertz and Riegel (2009); Dalferth (2010).

11 Musschenga defines assimilation as 'total immersion in the receiving society and accommodation to its dominant culture', and integration as 'a reciprocal process whereby the dominant group and the ethnic-cultural groups adopt certain elements of each other's culture, without disappearance of all cultural differences. A precondition for such a process to take place is the development of mutual respect and appreciation of the other culture' (Musschenga, 1998, p 202).

12 This document refers to the objectives relating to employment, innovation, education, social inclusion and climate/energy to be reached by 2020 (http://ec.europa.eu/europe2020/index_en.htm).

References

Bäckström, A. and Davie, G., with Edgardh, N. and Pettersson, P. (eds) (2010) *Welfare and Religion in 21st Century Europe: Volume 1. Configuring Connections*, Farnham: Ashgate.

Beresford, P. (2000) 'Service users' knowledges and social work theory: conflict or collaboration?', *British Journal of Social Work*, 30(4): 489–503.

Berger, P.L. (ed) (1998) *The Limits of Social Cohesion: Conflict and Mediation in Pluralist Societies: A Report of the Bertelsmann Foundation to the Club of Rome*, Boulder, CO: Westview Press.

Berger-Schmitt, R. (2000) *Social Cohesion as an Aspect of the Quality of Societies: Concept and Measurement, Volume 14*, Mannheim: Centre for Survey Research and Methodology, available at www.gesis.org/fileadmin/upload/dienstleistung/daten/soz_indikatoren/eusi/paper14.pdf.

Bernard, P. (1999) *Social Cohesion: A Critique*, CPRN Discussion Paper No. F/09, Ottawa: Canadian Policy Research Networks, available at awww.cprn.org/documents/15743_en.pdf.

Casanova, J. (2005) 'Immigration and the new religious pluralism: A European Union/United States comparison', Paper presented at the conference *The New Religious Pluralism and Democracy*, Georgetown University, Washington, DC, 21-22 April.

Casanova, J. (2009) 'Are we still secular? Exploring the post-secular: three meanings of "the secular" and their possible transcendence', Paper presented at the Institute for Public Knowledge, New York University, 22-24 October.

CDCS (European Committee for Social Cohesion) (2004) *A New Strategy for Social Cohesion*, Strasbourg: CDCS.

Chan, J., To, H.-P. and Chan, E. (2006) 'Reconsidering social cohesion: developing a definition and analytical framework for empirical research', *Social Indicators Research*, 75(2): 273-302.

Coser, L.A. (1998 [1956]) *The Functions of Social Conflict*, London: Routledge.

Dalferth, I.U. (2010) 'Post-secular society: Christianity and the dialectics of the secular', *Journal of the American Academy of Religion*, 78(2): 317-45.

Davie, G. (2012) 'A European perspective on religion and welfare: contrasts and commonalities', *Social Policy and Society*, 11(4): 589-99.

de Certeau, M. (1984) *The Practice of Everyday Life*, Berkeley, CA: University of California.

de Schoutheete, P. (2000) *The Case for Europe. Unity, Diversity, and Democracy in the European Union*, Boulder, CO: Lynne Rienner Publishers.

Dimeglio, I., Janmaat, J.G. and Mehaut, P. (2013) 'Social cohesion and the labour market: societal regimes of civic attitudes and labour market regimes', *Social Indicators Research*, 111(3): 753-73.

Durkheim, É. (1984 [1893]) *The Division of Labour in Society*, London: Macmillan.

Emerson, M.O. and Woo, R.M. (2006) *People of the Dream: Multiracial Congregations in the United States*, Princeton, NJ: Princeton University Press.

European Commission (1996) *First Cohesion Report*, Luxembourg: Office for Official Publication of the European Committees.

European Commission (2009) 'Discrimination in the EU in 2009. Special Eurobarometer', available at http://ec.europa.eu/public_opinion/archives/ebs/ebs_317_en.pdf.

European Commission (2010a) 'Eurobarometer 71. Future of Europe', available at http://ec.europa.eu/public_opinion/archives/eb/eb71/eb713_future_europe.pdf.

European Commission (2010b) 'A strategy for smart, sustainable and inclusive growth', Communication from the Commission: Europe 2020, available at http://ec.europa.eu/eu2020/pdf/COMPLET%20EN%20BARROSO%20%20%20007%20-%20Europe%202020%20-%20EN%20version.pdf.

Fitzpatrick, S. and Jones, A. (2005) 'Pursuing social justice or social cohesion? Coercion in street homelessness policies in England', *Journal of Social Policy*, 34(3): 389–406.

Fokas, E. (2009) *Welfare and Values in Europe: A Comparative Cross-Country Analysis*, Report for the European Commission funded Framework 6 Project on Welfare and Values in Europe: Transitions Related to Religion, Minorities and Gender, Brussels: European Commission.

Habermas, J. (2008) 'Notes on a post-secular society', available at www.signandsight.com/features/1714.html.

Hondagneu-Sotelo, P. (ed) (2007) *Religion and Social Justice for Immigrants*, New Brunswick, NJ: Rutgers University Press.

Janmaat, J.G. (2011) 'Social cohesion as a real-life phenomenon: assessing the explanatory power of the universalist and particularist perspectives', *Social Indicators Research*, 100(1): 61–83.

Jenson, J. (1998) *Mapping Social Cohesion: The State of Canadian Research*, CPRN Study No. F/03, Ottawa: Canadian Policy Research Networks, available at www.cprn.org/documents/15723_en.pdf.

Kearns, A. and Forrest, R. (2000) 'Social cohesion and multilevel urban governance', *Urban Studies*, 37(5/6): 995–1017.

Knauss, S. and Ornella, A.D. (eds) (2007) *Reconfigurations. Interdisciplinary Perspectives on Religion in a Post-Secular Society*, Berlin: LIT.

Labonte, R. (2004) 'Social inclusion/exclusion: dancing the dialectic', *Health Promotion International*, 19(1): 115–21.

Laiho, M., Pessi, A.B. and Helander, E. (2009) *Welfare and Values in Europe: Policy Recommendations on Three Levels – European Level and National (Regional/Local) Levels*, Report for the European Commission funded Framework 6 Project on Welfare and Values in Europe: Transitions Related to Religion, Minorities and Gender, Brussels: European Commission.

Laiho, M., Pessi, A.B. and Zrinščak, S. (2011) 'Welfare and values in Europe: from research to practise of social cohesion', *International Beliefs and Values Institute*, 3(1), available at http://bav.ibavi.org/index.php/beliefs-and-values/issue/view/12.

Levitt, P. (2007) *God Needs No Passport. Immigrants and the Changing American Religious Landscape*, New York, NY: The New Press.

Musschenga, A.W. (1998). 'Intrinsic value as a reason for the preservation of minority cultures', *Ethical Theory and Moral Practice*, 1: 201-25.

Parekh, B. (2006) *Rethinking Multiculturalism. Cultural Diversity and Political Theory*, Basingstoke: Palgrave Macmillan.

Pessi, A.B. (2008) 'Religion and social problems: Individual and institutional responses', in P. Clark (ed) *The Oxford Handbook of the Sociology of Religion*, Oxford: Oxford University Press, pp 941-61.

Prügl, E. and Thiel M. (eds) (2009) *Diversity in the European Union*, New York, NY: Palgrave Macmillan.

Ritzan, J., Easterly, W. and Woolcock, M. (2000) *On 'Good' Politicians and 'Bad' Policies: Social Cohesion, Institutions, and Growth*, Policy Research Working Paper 2448, Washington, DC: World Bank Publications.

Schreier, M. (2014) 'Qualitative content analysis', in U. Flick (ed) *The Sage Handbook of Qualitative Data Analysis*, London: Sage, pp 170-83.

Sen, A. (2007) *Identity and Violence: The Illusion of Destiny*, London: Penguin.

Soanes, C. and Stevenson, A. (eds) (2005) *Oxford Dictionary of English* (2nd edn), Oxford: Oxford University Press.

Tönnies, F. (2001 [1887]) *Community and Civil Society*, Cambridge: Cambridge University Press.

Ziebertz, H. and Riegel U. (2009) 'Europe: a post-secular society?', *International Journal of Public Theology*, 13: 293-8.

Zrinščak, S. (2006) 'Subsidiarity', in T. Fitzpatrick et al (eds) *International Encyclopaedia of Social Policy*, London: Routledge, pp.1366-9.

Part Two:
Thinking regionally: key case studies in welfare and religion in Europe

FIVE

The WaVE project as a record of religious and social transformations in northern Europe

Anders Bäckström

Introduction

Welfare and Values in Europe: Transitions Related to Religion, Minorities and Gender (WaVE), and its predecessor Welfare and Religion in a European Perspective: A Comparative Study of the Role of the Churches as Agents of Welfare within the Social Economy (WREP), focused on two aspects of European society that have been interconnected throughout history. Social care, as an expression of social concern, has always been central to religion (Glock and Stark, 1965; Smart, 1993). Similarly, nation states through different forms of governance have always had responsibility for caring for the poor, sick, disabled and elderly. This responsibility has however shifted over time, moving between public institutions (the state), the family, and religious, non-profit or private actors.

This 'interactive' relationship between the welfare state and religion was thought to have reached an end during the so-called golden decades of the welfare state in Europe following the Second World War. In the Nordic countries, and particularly in Sweden, this development was expressed in the high value placed on democracy, equality and private freedoms, alongside high levels of trust in societal institutions (Rothstein, 2011). This combination was increasingly associated with a secular view of society, as the World Values Survey (WVS) has shown.[1] Moreover, the Swedish (Nordic) approach was considered a model for the world to follow (Inglehart, 1997). The Swedes themselves perceived this way of working to be the culmination of civilisational development in the spirit of Fukuyama (1992), resulting in a feeling that their country was exceptional as far as social morality was concerned (Uvell, 2016).

At the same time, it has become increasingly clear that Sweden is subject to the same transformations that have characterised the western world since the 1980s. This is reflected in the increasing deregulation of welfare institutions (school, healthcare and social care) which has both social and ideological foundations. The former reflect the increased costs brought about by a variety of factors, including migration, social exclusion and the demands of an ageing population. The latter are based on a market approach, underpinned by a customer- and efficiency-oriented perspective in which the users of social welfare are viewed as 'clients' served within a cost-benefit perspective. In this context, the notion of 'civil society' was introduced in the 1990s as a unifying concept among groups and networks outside the realm of the state, the market and the family (Harding, 2012). The concept was launched as a response to increasing social costs and as an ideological answer to the decreasing role of the nation state and of the 20th-century folk movements (Jeppsson Grassman, 2010).

In the same way, migration and the appearance of new vulnerable groups have reinforced the role of religion as a social actor – a partner in cooperation with the state and civil society organisations. Individual requirements for enhancing existential security and happiness have also played a part. Therefore, the interaction between religion and the welfare state has once again become topical, but under the specific conditions of advanced industrial societies and their focus on governance. The nation state is looking beyond traditional definitions and borders, and has identified religion as one of several partners in a national conversation (Martikainen and Gauthier, 2013). In this chapter I argue that a new ecology of cooperation and conversation is playing a role in formulating a future social contract (Wijkström, 2012). A key question is how we can understand the role of religious voices in a conversation that is integral to the development of a democratic society, echoing a point made by Habermas (2006).

The WaVE and WREP projects are examples of a renewed research interest in the interaction between religion and the welfare state, in addition to the ever-present role of informal charitable social work. In this chapter, the focus is on the Swedish situation with its growing levels of civil society engagement, but noting its somewhat contradictory tendencies when it comes to the role of religious minorities. Comparisons will be made with Britain, with its emphasis on a mixed economy, and with Germany, where diaconal and other voluntary organisations have considerable influence in the areas of welfare. As Sweden becomes part of a global economic and cultural community, the strengths and weaknesses of the Swedish universal welfare model are revealed.

I start with the role of religion in the creation of distinct welfare regimes in Europe. I then present the difficulties in defining the underlying concepts of welfare, religion, minorities and gender in the WaVE project. Four theoretical issues follow, which form an important background to the two studies: values related to younger folk movements; conservative versus liberal approaches to social issues; different aspects of cooperation; and the appearance of a voluntary sector in Sweden. My main argument is that the welfare contributions of the Nordic majority churches lie in their integration into a typical Nordic 'cool' or inclusive culture of trust; thus their contribution to charity work should be seen as secondary. I also argue that the growing presence of religious minorities as a result of migration is regarded both as an asset (mirroring the benefits of a global vibrant economy) but also as a problem (expressing a distinctive form of religiousness that is foreign to Swedish culture).

Welfare and religion: the background

Three welfare regimes

The theoretical model underlying the WaVE project was developed by Gøsta Esping-Andersen (1990), who distinguished three dominant welfare regimes in Europe.[2] The Nordic social democratic regime is based on the state's responsibility for a universal allocation policy where citizenship is the basic criterion of financial support. The continental conservative regime is based on the family and on means-tested social provision. Social care and insurance provision depend on participation in the labour market. At the same time, the Catholic notion of subsidiarity, namely the idea of support at the lowest possible level in society, is fundamental. This idea has been implemented in a very consistent manner in Germany, even though the country is bi-confessional. The German system is built on a principle of social insurance that helps to finance the activities of voluntary organisations, the so-called 'Wohlfartsverbände'. The Catholic Caritas and the Protestant Diakonie Deutschland have a dominant position in the welfare market (Biendarra and Leis-Peters, 2012). The liberal Anglo-Saxon welfare regime is similar to the American private system, but with the key difference that healthcare and pensions in Britain are regulated by the state and available to all citizens. This model is characterised by a strong belief in individual freedom and private property, as well as by a certain scepticism towards the state and a preference for limiting the presence of the state in the welfare sector. The role of the market is also comparatively prominent, as illustrated by the role of private organisations in social welfare (Middlemiss Lé Mon, 2011).

Religion: the missing piece in welfare

Esping-Andersen paid little attention to the religious factor. The WaVE project considered this shortcoming in relation to the work of Manow (2004) and van Kersbergen and Manow (2009). Following their argument, the Lutheran countries of northern Europe, including Germany (Prussia), were the first to develop systems of welfare and social insurance, with Catholic and 'reformed' countries adopting these ideas rather later. Steered by the notion of the two kingdoms, the Lutheran churches legitimised this type of welfare regime through the theology of calling and trust in the state (Pettersson, 2011). The Catholic Church, on the other hand, actively tried to hinder the expansion of the state into aspects of society regarded as central to its own identity (notably the role of the family in social care). There were similar doubts in countries influenced by reformed theology (Switzerland and to some extent the Netherlands and England). This time, however, the hesitation was due to theological and political forms of individualism. Self-reliance, rather than social care, became the supreme virtue. This resulted in different religious and social developments in northern and southern, as well as continental, Europe. Against the supposition that the welfare state is solely a secular project, the WaVE project has highlighted that religion is a significant factor in the development of welfare regimes in Europe. That legacy is still observable, though is somewhat less visible in social scientific research.

What is welfare?

The WaVE project interview guide included seven questions that were put to the representatives of the majority churches, the religious minorities and the municipalities in all countries. The first question asked was: 'In your opinion, what is welfare?'[3] The interview schedule was initially formulated from a Nordic European perspective. It became increasingly evident, however, that the notion of welfare was practically unknown in southern Europe and thus difficult to define. In France, moreover, civil servants were not allowed to answer questions that made reference to religion. The first interesting finding, then, was that the concept of welfare as such varied considerably between northern, southern and eastern Europe and was, therefore, difficult to use as a general term.

The second finding concerned the gradual widening of the concept. Clearly welfare is about financial security through social insurance and financial assistance, especially in the Nordic context. At the same time, the idea of welfare has been broadened to entail a more nuanced sense of wellbeing, which has to do with the quality of an individual's life. This discovery connects closely to Erik Allardt's (1975) commonly used definition of welfare: 'to have, to love and to be'. 'Having' relates to financial and material security, while 'loving' and 'being' refer to social relations and to the individual's quality of life. It has become increasingly clear that welfare and wellbeing, as quality of life values, concern individual existential questions (Norris and Inglehart, 2004). This is an aspect of welfare that relates closely to the role of religious institutions as they meet the need for security and trust on the part of individuals. They also respond to existential questions associated with the vicissitudes of life (Jeppsson Grassman, 2010). This description comes close to the expanded definition of health by the World Health Organization.[4] In advanced post-industrial societies, the boundaries between these dimensions of welfare, wellbeing and health have become ever more fluid. The degree of post-industrial development is therefore significant when analysing the concept of welfare.

Religion beyond faith in God

A dilemma in researching the social (welfare) role of 'religion' is the lack of clarity surrounding the concept. As Zygmunt Bauman (1998) has so aptly expressed it, everyone knows what religion is until the concept has to be defined. In the Nordic countries, this ambiguity was already apparent in the 19th century with the pietist emphasis on individual conversion and the feeling of certainty with regard to salvation. This was an understanding that developed in contrast to a somewhat ossified state church and operated in parallel with movements or philosophies that criticised religion, aiming to free the individual from religious superstition. This ambivalence continues. As David Thurfjell (2015) states, the way religion is understood in the 20th century has been marked by opposition between two minorities: the highly religious and the highly anti-religious. The large in-between group that had a vague and largely immanent philosophy of life encompassing the values of modern society was defined as non-religious. For this in-between group, citizenship and membership in the national church have been closely linked; conversely a substantively defined belief in God has not been considered necessary (Martin, 2009). Thus the majority of Swedes do not regard themselves as religious, even if they are members of the Church of Sweden, baptise their children, and bury their relatives according to the rites of the Church. I argue that this in-between category represents a 'soft' or 'cool' religiosity that is not dependent on specific beliefs or religious commitment.[5] It stands in contrast to groups representing a 'hard' or 'hot' religiosity that favour scriptural beliefs, strong religious commitment and frequent practice. This is illustrated in Figure 5.1.

Figure 5.1: Four different types of religion

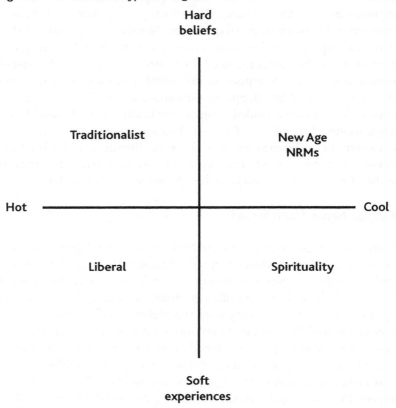

Note: NRMs are New Religious Movements.

This thinking connects to Grace Davie's model of vicarious religion, that is, the notion that religion is 'performed by an active minority but on behalf of a much larger number, who (implicitly at least) not only understand, but, quite clearly, approve of what the minority is doing' (Davie, 2013, p 22). It is a model that resonates well in northern Protestant Europe where religious commitment measured by church going and belief has always been low (Willander, 2014). A survey of the population in Sweden (2012) shows that a higher percentage feel a sense of belonging to the Church of Sweden (77%) than are members of the Church (65%) (Hollmer and Bäckström, 2013). This illustrates that cultural feelings of belonging are not necessarily connected to membership in the majority churches but to a general agreement about the values and rites performed by the churches. Abby Day (2011) has referred to this connectedness between culture and religion as 'believing in belonging'.

The figure also illustrates the fact that a 'hot' commitment can be combined with a 'soft' image of belief. It represents a form of religion that combines a liberal and inclusive understanding of the relationship between church and society. There are also groups that combine a 'cool' religious commitment with a 'hard' faith in external forces that control humanity, for example, fatalist determinism or astrology, which is captured under the umbrella of the New Age.

This overview raises a pertinent question: who is (religiously) 'different' (Woodhead, 2013)? In the Swedish (and English) cultural contexts, 'hot' and 'hard' forms of religiosity stand out in comparison with the dominant 'soft' and 'cool' forms. The latter, with its belief in both science and societal development, including the freedom of the individual, is what Nancy Ammerman (2005, 2007) calls 'golden rule religiosity'. Conversely – and based on the WVS data – Pettersson and Esmer (2005) note that groups with a 'cool' and 'soft' religiosity are 'different' or even exceptional in the global context, in contrast to groups with a 'hot' and 'hard' religiosity, which overall are closer to the norm.[6]

Religious minorities and the state

Europe has become an example of ethnic and religious diversity. The WaVE project shows that religious and ethnic pluralism can be observed in all of the local case studies, though more so in southern Europe and in Britain, and less so in Norway and especially in Finland. To be precise, in Sweden, over 20% of the population (or their parents) were born in another country, against 15% in Norway and less than 10% in Finland. These figures are, however, subject to change owing to extensive immigration during the refugee crisis in 2015 when approximately 162,000 refugees came to Sweden,[7] 31,000 to Norway and less than 10,000 to Finland.

As we have seen, the definition of a minority can be complex (see Chapter One in this volume). In Sweden, religious minorities consist both of congregations resulting from 19th-century revival movements, and faith communities brought by migration into Sweden since the 1970s. In 2015, there were five ethnic minorities and 42 religious communities approved by the state and entitled to financial support.[8] Religious pluralism is, however, more than the presence of diverse faith communities in a society. As James Beckford (2003) argues, the study of pluralism also reflects moral and political questions concerning acceptance in the public sphere. We need to ask, therefore, how religious diversity is perceived in the school or health systems, or in prisons.

A good example can be found in the case study in Gävle. Ninna Edgardh and Per Pettersson (2010) show that demands for special accommodation for religious or cultural reasons, such as separate physical education classes for boys and girls, may obstruct – or more accurately be thought to obstruct – the integration of minorities into the culture of the host country. This makes the human right to freedom of religion not only a complex but a key issue. The findings from Gävle suggest that Muslim communities assume both a bonding and a bridging role, according to Putnam's (2000) terminology, with no real signs of religious enclaves threatening the cohesion of society, as Klas Borell (2012) puts it. This observation, however, needs further investigation in light of the recent refugee crisis in Europe – the more so given the evident lack of religious literacy in social policy areas, such as social work and welfare (see Dinham, 2012).

Women as a bridge between religion and welfare

The WaVE study also shows that women have a dominant role as care providers throughout Europe. However, in the Nordic countries they are employed as civil servants in the state welfare sector, while in southern Europe they are mainly responsible for care within the family. In contrast, men are more often found in policymaking positions. There are clear trends in the research material pointing to social care as a female role – a tendency that includes the Scandinavian countries and churches. This is partly because women have a disproportionate role in both the religious and social sectors, a propensity identified in both the WREP and the WaVE enquiries (Bäckström et al, 2011, p 152).

The research also shows that the increasing employment of women is in tension with a growing need for informal care, especially at home (a situation known as the care deficit). This is especially evident in the south of Europe, where welfare is dependent on support offered by the family. The same problem is, however, also seen in Germany and

Britain, and even in Sweden, despite generous maternity leave. There are different tensions in relation to migrant women who are caught between the obligation to respect – and indeed to transmit – traditional values, while at the same time needing to integrate themselves (often through employment) into the host society. These dilemmas, which expose very clearly the friction between the freedom of religion on the one hand and the right to gender equality on the other, are explored further in Part Three.

These case studies respond to an increasingly urgent need. As Ninna Edgardh (2011) argues, the gender dimension and the issue of social care are all too often overlooked when analysing the role of religion in contemporary societies. It follows that both factors should be included in our enquiries if our understanding of religion is to be complete. For example, until recently, gender has been absent as a category both in debates about secularisation and in more recent discussions of the post-secular (Aune et al, 2008).

Four theoretical issues

In this section, I present our findings in relation to four theoretically significant themes that emerged in the course of the research process: the relationship between post-material values and 'younger' folk movements; the continuing tension between conservative and liberal approaches to the religion–society dichotomy; the increasing strains between professional and ideological aspects of cooperation; and the significance of a new voluntary sector in Sweden.

Post-material values and 'younger' folk movements

The different facets of Protestant individualism

The Nordic countries are characterised by tight bonds between 19th- and 20th-century folk movements and social democracy. In Sweden this cooperation is shown in the well-known concept of the people's or folk home (*folkhemmet*). Society is viewed as tantamount to a family home where everyone contributes, and both tasks and resources are allocated in a democratic, just and equal manner. From 1932 to 2006, moreover – with a few important exceptions at the end of the 1970s and the beginning of the 1990s – social democracy very largely shaped the idea of welfare for all citizens. This included considerable freedom for both women and men. In this context, Henrik Berggren and Lars Trägårdh (2015) refer to the paradox of individual freedom, itself connected to a high level of confidence in both social institutions and the state, as 'statist individualism'. According to this model, individuals are given considerable freedom by the state to develop their own lifestyle (women and men have been taxed separately since 1971) thanks to the security of the welfare system.

For this reason, statist individualism cannot be compared with Anglo-Saxon individualism, which is based on the idea that the state only interferes if individuals are not able to manage on their own. Nor can it be compared with the German model, where the individual is linked to the family, which is the main unit that interacts with the state. This Protestant-inspired individualism is, therefore, expressed differently in the welfare systems in Sweden, Britain and Germany. I argue that this model makes it possible to distinguish between a 'strong' and a 'cool' individualism. 'Strong' individualism is based on a 'look-after-yourself freedom' in which the state only engages if individuals are no longer able to manage by themselves, while 'cool' individualism is built on a rights-based freedom that enables the state to provide for the freedom of the individual by means of the welfare system. In the former, the role of the state is viewed as something negative; in the latter, the role of the state is welcomed.

The 'children of welfare' and new folk movements

The role of the folk movements in Sweden is, however, shifting. This change is part of a broader discussion about the renegotiation of the social contract in light of a growing emphasis on the market and freedom of choice (Wijkström, 2012). This transformation was studied for the first time in a project entitled *Framtida folkrörelser (Future Folk Movements)* (Pettersson, 1992). It was based on data collected from a comprehensive survey as well as on Ronald Inglehart's (1977) well-known theory of the silent revolution of values through generational shifts. The theory argues that the development of values in society evolves from collective values, strict social morality and faith-based life views to private and tolerant values associated with freedom and increasingly secular outlooks (Pettersson, 1992, p 34). This shift of values results in a decrease in traditional folk movements (including political parties and churches); at the same time new movements and networks founded on – for example – environmental causes, peace and women's issues are growing in scope and influence. This means that the 'children of welfare' have a different perspective on social issues from their parents. This development is particularly apparent in northern Europe, as the WVS studies have shown.

The question at stake is the following: what does this change of values mean for the robustness of the Swedish welfare system? Are we experiencing a new shift in the relationship between public institutions (the state), the family, and religious, non-profit or private actors and if so, in what direction? How will the next generation (the 'grandchildren of welfare') define the idea of individual freedom in relation to (say) environmental and social issues? Is there, in other words, a need to bring the theory of post-material values up to date, taking into account recent changes in Northern Europe?

The continuing tension between conservative and liberal approaches

The question of how different theological orientations influence the churches' vision of their role in society was highlighted in the development of liberation theology in the 1960s (Cox, 1966; Boff and Boff, 1987). The same point was illustrated a decade later in studies arguing for vertical traditional versus horizontal liberal orientations among Catholic priests and Catholic communities (Schmidtchen, 1973). A similar tendency was revealed in Protestant Sweden by Anders Bäckström (1983). Finally, Peter Beyer (1994) argues that because of the pressures of globalisation, theological divisions *within* religious communities have become more pertinent, than divisions *between* religious communities.

The question of a vertical versus a horizontal view of the social role of the churches was analysed in a 1992 survey among priests, deacons and lay chair holders of parochial church councils in Sweden (Bäckström, 1994). The survey revealed that majority religions have a complementary function in relation to the welfare state. Within this majority view, however, there are three distinctive perspectives regarding the social work of the Church: the relationship was viewed, first, as a public responsibility; second, as a private religious issue; and, third, as the professional activity of an institution. These findings indicate that there are different objectives in the welfare activities of the local parish: a socially active and critical role; a spiritual role which is primarily faith-based; and a professional outreach role intended for people in need of support. Such divisions illustrate the idea of competing horizontal and vertical views, but it also hints at a compromise between the vertical and horizontal functions, discovered in the Church of Sweden's professional ethos, partly evidenced by the large number of people it employs.[9]

Broadly speaking, the WaVE project reveals the same tendency, showing that conservative (often evangelical) groups are more interested in running their own schools and developing their own 'welfare industry' (vertical orientation), as Jan Vranken (2013) puts it; conversely, liberal groups aim to develop a relationship with the social authorities (horizontal orientation). The tension between these two orientations can be found in all of the countries and in all of the religious communities within the WaVE project, but in different stages of development. It also reveals how complex the whole issue becomes when religious minorities are involved. Migrant communities tend to develop strategies of their own for the care of older and younger family members, which renders the conservative–liberal or vertical–horizontal dichotomy less prominent.

The increasing strains between practical and ideological aspects of cooperation

The research programme From State Church to Free Folk Church (1997–2003) was launched in the 1990s (Bäckström, 1999). Two studies within this programme investigated the relationship between welfare and religion. The first (developed in this section) focused on patterns of cooperation in social initiatives between the local church and the municipality in six towns and villages in Sweden (Bäckström, 2001). The study highlighted different dimensions of cooperation. The second (developed in the following section) focused on all social and voluntary activities taking place within faith-based communities in one locality in Sweden (Jeppsson Grassman, 2001). It underscored the difference between voluntary work in the Nordic countries and that in other welfare regimes.

The first study confirmed the image of separate areas of competence, in which the Church of Sweden, along with other faith communities, complements state welfare provision (Bäckström, 2001). The findings indicate that the contributions of faith communities are primarily symbolic, moral/ethical and pedagogical, with a focus on the fundamental value of the environment and individual integrity, as well as on cultural belonging and feelings of security (Bäckström et al, 2004). Further, the Church's contribution to social welfare was seen as somewhat ad hoc, reflecting the practical aspects of social care, its role as a critical voice and the innovative role of faith communities.

The study also revealed that cooperation has at least two meanings. On the one hand, cooperation can take place through specific interactions between different professional institutions, such as churches, schools, police, prisons, and healthcare and emergency services (especially when they respond to a crisis). In this mode, it builds on different competences in a specialised society. On the other hand, cooperation may also refer to consensus building about the welfare and wellbeing of the individual in its broadest sense. In this sense, it develops the values-based and values-driven relationships between the institutions listed above beyond their various specialisations and social function. It is this that I term a growing ecology of cooperation, which I see as part of the deregulation of late-modern societies where new and hybrid models of conversation and collaboration are able to develop (Wijkström and Zimmer, 2011).

Sweden is a good example of the tension between the two models of cooperation, both of which introduce religion as a cooperative partner, but in different ways. The first model illustrates a cooperation based on the modern idea of differentiation (the growing separation between state and church), while the second illustrates growing cooperation as part of a new mode of conversation (the growing convergence between state and religion). Migration has brought this tension to the fore as local authorities are trying to find the best ways of cooperating with religious minorities, while at the same time trying to remain neutral.

The significance of a new voluntary sector in Sweden

The second study mentioned in the previous section focused on the social work of faith-based communities in one municipality in Sweden (Jeppsson Grassman, 2001). This study, and others that followed, shattered the notion that a strong welfare state results in an underdeveloped associational life as measured though membership and civic involvement. For example, 86% of Swedish people are members of associations and organisations and 48% are active members of at least one association – especially sports clubs, trade unions and cultural associations (Jeppsson Grassman and Svedberg, 1999; von Essen and Svedberg, 2010; Hollmer, 2014). These figures are the highest in Europe regarding voluntary engagement (Jeppsson Grassman, 2010). This can be explained partly by the tradition of folk movements and similar associations discussed above and partly by the state's significant financial support for such organisations. This tradition is regarded as central to the values of democracy in Sweden.

The 1990s stand as the decade when Swedish society shifted from the logic of an industrial society, with citizenship at its core, to the logic of a service society, in which service relations between individuals moved centre-stage – with a marked emphasis on the values of freedom and quality of life. Eva Jeppsson Grassman (2014) argues, however, that the 1990s – a time of high expectations regarding the social role of the non-profit sector – should be viewed simply as phase one of the development of civil society in Sweden. Phase two took place between 2005 and 2015 and marked a shift to lower and more realistic expectations and to a more critical view of the non-profit sector. The WaVE project was carried out during the shift from phase one to phase two. It was based on the idea that deregulation gives civil society more space (Bäckström, 2003). Today it has become clear that this deregulation is indeed about the increased role of the market, but that it also concerns the state's growing interest in regulating both the market and civil society by means of quality control (Linde, 2014).[10]

It is equally clear that there has been a change in public attitudes towards the non-profit sector as a provider of welfare. In 1992, only 8% were in favour of this shift compared with 48% in 2012 (Jeppsson Grassman, 2014). Behind this change of attitude lies a conscious effort by the conservative governments in Sweden (2006-14) to strengthen commercialisation and to invite civil society actors to participate, through both an Agreement of Collaboration in 2008 and through an explicit change in the law relating to civil society in 2009.[11]

This change of attitude reflects an ongoing transformation of society that Tommy Lundström and Filip Wijkström (1995) have captured in the phrase 'from voice to service'. It summarises the development from a welfare society, dominated by folk movements and an emphasis on the social community, to a market-oriented service society. In such a society, non-profit organisations have been steered towards a greater professionalisation in social service provision. This has resulted in an extensive and continuing debate on how non-profit organisations can maintain their ideological specificity if they are to become contract-driven providers of welfare.

The countries included in the WaVE project have all been affected by increased costs. Most European governments are dealing with this through the privatisation of welfare institutions, seeking to make care more efficient by applying the rules of competition and the market. The Swedish and English systems show some similarities in this respect, and in Germany the for-profit sector is also expanding at the expense of diaconal non-profit organisations (Leis-Peters, 2014; Middlemiss Lé Mon, 2015). Since 2010, however, it has become increasingly clear that non-profit (and faith-based) actors in Sweden do not always follow the expectations of the government.[12] Social commitment is self-evident (SKU, 2009, 2013) but to function as a welfare industry is a step too far. Welfare is still regarded as the responsibility of the state. Behind this reluctance, moreover, there is a visible ambivalence: between a market logic, on the one hand (where religious and cultural specificity risks being eradicated on account of money being the main consideration), and a social–community or solidarity logic on the other (where charitable care provides an added value that is difficult to measure in financial terms). This ambivalence illustrates a major dilemma: is 'religion' to function primarily as an entrepreneurial activity or as an arena for voluntary and social work?

The relationship between religion and welfare is not, therefore, a zero-sum game. A stronger state with a strong economy does not necessarily result in smaller associations and a deprived religious life; on the contrary, it gives people more freedom to create their own beliefs and social commitments. This is clearly illustrated by the fact that altruistic motives and charitable giving are top priorities in the Nordic countries, to the extent that giving is considered essential as it strengthens one's self-esteem. In 2015, 74% of the population in Sweden gave money to a charity.[13]

The need for a renewed conversation in a 'cool' culture of trust

The WaVE research reveals societal challenges that have both social and ideological connotations. The project also shows that these challenges form similar patterns in the towns and case studies under investigation. The responses to these challenges differ, however, depending on their historical conditions and contexts. A second point runs parallel. The complexity of the changes that are occurring today suggests that there is a danger of studying the place of religion within them with approaches that belong to the past (Woodhead, 2012). Or, put differently, the uncertain boundaries between the welfare state and religion that we see today demand greater imagination in research than we are used to (Davie, 2013). This is an important lesson learnt from the welfare and religion projects.

In the following section, I reflect on the issues raised so far. I also point to the need for future research in order to understand the continuing connections between welfare and religion, and the need to sustain a 'cool' culture of trust that makes room for minority religious voices.

Multiple roads to modernity

In his important work on secularisation, David Martin (1978, 2011) pointed to the importance of cultural specificities when he referred to the idea of religion playing different roles in different pathways to modernity. Looking at the French, American and Russian revolutions, we can see how three explicitly secular states have dealt with religion in very different ways. In the United States, religious freedom and the participation of religious communities in the building of the nation have always been key issues, resulting in a 'passive secularism', as Kuru (2009) calls it. In France, freedom *from* religion is the overriding goal, leading to a much more 'assertive secularism' and to the political goal of the privatisation of religion. In Russia, religion (Christianity) was first viewed as 'the opium of the masses' but is now, according to President Vladimir Putin, Europe's bedrock. In the Nordic countries, it is the *absence* of a revolution that explains the cooperation between the church and the state throughout the 20th century, which may be considered a type of pragmatic secularism in a 'cool' or broad understanding of culture. Sweden is an example of a 'pragmatic freedom' both towards and away from religion; at one and the same time, it embodies both cultural integration and individual autonomy. It is quite clear, therefore, that the secular solutions that have emerged in the 20th century are far from homogenous.

Parallel developments in religious and social life

A further finding of the WREP and WaVE projects is the relationship between Esping-Andersen's typology of welfare regimes and the analyses of secularisation developed by David Martin and mentioned in the previous section. Crucially, Martin's variations mirror very closely the regime types identified by Esping-Andersen and illustrated in the WaVE case studies. In many ways this is hardly surprising given that both theories draw on the same underlying alignments and cleavages in European society, initially identified by Seymour Lipset and Stein Rokkan (1967). This connection was first observed by Grace Davie (2012, p 5) who wrote:

> Placing Gøsta Esping-Andersen alongside David Martin symbolises one of the important achievements of WREP: that is to bring together two very different bodies of literature from two fields of European social science which are seldom read by the same people. Striking parallels emerge which are as relevant now as they were when first developed.

'Cool' trust and religiosity

Rather different are the WaVE findings concerning the state – specifically that trust in the state also includes trust in the Nordic folk churches as part of the national project in the 20th century (Bäckström, 2014, 2016). This culture of trust is rooted in history and is one of the prerequisites for the freedom and security (both financial and cultural) that are central to the rights of the individual. According to Henrik Berggren and Lars Trägårdh (2015, p 435) – and as already explained – this trust should not be seen as 'hot' (that is, connected to traditional family values or exclusive faith communities); rather, it is 'cool' (underpinned by rules – the law – in society as a whole). The values of democracy, human rights and human dignity are seen as fundamental. Thus the Swedish model of a 'cool' trust in the welfare state is connected to a 'cool' religiosity, which is part of the more general culture of trust. The Swedish/Nordic model is, however, challenged, on the one hand by 'hot' religious minorities, both 19th century and more recent, and, on the other by 'hot' versions of secularism. This explains two things: the tendency towards polarisation in the debate about religion and the inclination to render the dominant culture of trust, which includes a 'cool' or inclusive religiosity, invisible.

The weakness of the universal welfare model

In short, the strength of the universal model of welfare is also its weakness. The model cannot easily accommodate cultural or religious specificities. Unsurprisingly, migration into Sweden has challenged the tight, but nonetheless understated, bonds between the state and the individual, as different social patterns (for example, extended families or 'clans') are introduced into society (Demker, 2013). In particular, the universal welfare model has difficulty accommodating a 'hot' cultural identity, which includes collectivist attitudes or beliefs that deviate from the secular norm of the majority. This combination of a 'cool' trust in the state, 'cool' religiosity and 'cool' interpretation of culture, with an emphasis on the freedom of the individual with certain duties and responsibilities, results in the following paradox: those who, in a democratic context, deviate from a basically tolerant world view, challenge – simply by their existence – this understanding of tolerance. This explains why diversity is perceived to be a necessary condition for cultural and economic prosperity, but only as long as it does not include cultural identities that challenge the norm. This issue is particularly relevant to religious traditions that have arrived in Sweden in recent decades, especially Islam.

Tolerance and diversity

In Sweden, religious pluralism is a reality: about 150 languages are spoken and the entire world map of religion is represented in the country. Diversity will remain a key issue in Swedish society for the foreseeable future. The question is how people can learn to live together as comfortably as possible (Mahmood, 2013). The political legitimation of religious diversity is, however, still being developed. The Swedish idea of tolerance demands acceptance of all minorities wanting to become part of Swedish culture. As Hans Joas (2014) argues, however, there is a risk that a European rejection of the community-based approach among the newly arrived refugees may trigger an oppositional identity, which may become more religious than it was in the home countries. This could also create dreams of a better world (kingdom) that may be expressed in extremist forms. Such a situation is likely to create an introverted cultural climate that manifests itself in nationalist political movements. The so-called multi-religious threat to secular homogeneity, along with neoliberal economic tendencies, provokes in turn nostalgic flashbacks of an ethnically homogenous welfare state, with its national church, as a utopian goal for certain groups of society. The uncertainty that informs the current situation feeds into populist and nationalist ideas in the whole of Europe, including the Nordic countries.[14]

Religion and the secular

Whatever the case, the defining feature of late-modern society is its pluralism – a state of affairs that some researchers have called the post-secular condition (Sigurdson, 2009; Ziebertz and Riegel, 2009). Craig Calhoun (Calhoun et al, 2011, p 5) reminds us, however, that secularism is a political concept, the idea of which is to separate religion from the public sphere. The historical process that we call secularisation, which includes the transfer of authority from institutions to the individual, is often confused with the political idea or ideology of secularism (Casanova, 2011). For democracy to develop, it is the acceptance of pluralism rather than secularism that is required (Berger, 2001).

Indeed in a religiously and socially diverse society, secularism may become an obstacle that prevents religious communities from taking part in public life. Conversely, a plural society has the capacity to create the political freedom for religion to develop in different ways (Joas, 2014). In a society with several value systems, secularism is reduced to one of several basic understandings. This makes it possible for a religious discourse to be present in public conversation and for religious actors to politicise both their own religion and the place of other institutions in society (Demker, 2016).

What we see today is that religion is given space in the public conversation, together with science, politics, law and culture, with the aim of promoting a good society for all citizens. In this chapter, I have suggested that Swedish society is on the road to becoming a global society in which diversity, as a resource for democracy, increasingly needs to include religious voices. The goal is to promote a social order that is held together by a shared commitment on the part of most citizens and is not disrupted or antagonised by ideological or theological constraints. This explains the entirely positive tendency, as Danièle Hervieu-Léger (2006) argues, to look for commonalities behind different world views and institutions – an important principle of inter-faith dialogue.

Conclusion

Who is going to do what, for whom and for what reason? This challenge is accentuated by increased migration flows. Uncertainty around the fundamental concepts of welfare and religion in relation to (religious) minorities further complicates the situation. Gender issues are also important in that women are more affected by these changes than men. The WaVE project shows that although similar developments are taking place in each of the countries under review, marked differences in their respective welfare models remain in spite of these changes. This means that religion, both in its majority and minority roles, functions differently in different parts of Europe.

The interaction between religion and the welfare state is now evident at three levels of Swedish society. First, it combines a 'cool' religiosity with a 'cool' culture of trust that is supported by Lutheran ideas of a calling that applies to, and supports, every individual. The historical majority churches and their rites still contribute to welfare by strengthening a sense of cultural identity, security and social cohesion. Second, at the meso level, churches, religious minorities and networks function both as a voice and as social actors through the activities of local parishes and congregations (a social community logic), and as providers of welfare services (an instrumental service logic). Finally, at the individual level, personal welfare or wellbeing takes shape through support to individuals relating to existential questions (meaning making), but also through informal networks of care. The latter, interestingly, resonate well with the ethos of religious minorities and their care for family members.

Key questions remain, however. Do universal welfare systems have a greater ability to create conditions for integration, or do welfare systems with less state involvement function better? Has the neoliberal era reached its peak given that new constellations are continuing to develop? The free market logic, which some viewed as a 1980s vision of a better society, appears today as an obstacle as well as an asset to economic equality and poverty reduction.[15] We should also ask whether the 'grandchildren' of the welfare society born in the 1990s, who have experienced prosperity and health but also the social and environmental challenges of the 21st century, will adopt stricter values towards social and economic issues. Finally, what is the fate of these values? Will their dominant expressions be social democratic, liberal or nationalist (populist)?

In the introduction to this chapter, I suggested that the development of a strong welfare state during the years following the Second World War led to the perception that the interaction between religion and the welfare state was coming to an end. We have seen that this understanding was ideologically based, rather than built on an accurate description of reality. Today, it is more accurate to say that religion has been present throughout the 20th century, although functional differentiation and political understandings of secularism have all too often rendered it invisible.

I have argued that new partnerships are emerging. These collaborations must include different stakeholders in order to strengthen the confidence that characterises 'cool' cultures of trust. This new 'ecology of conversation' is transnational and shapes policy alongside rather more traditional decision making; it is a crucial factor behind the new relationships of communication and decision making. Gaining knowledge about how religion is part and parcel of this diverse ecology and how the state manages this diversity is an important task for future research.

Notes

[1] See www.wvs.org

[2] A welfare regime is regarded as an ideal type and does not relate to specific countries. According to Gøsta Esping-Andersen, a 'regime' refers to the way in which welfare production is allocated between state, market and household in a

variety of European countries. For a summary of critiques of Esping-Andersen's typology, see Jeppsson Grassman (2010, p 28).

3   These questions are presented, together with a number of methodological considerations, in Edgardh Beckman et al (2006) and Bäckström et al (2010). See also Chapters One and Four of this book.

4   'Health is a state of complete physical, mental and social well-being and not merely the absence of disease or infirmity'; see www.who.int/about/definition/en/print. html

5   The Swedish word *sval* is translated as 'cool'. It refers to an inclusive (mild) religiosity that is closely related to spirituality.

6   See Chapter Nine in this book for a further discussion of Pettersson and Esmer (2005) and the idea of religious and cultural difference.

7   About 80,000 will, however, be returned to their countries of origin; see www. thelocal.se/20160128/sweden-to-hire-planes-to-send-back-80000-migrants

8   The Commission for Government Support to Faith Communities (see www. sst.a.se). This is a state authority responsible for granting financial support to religious communities. It is also tasked with implementing the values of democracy through training courses. In 2015, the aid it offered was estimated to be 92 million SEK.

9   In 2015, there were 22,000 employees in the Church of Sweden. Similar results were found in Norway; see Angell (2010).

10   The privatisation of schools, healthcare and social care, undertaken in Sweden since 1992, is marginal in the non-profit sector, with a share increase from 2% to 3% of the market. On the other hand, for-profit companies and organisations have greatly increased their share, especially in the school sector and in elderly care, to approximately 20% in 2013 (Blomqvist et al, 2014).

11   See www.overenskommelsen.se; En politik om det civila samhället 2009/10: 55 (A Policy for the civil society 2009/10: 55) www.regeringen.se/49b70c/ contentassets/626c071c353f4f1d8d0d46927f73fe9c/en-politik-for-det-civila-samhallet-prop.-20091055. These agreements resulted in the Swedish Agency for Youth and Civil Society, a state authority established in 2012. The effect of these agreements is uncertain (Linde, 2014).

12   See www.socialforum.se

13   The total amount donated to charities in 2014 was 14.3 billion SEK (6 billion from the general public, 5 billion from the Swedish International Development Cooperation and other organisations, 2 billion from the People's Postcode Lottery and 1 billion from private companies); see www.frii.se.

14   In 2016, nearly 20% of European citizens voted for a far right or left populist party, while one third of European governments included a populist party (Johansson Heinö and Svanborg-Sjövall, 2016).

15   See Piketty (2014), which has sold more than 1.5 million copies. During an interview with Sweden's former Prime Minister Fredrik Reinfeldt, former Prime Minister of Britain Tony Blair characterised market forces as bad masters but good servants; see www.svtplay.se/video/11779766/toppmotet/toppmotet-avsnitt-3?tab=senast

References

Allardt, E. (1975) *Att Ha, att Älska, att Vara. Om välfärd i Norden* (*To Have, to Love, to Be. Welfare in the Nordic Countries*), Lund: Argos.

Ammerman, N.T. (2005) 'Religion, the state and the common good: shifting boundaries in Europe and the United States', in A. Bäckström (ed) *Welfare and Religion. A Publication to Mark the Fifth Anniversary of the Uppsala Institute for Diaconal and Social Studies*, Diakonivetenskapliga institutets skriftserie 10, Uppsala: Uppsala Institute for Diaconal and Social Studies, pp 21-34.

Ammerman, N.T. (ed) (2007) *Everyday Religion. Observing Modern Religious Lives*, Oxford: Oxford University Press.

Angell, O.H. (2010) *Kva tyder diakonen for den lokale diakonien? Sammanhengen mellom diakonal profil og det å ha diakon i norske kyrkjelydar* (*What does the Deacon Mean for Local Diaconal Work?*), Oslo: Diakonhjemmet Høgskole.

Aune, K., Sharma, S. and Vincent, G. (eds) (2008) *Women and Religion in the West: Challenging Secularization*, Farnham: Ashgate.

Bäckström, A. (1983) *Religion som yrke* (*Religion as an Occupation*), Stockholm: Verbum.

Bäckström, A. (1994) *För att tjäna. En studie av diakoniuppfattningar hos kyrkliga befattningshavare* (*To Serve: A Study of the Diaconate and Diaconal Work in the Church of Sweden*), Uppsala: Svenska kyrkans utredningar, 1.

Bäckström, A. (1999) *From State Church to Free Folk Church. A Sociology of Religion, Service Theoretical and Theological Analysis in the face of Disestablishment between the Church of Sweden and the State in the year 2000*, Stockholm: Verbum.

Bäckström, A. (2001) *Svenska kyrkan som välfärdsaktör i en global kultur: En studie av religion och omsorg* (*The Church of Sweden as a Welfare Provider in a Global Culture. A Study of Religion and Social Care*), Stockholm: Verbum.

Bäckström, A. (ed) (2003) *Welfare and Religion in a European Perspective: A Comparative Study of the Role of the Churches as Agents of Welfare within the Social Economy*, Uppsala: Diakonivetenskapliga institutets skriftserie, 4.

Bäckström, A. (ed) (2014) *Välfärdsinsatser på religiös grund. Förväntningar och problem* (*Welfare Efforts on Religious Grounds. Expectations and Problems*), Skellefteå: Artos.

Bäckström, A. (2016) 'En osynlig kyrka i en synlig tillitskultur' ('An invisible church in a visible culture of trust'), in A. Bäckström and A. Wejryd (eds) *Sedd men osedd. Om folkkyrkans paradoxala närvaro inför 2020-talet* (*Seen but Unseen. On the Paradoxical Presence of the Folk Church in the 2020s*), Stockholm: Verbum, pp 29-48.

Bäckström, A. and Davie, G., with Edgardh, N. and Pettersson, P. (eds) (2010) *Welfare and Religion in 21st Century Europe: Volume 1. Configuring the Connections*, Farnham: Ashgate.

Bäckström, A., Davie, G., Edgardh, N. and Pettersson, P. (eds) (2011) *Welfare and Religion in 21st Century Europe: Volume 2. Gendered, Religious and Social Change*, Farnham: Ashgate.

Bäckström, A., Edgardh Beckman, N. and Pettersson, P. (2004) *Religious Change in Northern Europe. The Case of Sweden*, Stockholm: Verbum.

Bauman, Z. (1998) 'Postmodern religion', in P. Heelas, with D. Martin and P. Morris (eds) *Religion, Modernity and Postmodernity*, London: Blackwell, pp 55-78.

Beckford, J.A. (2003) *Social Theory and Religion*, Cambridge: Cambridge University Press.

Berger, P.L. (2001) 'Postscript', in L. Woodhead, with P. Heelas and D. Martin (eds) *Peter Berger and the Study of Religion*, London: Routledge, pp 189-98.

Berggren, H. and Trägårdh, L. (2015) *Är svensken människa? Gemenskap och oberoende i det moderna Sverige* (*Are Swedes Human? Community and Independence in Modern Sweden*), Stockholm: Norstedts.

Beyer, P. (1994) *Religion and Globalization*, London: Sage.

Biendarra, I. and Leis-Peters, A. (2012) 'Overview of the national situation in Germany', in A. Bäckström (ed) *Welfare and Values in Europe: Transitions Related to Religion, Minorities and Gender. Volume 2: Continental Europe: Germany, France, Italy, Greece*, Studies in Religion and Society 5, Uppsala: Acta Universitatis Upsaliensis, pp 13-54.

Blomqvist, P., Mankell, A. and Winblad, U. (2014) 'Varför så få ideella aktörer inom äldreomsorgen?' (Why is there no third sector in Swedish elderly care?), in A. Bäckström (ed) *Välfärdsinsatser på religiös grund. Förväntningar och problem* (*Welfare Efforts on Religious Grounds. Expectations and Problems*), Skellefteå: Artos, pp 165-93.

Boff, L. and Boff, C. (1987) *Introducing Liberation Theology*, Tunbridge Wells: Burns & Oates.

Borell, K. (2012) *Islamofobiska fördomar och hatbrott. En kunskapsöversikt* (*Islamophobic Prejudice and Hate Crimes. An Overview*), Stockholm: Nämnden för statligt stöd till trossamfundens skriftserie, 1.

Calhoun, C., Juergensmeyer, M. and VanAntwerpen, J. (eds) (2011) *Rethinking Secularism*, Oxford: Oxford University Press.

Casanova, J. (2011) 'The secular, secularizations, secularisms', in C. Calhoun, M. Juergensmeyer and J. VanAntwerpen (eds) *Rethinking Secularism*, Oxford: Oxford University Press, pp 54-74.

Cox, H. (1966) *The Secular City: Secularization and Urbanization in Theological Perspective*, London: SCM Press.

Davie, G. (2012) 'A European perspective on religion and welfare: contrasts and commonalities', *Social Policy and Society*, 11(4): 589-99.

Davie, G. (2013) *The Sociology of Religion. A Critical Agenda* (2nd edn), London: Sage.

Day, A. (2011) *Believing in Belonging. Belief & Social Identity in the Modern World*, Oxford: Oxford University Press.

Demker, M. (2013) 'Religion är en del av den gemensamma medborgerliga offentligheten' ('Religion as part of a common civic public sphere'), in H. Stenström (ed) *Religionens offentlighet. Om religionens plats i samhället* (*Making Religion Public. On the Place of Religion in Society*), Skellefteå: Artos, pp 115-24.

Demker, M. (2016) 'Vilken plats vill kyrkan ha i den offentliga debatten?' ('Prospects for a transformed church in public debate?'), in A. Bäckström and A. Wejryd (eds) *Sedd men osedd. Om folkkyrkans paradoxala närvaro inför 2020-talet* (*Seen but Unseen. On the Paradoxical Presence of a Folk Church in the 2020s*), Stockholm: Verbum, pp 53-65.

Dinham, A. (2012) *Faith and Social Capital After the Debt Crisis*, Basingstoke: Palgrave Macmillan.

Edgardh, N. and Pettersson, P. (2010) 'The Church of Sweden: A Church for all, especially the most vulnerable', in A. Bäckström and G. Davie, with N. Edgardh and P. Pettersson (eds) *Welfare and Religion in 21st Century Europe, Volume 2. Gendered, Religious and Social Change*, Farnham: Ashgate, pp 39-56.

Edgardh, N. (2011) 'A gendered perspective on welfare and religion in Europe', in A. Bäckström and G. Davie, with N. Edgardh and P. Pettersson (eds) *Welfare and Religion in 21st Century Europe: Volume 2. Gendered, Religious and Social Change*, Farnham: Ashgate, pp 61-106.

Edgardh, N., Ekstrand, T. and Pettersson, P. (2006) 'The Church of Sweden as an agent of welfare – The case of Gävle', in A.B. Yeung, with Edgardh Beckman, N. and Pettersson, P. (eds) *Churches in Europe as Agents of Welfare – Sweden, Norway and Finland*, Uppsala: Uppsala Institute for Diaconal and Social Studies 11, pp 20-85.

Esping-Andersen, G. (1990) *The Three Worlds of Welfare Capitalism*, Cambridge: Polity Press.

Fukuyama, F. (1992) *The End of History and the Last Man*, London: Penguin Books.

Glock, C.Y. and Stark, R. (1965) *Religion and Society in Tension*, Chicago, IL: Rand McNally.

Habermas, J. (2006) 'Religion in the public sphere'. *European Journal of Philosophy*, 14(1): 1-25.

Harding, T. (2012) *Framtidens civilsamhälle* (*The Future Civil Society*), Stockholm: Elanders.

Hervieu-Léger, D. (2006) 'In search of certainties: the paradoxes of religiosity in societies of high modernity', in *The Hedgehog Review. Critical Reflections on Contemporary Culture. After Secularization*, 8(1-2): 59-68.

Hollmer, M. (2014) 'Samband mellan aktivitet i civilsamhället och tilltro till privata aktörer i välfärden' (The connection between activity in civil society and attitudes towards private welfare providers), in A. Bäckström (ed) *Välfärdsinsatser på religiös grund. Förväntningar och problem* (*Welfare Efforts on Religious Grounds. Expectations and Problems*), Skellefteå: Artos, pp 111-37.

Hollmer, M. and Bäckström, A. (2013) *Svenska kyrkan och välfärden. En undersökning av attityder* (*The Swedish Church and Welfare: A Survey of Attitudes*), Studies in Religion and Society 10, Uppsala: Acta Universitatis Upsaliensis.

The Impact of Religion: Challenges for Society, Law and Democracy, Swedish Research Council Programme 2008-2018 (www.impactofreligion.uu.se).

Inglehart, R. (1977) *The Silent Revolution. Changing Values and Political Styles among Western Publics*, Princeton, NJ: Princeton University Press.

Inglehart, R. (1997) *Modernization and Postmodernization. Cultural, Economic, and Political Change in 43 Societies*, Princeton, NJ: Princeton University Press.

Inglehart, R. (2007) 'Mapping global values', in Y. Esmer and T. Pettersson (eds) *Measuring and Mapping Cultures: 25 Years of Comparative Value Surveys*, Leiden: Brill: 11-32.

Jeppsson Grassman, E. (2001) *Socialt arbete i församlingens hägn* (*Social Work Within the Parish*), Stockholm: Verbum.

Jeppsson Grassman, E. (2010) 'Welfare in western Europe: existing regimes and patterns of change', in A. Bäckström and G. Davie, with N. Edgardh and P. Pettersson (eds) *Welfare and Religion in 21st Century Europe: Volume 1. Configuring the Connections*, Farnham: Ashgate, pp 25-37.

Jeppsson Grassman, E. (2014) 'Vilken väg? Svenska kyrkans omsorg i en tid av välfärdsförändringar' ('Which way? The Church of Sweden and its care work in a time of welfare change'), in A. Bäckström (ed) *Välfärdsinsatser på religiös grund. Förväntningar och problem (Welfare Achievements on Religious Grounds. Expectations and problems)*, Skellefteå: Artos, pp 285-303.

Jeppsson Grassman, E. and Svedberg, L. (1999) 'Medborgarskapets gestaltningar. Insatser i och utanför föreningslivet' ('Portrayals of citizenship. Actions inside and outside the life of associations'), in *Civilsamhället, Statens Offentliga Utredningar 84 (Civil Society, Government Official Report 84)*, pp 121-80.

Joas, H. (2014) *Faith as an Option. Possible Futures for Christianity*, Stanford: Stanford University Press.

Johansson Heinö, A. and Svanborg-Sjövall, K. (2016) 'Så bör den auktoritära populismen bemötas' ('How to counter authoritarian populism'), *Dagens Nyheter*, 19 June, p 6.

Kuru, A.T. (2009) *Secularism and State Politics toward Religion. The United States, France and Turkey*, Cambridge: Cambridge University Press.

Leis-Peters, A. (2014) 'På väg mot en tysk (välfärds) modell? Reflektioner kring möjliga nya vägval för Svenska kyrkan' ('Towards a German (welfare) model? Reflections on possible new directions for the Church of Sweden'), in A. Bäckström (ed) *Välfärdsinsatser på religiös grund. Förväntningar och problem (Welfare Achievements on Religious Grounds. Expectations and Problems)*, Skellefteå: Artos, pp 259-81.

Linde, S. (2014) 'Dialog eller styrning? Om relationen mellan staten och de idéburna organisationerna, med särskilt fokus på Överenskommelsen och Svenska kyrkan' ('Dialogue or control? The relationship between the state and non-profit organisations, with particular emphasis on consensus and the Swedish Church'), in A. Bäckström (ed) *Välfärdsinsatser på religiös grund. Förväntningar och problem (Welfare Achievements on Religious Grounds. Expectations and Problems)*, Skellefteå: Artos, pp 195-220.

Lipset, S.M. and Rokkan, S. (eds) (1967) *Party Systems and Voter Alignment: Cross-National Perspectives*, New York, NY: Free Press.

Lundström, T. and Wijkström, F. (1995) *Från röst till service? Den svenska ideella sektorn i förändring (From Voice to Service? The Swedish Voluntary Sector in Change)*, Stockholm: Ersta Sköndal högskola.

Mahmood, Q. (2013) 'Att gå från en etnisk till en pluralistisk nationalism' ('From an ethnic to a pluralist nationalism'), in J. Strömbeck (ed) *Framtidsutmaningar: de nya Sverige (Future Challenges: The new Sweden)*, Stockholm: Fritzes, pp 107-19.

Manow, P. (2004) *The 'Good, the Bad and the Ugly'*. *Esping-Andersen's Welfare State Typology and the Religious Roots of Western Welfare State*, Working Paper 04/05, Cologne: Max-Planck-Institut für Gesellschaftsforschung.

Martikainen, T. and Gauthier, F. (eds) (2013) *Religion in the Neoliberal Age. Political Economy and Modes of Governance*, Farnham: Ashgate.

Martin, D. (1978) *A General Theory of Secularization*, Oxford: Blackwell.

Martin, D. (2009) 'The relevance of the European model of secularization in Latin America and Africa', in H. Joas and K. Wiegandt (eds) *Secularization and the World Religions*, Liverpool: Liverpool University Press, pp 278-95.

Martin, D. (2011) *The Future of Christianity. Reflections on Violence and Democracy, Religion and Secularization*, Farnham: Ashgate.

Middlemiss Lé Mon, M. (2011) 'Overview of the national situation in England', in A. Bäckström (ed) *Welfare and Values in Europe: Transitions Related to Religion, Minorities and Gender, Volume 1. Northern Europe: Sweden, Norway, Finland, England*, Studies in Religion and Society 4, Uppsala: Acta Universitatis Upsaliensis, pp 217-48.

Middlemiss Lé Mon, M. (2015) *Frivilligarbete inom och för kyrkan. En lösning av de problem som kyrka och samhälle står inför? (Voluntary Work in and for the Church. A Solution to the Problems Faced by the Church and Society?)*, Stockholm: Forum-idéburna organisationer med social inriktning.

Norris, P. and Inglehart, R. (2004) *Sacred and Secular. Religion and Politics Worldwide*, Cambridge: Cambridge University Press.

Pettersson, P. (2011) 'Majority churches as agents of European welfare: A sociological approach', in A. Bäckström and G. Davie, with N. Edgardh and P. Pettersson (eds) *Welfare and Religion in 21st Century Europe: Volume 2. Gendered, Religious and Social Change*, Farnham: Ashgate, pp 15-59.

Pettersson, T. (1992) 'Välfärd, värderingsförändringar och folkrörelseengagemang' ('Welfare, value changes and commitment in folk movements'), in S. Axelson and T. Pettersson (eds) *Mot denna framtid. Folkrörelser och folk om framtiden (Towards the Future. Folk Movements and People on the Future)*, Stockholm: Carlssons, pp 33-133.

Pettersson, T. and Esmer, Y. (2005) *Vilka är annorlunda? Om invandrares möte med svensk kultur (Who is different? Immigrant Encounters with Swedish Culture)*, Integrationsverkets rapportserie. Stockholm: Stockholms Stadsbibliotek.

Piketty, T. (2014) *Capital in the Twenty-First Century*, London: Belknap Press.

Putnam, R.D. (2000) *Bowling Alone. The Collapse and Revival of American Community*, New York, NY: Simon & Schuster.

Rothstein, B. (2011) *The Quality of Government: Corruption, Social Trust, and Inequality in International Perspective*, Chicago, IL: University of Chicago Press.

Schmidtchen, G. (1973) *Priester in Deutschland. Forschungsbericht über die im Auftrag der Deutschen Bischofskonferenz durchgefürte Umfrage unter allem Welt- und Ordenspriestern in der Bundesrepublik Deutschland (Priests in Germany. Research Report on a Survey carried out on Behalf of the German Bishop's Conference among Priests in the Federal Republic of Germany)*, Freiburg: Herder.

Sigurdson, O. (2009) *Det postsekulära tillståndet. Religion, modernitet, politik (The Post-Secular Condition. Religion, Modernity, Politics)*, Munkedal: Glänta Produktion.

SKU (Svenska Kyrkans Utredningar) (Church of Sweden Studies) 2009: 2 and 2013: 3.

Smart, N. (1993) *Religions in the West*, Englewood Cliffs, NJ: Prentice Hall.

Thurfjell, D. (2015) *Det gudlösa folket. De postkristna svenskarna och religionen (The Godless People: Post-Christian Swedes and Religion)*, Stockholm: Molin & Sorgenfrei Förlag.

Uvell, M. (2016) 'Ryktet om svenskens tolerans är överdrivet' ('The rumour of Swedish tolerance is exaggerated'), *Dagens Nyheter*, 21 February.

van Kersbergen, K. and Manow, P. (eds) (2009) *Religion, Class Coalitions and Welfare States*, Cambridge: Cambridge University Press.

von Essen, J. and Svedberg, L. (2010) 'Organisationer och engagemang i det svenska civilsamhället' ('Organisations and commitment in Swedish Civil Society'), in J. von Essen (ed) *Det svenska civilsamhället – en introduktion (Swedish Civil Society – An Introduction)*, Stockholm: Forum för frivilligt socialt arbete.

Vranken, J. (2013) 'Faith-based NGOs and social exclusion in European cities: what is in it for policy action?', in A. Row, and P. Pettersson (eds) *Consolidating Research on Religion: Moving the Agenda Forward*, Studies in Religion and Society 8, Uppsala: Acta Universitatis Upsaliensis, pp 1-14.

Wijkström, F. (ed.) (2012) *Civilsamhället i samhällskontraktet. En forskarantologi om vad som står på spel (Civil Society in the Social Contract. An Anthology of What is at Stake)*, Stockholm: European Civil Society Press.

Wijkström, F. and Zimmer, A. (eds) (2011) *Nordic Civil Society at a Cross-Roads. Transforming the Popular Movement Tradition*, Baden-Baden: Nomos.

Willander, E. (2014) *What Counts as Religion in Sociology? The Problem of Religiosity in Sociological Methodology*, Uppsala: Uppsala University.

Woodhead, L. (2012) 'Introduction', in L. Woodhead and R. Catto (eds) *Religion and Change in Modern Britain*, London: Routledge, pp 1–33.

Woodhead, L. (2013) 'Who is different?', Paper presented at the Impact of Religion Conference, Uppsala University, 20–22 May.

Ziebertz, H.G. and Riegel, U. (2009) 'Europe: a post-secular society?', *International Journal of Practical Theology*, 13(2): 293–308.

SIX

The intersections of state, family and church in Italy and Greece

Margarita Markoviti and Lina Molokotos-Liederman

Introduction

This chapter focuses on the intersection of state, family and church in southern Europe, based on the examples of Italy and Greece and the findings of the Greek and Italian case studies from the Welfare and Values in Europe: Transitions Related to Religion, Minorities and Gender (WaVE) project. Although our starting point is the WaVE case studies, we examine them in the context of the current situation to highlight recent socioeconomic and political developments since the completion of the project in 2009, notably the escalation of both the economic crisis and the refugee crisis since 2012. We draw our data from both the WaVE Greek and Italian case studies and additional materials on the responses to the economic crisis of majority churches: the Catholic Church in Italy and the Orthodox Church in Greece.

We first examine the shared characteristics between the Greek and Italian situation, compared with northern and western Europe. These consist of common cultural, social, economic and political traits and legacies, including asymmetrical paths to modernisation, uneven development of the welfare state and social policy, the importance of the family in the context of the 2009 economic crisis and recent waves of immigration.

We then look at the specificities of the Greek and Italian cases, first in terms of the size and development of their economies, and more specifically in terms of the different scales of economy. (Although both countries have significant agricultural production and tourism, Italy, compared with Greece, is the third largest economy in the Eurozone and a G7 member with much higher industrial production and exports.) We also examine their distinctive religious traditions, especially in relation to the delivery of social welfare, with the aim of exploring how the similarities and differences between Greece and Italy are translated and reflected in majority churches' responses to the recent economic and immigration crisis. Specifically, in the Italian case with regard to Catholicism, the principle of subsidiarity and the development of social action have developed in different ways from the Christian Orthodox concept of diaconia and its particular approach to social service.

Italy and Greece: common and distinct trajectories as part of a southern European pattern

Social, economic and political patterns

The shared features and enduring characteristics of the southern European countries of Portugal, Italy, Greece and Spain, known by the unfortunate acronym as 'PIGS', include not only geographical proximity, but also the fact that, together with the EU's eastern European members, they have the least affluent and least developed economies (Therborn, 2015). Structural familialism, namely, the enduring key role of family households and family ties, their strongly gendered labour markets (with significant gender gaps in employment), and the common 'architecture' of their welfare systems, accompanied by persistent unemployment and clientelist practices, are just a few features the southern European cluster of countries have in common (Mari-Klose and Moreno-Fuentes, 2015, p 5).

The Greek crisis of 2009, which began in the aftermath of the global financial crisis of 2008, and the endurance of public debt have accentuated what might be called Europe's north–south divide, and the political and economic marginalisation of southern Europe from western and northern Europe. These developments seem to seriously challenge the idea of a unified and converging Europe, as the road to Europeanisation has proved to be distinct for each member state of the European Union (EU). While Italy was one of the founding members of the European Economic Community (EEC) in 1958, Greece, Spain and Portugal joined following the consolidation of democracy (Greece in 1981 and Spain and Portugal in 1986). Their membership in the EU was an attempt, among others, to minimise the political, socioeconomic and cultural differences or gaps between the north and south of Europe (Trautsch, 2013). However, some three decades later, the economic crisis has challenged the assumption of a consistent path to southern European modernisation, compared with that in northern and western Europe.

Italy and Greece form a pair of neighbouring south-eastern European countries and part of the EU's south-eastern periphery. They share many characteristics, but are also separated by underlying differences primarily in relation to northern and western Europe and, to a certain extent, to south-western Europe (Portugal and Spain), which have their own specific characteristics (Trautsch, 2013). Despite their geographic proximity, Greece and Italy have followed separate historical trajectories in the recent centuries. In the first place, while Greece was part of the Ottoman Empire between the 15th and 19th centuries, Italy experienced no such Ottoman influence or domination.[1] As the two countries entered late modernity in the 20th century, they both experienced periods of authoritarian rule and subsequently a transition to democracy. The fact that the Colonels' dictatorship in Greece was relatively short-lived but more recent (from 1967 to 1974) meant that the country had less time to make the transition from authoritarianism to democracy from the 1970s onwards (Sotiropoulos, 2004), unlike the more prolonged yet much earlier period of authoritarian rule in Italy (from 1922 to 1943), which allowed more time for the transition towards democratic rule from the 1940s onwards. These tumultuous developments have left deep scars in both these countries' histories, including deep ideological polarisation and rifts that remain to this day. Sartori has famously described post-war Italian political structure in terms of 'polarised pluralism' (Sartori, 1976), which led, after 1994 and the 'clean hands' scandal,[2] to a period of consolidation of a bipolar system by 2001, reflecting the considerable ideological distances in Italian society (Donovan, 2011). Though the recent economic and social crisis has to a certain degree led to the fragmentation and transformation of the Greek political system, the persistence of ideological polarisation in the country is understood to be largely the legacy of intense, destabilising political conflict and political division from 1916 to the restoration of democracy in 1974 (Diamandouros and Gunther, 2001).

Despite the discrepancies in the size of their economies, Greece and Italy share some key features in their socioeconomic histories: delayed industrialisation,[3] labour rigidity and low labour productivity, public deficits and high levels of public debt, weak tax collection, influx of undocumented immigrant labour, inefficient public infrastructure and under-funded social welfare provision by the state (Gal, 2010; Trautsch, 2013), in addition to the existence of a large, informal economic sector, a 'grey' or 'black' market economy, which has largely determined the degree to which the state is capable of implementing effective social policy or planning (Morin, 1990; Katrougalos and Lazaridis, 2003; Petmetsidou and Tsoulouvi, 1992, cited in Symeonidou, 2013). Additionally, the growth of consumer societies and strong consumerist patterns of behaviour, lying on a foundation of a weak productive economic base, especially in the case of Greece, did not justify the overactive consumption patterns that led to high levels of private and public debt (Trautsch, 2013). The points of convergence expand to the political sphere of the two countries and concern the politicisation of top administrative ranks, enduring political clientelism, the absence of a European civil service or governing elite, and an interventionist yet administratively weak state, including chronic budget deficits (Sotiropoulos, 2004, p 405; Trautsch, 2013, p 2). These similarities in the social, economic and political fields of Italy and Greece are significant, not only because they allow us to categorise and draw comparisons, but also because of the effects these have on welfare provisions and the type of social policies in the two countries.

The enduring presence of clientelism

The enduring presence of clientelism and patronage[4] is a common behavioural and structural pattern that has permeated Greek and Italian political, social and economic fields. The influence of historical, structural and institutional circumstances in both countries created fertile grounds for the endurance of political clientelism both at the bottom (between political parties and society) and at the top (bureaucratic clientelism between governing elites and public bodies) (Sotiropoulos, 2004).

Italian and Greek political clientelism at the bottom, which manifested itself in the reciprocal and transactional relations between political parties and society, was partly responsible for the sharp increase in state employment growth that took place in the 1980s, which grew to be larger and more costly than in western and northern Europe (Sotiropoulos, 2004). State and welfare institutions turned into employment agencies 'catering to the economic needs of the political clienteles of alternating governing elites, [and] taking particular care of the working population already safely employed in the public sector' (Sotiropoulos, 2004, pp 412-13; see also Gal, 2010). In Greece, where the origins of clientelism are often attributed to the country's former Ottoman domination and the 'oriental values' of its Ottoman and Byzantine past (Papakostas, 2012, p 84), such practices of favouritism precluded the development of a collective consciousness and a broad consensus on social policy matters (Symeonidou, 2013).

Under the shadow of political clientelism at the top, political parties in Greece and Italy have used clientelism extensively, including in state building (Piattoni, 2001). In Greece, despite the efforts to build a state bureaucracy based on laws and regulations, public officials and politicians remained subject to the pressures of partisanship and partisan affiliation, which recreated dynamics originating in the tradition and crucial role of families and villages (Papakostas, 2012). In Italy, which does not share the centralised features of the Greek state, clientelism is more uneven geographically; just as the economy developed along a clear north–south divide, with clientelist practices that were more prevalent in the south compared with the north of Italy (Caciagli, 2006). Hiring civil servants on partial criteria that put merit aside contributed to the development of a politicised civil service, which is partly responsible for the enduring lack of well-educated civil servants, administrative elites of a certain social status, and efficient bureaucracies in both Greece and Italy (Sotiropoulos, 2004; Gal, 2010). This led to the development of inefficient administrative bureaucracies, coupled with ongoing resistance to reform, especially as patronage in the two countries has functioned as a substitute for the welfare state, providing vertical, informal channels of articulation of demands (Tsoukalas, 1986).

Since the 1990s, there have been ongoing efforts towards administrative decentralisation as a result of EU pressure,[5] the professionalisation of civil servants and the drawing of a clearer demarcation line between politics and public administration, but progress so far has been slow and uneven (Sotiropoulos, 2004). A lot of work remains to be done in building accountable governance systems, which suggests that the ongoing and fluctuating gap between southern European countries, such as Greece and Italy, and northern and western Europe, remains (Tassinari, 2014).[6]

Social policy and the welfare system

The Italian and Greek welfare systems, which belong to the Mediterranean or southern model (Ferrera, 2005), are typically described as underdeveloped versions of the conservative/corporatist system, based on Esping-Andersen's 1990 classification (Esping-Andersen, 1990), together with a strong presence of clientelist tendencies in the funding and delivery of social protection. Indeed, the clientelist patterns of behaviour described in the previous section are manifested in the welfare sectors of both countries in the form of reciprocal patron–client relations between social administrations and beneficiaries in the distribution of resources and benefits. This has a direct influence on both the structuring of state welfare institutions and the practice of social welfare provision (Ferrera, 2005; Gal, 2010;

Matsaganis, 2013). Such clientelist tendencies persisted despite the expansion of social welfare in the 1970s and 1980s[7] and the increased social spending on pensions, unemployment benefits and social rights following authoritarian rule and the transition to democracy (Sotiropoulos, 2004).

In general, southern European welfare systems are considered to have developed unevenly, while trying to 'catch up' with western and northern Europe as part of a process of Europeanisation (Gal, 2010, p 285). In addition, their expansion took place during a period in which the legitimacy of the welfare state in Europe was starting to weaken, with calls for fiscal constraints, modernisation and reform, including the containment of costs of social programmes and the tightening of social budgets (Petmesidou and Guillen, 2014). This resulted in the emergence of rudimentary welfare systems and fragmented forms of social welfare provision that were dependent on employment and the male breadwinner model as a precondition for social coverage. Passive or reactive social models and policies with emphasis on cash transfers came at the expense of service provision and underdeveloped social policy areas (Calzada and Brooks, 2013).

In spite of these common trends, however, the welfare states of Greece and Italy are distinct in one underlying way: according to a typology adopted by the European Commission,[8] Greece's welfare structure (together with those of Spain and Portugal) is still in its infancy, while the Italian system is part of a group of the more mature European welfare states based on insurance, such as France, Belgium and Germany (Katrougalos and Lazaridis, 2003). An additional diverging point in the welfare systems of the two countries relates to the respective type of territorial politics and devolution stages. In the case of Italy, territorial variations translate into 'conflicting models of welfare', with vast discrepancies in benefits and social priorities between different regions or municipalities along political lines (Cancellieri and Longo, 2012). In contrast, the highly centralised, unitary organisation of both the political system and the welfare state in Greece has precluded such territorial variations (Symeonidou, 2013),[9] though the inequalities of peripheral development can result in fragmented social policies as gaps in infrastructure and social protection are evident in poorer regions (Katrougalos and Lazaridis, 2003). A further particularity of the Greek case concerns the progressive division between the capital, Athens, with the highest concentration of labour and industry on the one hand, and the rest of Greece, or the periphery, on the other (Papademetriou and Emke-Poulopoulos, 1991).

Welfare systems, such as the ones in Italy and Greece that are inadequately funded, lack coordination and are based on cash transfers favouring working people who are already part of the labour market, rather than those with precarious employment, run the risk of being unable to respond effectively to new challenges and risks, such as precarious employment, unemployment, the social transformations of the family unit, low birth rates and an ageing population (Cancellieri and Longo, 2012; Fokas, 2012). The development of overall weak systems of social protection and state support for families, and the limited success in alleviating poverty and income inequality, as well as low levels of female labour participation, became the weakest, and most persistent, links of the southern European or Mediterranean social welfare systems (Ferrera, 2005; Gal, 2010; Moreno and Mari-Klose, 2013). Poverty and income inequality therefore remained much higher in most southern European countries compared with the rest of Europe, even before the economic crisis of 2009 (Petmesidou, 2013b; Matsaganis, 2013). After 2009, the social consequences of the economic crisis, such as unemployment, precarious work opportunities, job insecurity, and reduced income levels and homelessness, coupled with state cutbacks in social protection and public healthcare services, and increased taxation, magnified the already significant weaknesses of the welfare systems.

Family and gender in social welfare

While the public welfare sector in Greece and Italy is founded on universal healthcare and education, social protection is conditional on labour market participation. Therefore, paid work, primarily through the male breadwinner model, is a precondition for any type of social rights, insurance and benefits, with a tendency towards cash transfers rather than provision of social services, targeted primarily at families (Cancellieri and Longo, 2012). The uneven and fragmented characteristics in the Italian and Greek welfare systems have left a large vacuum in welfare provision. This has typically been filled by the family, which compensates for the lack of state social services (Gal, 2010; Calzada and Brooks, 2013; Petmesidou, 2013). Researchers have therefore considered the southern European welfare systems to be part of the Mediterranean typology of the 'familist regime', where the family – and not the state – acts as a social safety net (Ferrera, 2005; Petmesidou, 2013, p 179). This constitutes one of the strongest common elements between the Italian and Greek welfare systems. As a provider of social care to its members and extended family members, the Mediterranean family has preserved its integrity (Moreno and Mari-Klose, 2013) and acts as a generous welfare broker and provider, pooling resources in a number of areas, ranging from childcare and care for the elderly and disabled, to employment within family-owned enterprises and housing, as well as direct or indirect income support (Ferrera, 2005; Moreno, 2006). In this sense, family solidarity has acted historically as an informal social shock absorber and source of intergenerational 'household micro-solidarity' (Moreno and Mari-Klose, 2013, pp 494-5). However, such high levels of family-based social care in the Mediterranean are not unique to southern Europe. Indeed in Chapter Seven, Siniša Zrinščak argues that in post-communist countries family ties and loyalties are also very strong, with similar explicit and implicit forms of familialism, and with specific caring responsibilities for the family as a fundamental social institution as a result of the loopholes and gaps in social care left by the respective state welfare systems.

The explicit familialism that we observe in southern Europe is based to a great extent on the morality of intra-family solidarity, namely the 'moral responsibility' for the family (typically women) to look after family members, rather than outsourcing this responsibility to the state. This conceptualisation of solidarity is based not only on moral grounds and a sense of duty and dignity, but also on the view that families can provide better care than the state (Moreno, 2006, p 76; Calzada and Brooks, 2013). It may further relate to the social stigma that has been traditionally associated in certain cultures with receiving social welfare services from state institutions rather than from family members (Katrougalos and Lazaridis, 2003). In fact, a crucial consequence of the family in its role as a social safety net is the creation of gendered perceptions and divisions, as family solidarity entails rigid and 'appropriate' gender roles, with the man acting as the main breadwinner and the woman as the primary care provider with domestic responsibility for the household. Household micro-solidarity is practically synonymous with the care offered by women who, on the one hand, automatically become the official or main providers of care work for family members, but, on the other, act as informal (unpaid) care workers within the extended family, acquiring the role of 'compulsory altruists' (Symeonidou, 2013, p 84).

A key factor that has helped maintain and legitimise this interdependence between the welfare model, the endurance of the family and the gendered relationships within it is also linked to a religious tradition. Researchers have observed that both Catholic and Orthodox forms of Christianity have stronger ties to the community, the family and the institution of marriage, compared with the more individualistic ethic of Protestantism (Gal, 2010; Moreno and Mari-Klose, 2013). This in turn has legitimised and reinforced a gendered division of labour where women have a pivotal role and typically fill the loopholes left by state welfare services.

The role of the family as a social security net sets southern Europe and post-communist countries apart from northern and western European countries. This leads to two intertwined questions: whether the family solidarity that is particularly strong in southern Europe has been a result of, and response to, the gaps of the state welfare sector; and/or whether the strong presence of the family as a social safety net has been a cause of, or factor in, the structural weaknesses of the southern European welfare regimes (Trautsch, 2013). In other words, did assumptions about the traditional role of women and the family in social care encourage the state to limit its spending in areas usually covered by the family, taking the self-reliance of families for granted and simply assuming that these areas would be covered by the family as a de facto alternative to state welfare provision (Moreno, 2006, p 76; Gal, 2010)? Furthermore, has the crucial role of the family as a safety net in social welfare reinforced the 'who you are related to' syndrome, and rendered the state reluctant to invest further in welfare service provision, thereby perpetuating serious gaps in the state welfare system (Moreno, 2006; Moreno and Mari-Klose, 2013)? The answers probably lie somewhere in between these two poles, with the family and the state being strongly intertwined in the southern European context.

All over Europe, transformations in the institution of marriage and the size and structure of the family unit (with an increasing number of one-parent families and cohabitation arrangements), declining birth rates, and the growing participation of women in the labour market, are challenging traditional caring arrangements and are transforming social expectations and practices in the area of care (Moreno and Mari-Klose, 2013). The structure of the Mediterranean family is also starting to fade, and the family unit, which has typically been a very important source of support and coping mechanism, is under pressure (Calzada and Brooks, 2013). Moreover, given the economic crisis, female employment, often considered more of a private choice but gradually becoming a necessity, has implications for care responsibilities within the family and duties in the workplace. Researchers often refer to the 'double-shift' burden of Mediterranean women (or 'superwomen', according to Moreno, 2006, p 76), resulting from both unpaid care responsibilities for family members and paid employment (Bugra, 2012, p 11). The result is a trade-off between motherhood and working outside the home: an erratic career or no career at all (withdrawing from the labour market), having fewer children, or employing immigrant women for domestic work (Moreno, 2006, p 75).

These developments in the division of labour with regard to caring responsibilities along gender lines bring to the forefront more specific questions pertaining to care and the role of formal and informal care workers. The resulting vacuum in the provision of social care has led to the emergence of the demand for care work, usually provided by female immigrant domestic workers, who are often favoured as the preferred means of social care provision over those provided by the state (Gal, 2010; Calzada and Brooks, 2013; Moreno and Mari-Klose, 2013). In this respect, some researchers talk about the weakening of traditional or formal familialism as part of a process of 'de-familialisation of care' in favour of the emergence of a new social care market (Da Roit et al, 2013, 2015; Moreno and Mari-Klose, 2013, p 510).

The intersection of family, gender and religion in welfare

Given the historically passive state intervention in social welfare in southern Europe, state budget cuts and the severe effects of the economic crisis, the family finds itself overburdened and increasingly unable to support and care for relatives. An enormous burden and mounting pressure has been created for families, as they have been left alone to take care of the needs of children and old or vulnerable family members. While the family is increasingly unable to act as a social safety net (Calzada and Brooks, 2013), the state is gradually retrenching from social service provision, leaving this area to the private sector (for-profit companies) and the voluntary or third sector. Researchers therefore refer to a growing 'welfare pluralism' or 'welfare mix', in which the social welfare landscape can be compared to a mosaic, comprising the state/public and private sector, the family and voluntary organisations (Schartau, 2009; Rose, 2011). This is where faith-based organisations (that is, churches and other faith-based organisations) operate as sources of additional social support and solidarity. In that sense, faith-based organisations, especially majority churches, seem to be complementing the welfare function of the family in what could arguably be called the role of a 'second family'.

Majority churches as welfare actors in Italy and Greece

The role of faith-based organisations, including majority churches, relates more broadly to the question of how religious organisations, with their specific values of philanthropy, establish social welfare institutions, and thus influence the structure of welfare systems, social policy and delivery of social services. The economic crisis that began in 2009 has prompted a 'redeployment' of the social role of religion, including majority churches, in redefining the relationships between religious actors and the public sector in social policy implementation and social welfare provision (Itçaina, 2015). Indeed, majority churches in Greece and Italy do their best to fill the large social welfare gaps left by the state, especially when the family is no longer able to offer support, by playing an active role in the development and implementation of social services. Churches provide a range of social services when social support is either not offered by the state, or when remote geographical regions are not served by the state.

More immediately, majority churches are also intervening in a more recent challenge that the welfare systems in Italy and Greece have been facing, namely the mass influx of immigrants, which has been increasing since 2013 and reached a peak in 2015-16. Because of the geopolitical position of the two countries at the southern borders of Europe, Italy and Greece are on the frontline of this crisis, serving as the main points of entry for migrants and refugees from the Middle East and Northern Africa on their way to western and northern Europe.

These unprecedented refugee and immigration numbers have caught Europe unprepared, and have exposed the complete lack of any common policy or coordination regarding the handling of this humanitarian crisis.[10] Consequently, this has left the burden in the hands of the Italian and Greek governments – two transition, not destination, countries[11] that have been asked to supervise the relocation schemes, which are reserved for refugees primarily from Syria and Eritrea,[12] to act in effecting mass returns following an EU agreement with Turkey and, last but not least, to organise (temporary) migrant detention centres in selected spaces and areas[13] (for example, the Idomeni camp on the Greek northern border with the former Yugoslav Republic of Macedonia). The sheer number of refugees and migrants has also caught the current social infrastructure of the two countries unprepared and rendered them unable to cope in the processing and regularisation of refugees and migrants who face structural barriers to registration, application processing, and access to health and social care. Employment and overall social integration, on account of poorly formulated and implemented immigration policies, together with structural and bureaucratic obstacles, are further challenges that add huge pressures to already weakened welfare systems in both countries. While the economic crisis in Italy and Greece led the European Commission in August 2015 to approve a 2.4 billion Euro emergency aid package (with 560 million Euros earmarked for Italy and 473 million Euros for Greece) to subsidise their migrant rescue efforts, many policymakers claim that these funds fall far short given the growing magnitude of the problem (Reuters, 2015).

In response to both the economic and refugee crisis, third-sector organisations, including majority churches, are increasingly trying to fill in the gaps. Faced with such a dire social situation, there are very strong signs of volunteer activities and social mobilisation on the part of civil society (Fokas, 2012). This is an interesting development, especially in a country such as Greece where civil society and the culture of volunteerism have historically been weak (Clarke et al., 2015; Roumeliotis and Jones, 2010). Albeit concluded before the onset of the recent and more intense influx of immigrants and the humanitarian crisis, the WaVE case study reports on Italy and Greece nevertheless reflect to different extents the tensions in the interaction between majority (including majority churches) and minority populations in the context of immigration policies and welfare provisions. An interesting point in common is the fact that in both countries immigration has become to a large extent an 'Islamic' immigration issue, influencing national debates about Muslim integration, the international threat of terrorism (Frisina and Cancellieri, 2012), the public and social role of religion, and church–state relations, especially in the case of Greece (Kokosalakis and Fokas, 2012).

The following sections look more carefully at the religious traditions in Greece and Italy. Specific structural and historical factors help explain differences in the conceptualisation, development and delivery of the social welfare work offered by Italian Catholic and Greek Orthodox churches and their role in the context of growing immigration.

Italy

The Italian Catholic Church, albeit independent from the Italian state, enjoys particular privileges that emanate from the 1984 'framework of agreement' between the Catholic Church and the state. For example, it guarantees the appointment of key figures who have ecclesiastical functions, and the official civil acknowledgement of religious holidays, as well as the teaching of the Catholic religion in schools (Cancellieri and Longo, 2012). As a result of its institutionally favourable position in the country, and through its presence in the public sector and roots in civil society, the Church continues to exercise direct influence on how Italian society organises itself (Driessen, 2014).

The Catholic Church's social work is founded on the principle of subsidiarity, namely the precedence of intermediate and independent or third-party welfare bodies (including the Catholic Church and other faith-based organisations) over public providers in the implementation of social policies and development and delivery of welfare services (Cancellieri and Longo, 2012). Originally developed in the 1890s[14] as a key foundation of Catholic social teaching, the concept of subsidiarity was further emphasised by Pope Benedict in 2006 in his encyclical *Deus Caritas*. Here subsidiarity is a principle that 'generously acknowledges and supports initiatives arising from the different social forces and combines spontaneity with closeness to those in need' (Ratzinger, 2006).[15] Following Law 328/2000, which among others recognised the role of private associations, including church associations, in welfare provision, state authorities in Italy have turned to the third sector as part of an 'externalisation of welfare services trend' (Muehlebach, 2012; Ozzano and Giorgi, 2016, p 26). This is part of a larger, accelerated process of decentralisation in various policy areas, among which are social care and healthcare, that favours more regionalism in Italy, with the delivery of social services falling under the jurisdiction of local/regional authorities and municipalities (Cancellieri and Longo, 2012; Ozzano and Giorgi, 2016). Decisions are to be taken at a local level with a strong appreciation of the role of intermediary third-sector (non-profit) organisations, such as voluntary organisations, including church-related organisations, fraternal groups and parish churches. But this has also raised concerns over territorial inequalities and variations, depending on the human and material/financial resources of local areas (Cancellieri and Longo, 2012).

The principle of subsidiarity combined with the process of decentralisation in Italy (and also in Europe as a whole) has given renewed legitimacy to religious organisations and increased their role in the area of welfare. This has helped to erode further the top–down hierarchical organisation of the Catholic Church, which was already weakened by the Second Vatican Council (1962-68), leading to greater decentralisation and the autonomy of local churches. Following state budget cuts, the Catholic Church's role in the Italian welfare sector has become even stronger, thus encouraging the growth of intermediary bodies in the implementation of social welfare policies (Cancellieri and Longo, 2012).[16]

The Italian Catholic Church has developed a broad and officially recognised network of charitable organisations and, through its social arm Caritas-Diakonia, it has become a crucial welfare partner for local authorities in dealing with poverty and emergency situations. The

Church uses its local or regional knowledge to highlight new areas of need and provide data to state authorities through a broad range of Catholic organisations, from direct-affiliation organisations, such as Caritas-Diakonia, to other church-related and faith-based organisations and informal parish groups (Itçaina, 2015). Caritas can therefore often play the role of data provider and social whistle-blower (Itçaina, 2015, p 16). At the same time, Catholic organisations provide basic social welfare services (such as distributing primary goods and services, and offering housing) as primary care providers with a vanguard role (using Pettersson's typology of different functions – Pettersson, 2011). In addition, and beyond charity, the Catholic Church's social action expands towards social activism and advocacy (poverty, human rights, social justice and global peace), including innovative programmes that promote empowerment and social inclusion, and use conditional forms of assistance (for example, food and housing in exchange for job search or community engagement – see the case study of third-sector organisations in the Emilia Romagna region of Italy by Xabier Itçaina, 2015). Catholic organisations have, therefore, engaged in social advocacy work such as campaigning for residence and work permits for the regularisation process for migrants, developing legislative and policymaking proposals, and offering expertise on poverty and social exclusion. As such, Catholic third-sector activism, especially when working with immigrants, is close to secular local and transnational global justice and peace movements working with migrants (Itçaina, 2015). The recent immigration crisis has not found the Catholic Church in Italy entirely united, however. Much as in the case of the Orthodox Church in Greece (discussed in the next section), prelates of the Catholic Church in Italy have expressed their scepticism about providing care and support to migrants by publicly sharing the views of xenophobic politicians – such as Mattero Salvini, leader of the Northern League Party – that Italians must put their own interests first.[17]

Such activism is not limited to the majority church in Italy, as other religious communities also engage in forms of welfare provision. In response, for instance, to the immigration and humanitarian crisis, the Federation of Protestant Churches in Italy – including the Methodist and Waldensian Churches – launched a programme entitled Mediterranean Hope, which sought to secure and improve the conditions for migrants who have risked their lives crossing the Mediterranean (primarily in the boats of smugglers), by offering them accommodation, helping with their integration into the Italian population, and successfully putting pressure on the government to implement the issue of 'humanitarian' visas for vulnerable individuals.[18] Similarly, the Italian Islamic Religious Community (CO.RE.IS.), the main organisation that gathers Italian Muslims together, has set up two working groups, one related to education and another one to health, which on the one hand, help institutions understand the religious needs of immigrants, and, on the other, help the latter to understand the legal and technical needs of institutional and public structures.

Nonetheless, as the study by Annalisa Frisina and Adriano Cancellieri on Padua shows (Frisina and Cancellieri, 2012), there is a particular field in which welfare, religion and gender roles seem to clash in Italy: namely reproductive health. The study investigated access and availability of local welfare services to immigrants by focusing on reproductive health, a type of welfare service that immigrant women use widely. Considering the discourse and practices of the social actors involved, the findings show that institutional Catholicism plays a predominant role in local welfare, and that when it comes to reproductive health the Italian welfare regime is predominantly conservative. Within this perspective, cuts in social spending and the negative portrayal of migrants by the mass media (as undesirables to be expelled) have rendered the provision of health services, especially to irregular migrants, a particularly challenging problem. As a result, the view that seemed to prevail in the Padua case study was that social rights are not for everyone, but should be granted only to certain groups, such as legal migrants and autochthonous citizens. The field of reproductive health is therefore very revealing as it includes issues that pertain in particular to women, ranging from childcare services to abortion. Furthermore, in spite of the presence of progressive Catholics within the Italian welfare system, the active role of institutional Catholicism played by a number of conservative private social organisations (mainly those affiliated to the pro-life movement) creates very real tensions in this field (these are developed in detail in Chapter Eleven).

Despite the Italian Catholic Church's significant social action in the area of welfare, opinions with regard to its intervention in the economic crisis differ. Xabier Itçaina focuses on the (predominantly secularised) region of Emilia-Romagna and argues that the crisis has strengthened the role of the Catholic Church as service provider in public welfare (Itçaina, 2015). At the same time, however, the Catholic Church has been criticised for using only a small percentage of its revenue to provide social welfare actions and for not deploying all of its economic and social capacity to act effectively in a time of crisis and social collapse. While Catholic associations such as Caritas have campaigned to defend the interests of the victims of the economic crisis, they have also been criticised for offering weak, symbolic and ineffective initiatives. As in the case of the Orthodox Church in Greece, the burning issue of clerical wealth has also emerged in Italy since 2008, as critics have attacked the ambiguous legislation relating to the Catholic Church's tax exemption on its commercial property.[19]

Greece

A similar situation can be observed in Greece, as the impact of the economic crisis has put additional pressures on the Orthodox Church of Greece (OCG) to increase its social charitable work in social welfare. This has happened in a context where the Church already has a significant place in the Greek welfare system, originating in the philanthropic role of the Church during the Byzantine era and the establishment of the modern Greek state in the 19th century, when the Church represented a model of philanthropy and, together with the family, catered for welfare needs (Fokas, 2012). In fact, the Greek state and the OCG often work in partnership, as the latter's 'prevailing position', confirmed by Article 3 of the Constitution of 1975, reflects its symbolic nature as civil religion, as well as an overall organisational and economic role in the country's affairs. The Orthodox Church is, moreover, considered by law (Law 590/1977) as an official and *de jure* partner of the state in social protection (Kokosalakis and Fokas, 2012; Petmesidou and Polyzoidis, 2013).

We might argue that the principle of subsidiarity in Greek Orthodoxy took shape and form in the Church's decentralised structure, and more particularly in its decentralised welfare provision (Fokas, 2012). However, Orthodox social service, or diaconia, is different. The values of Eastern Orthodoxy and its relatively limited engagement in social activism were not conducive to the development of institutionalised voluntary action (Petmesidou and Polyzoidis, 2013). Furthermore, national Orthodox churches are autocephalous entities under the authority of autonomous patriarchates, with the right to elect bishops within each administrative jurisdiction. There is no predominant centralised and hierarchical administrative structure, such as we find in the Catholic Church in the figure of the Pope and the authority of the Vatican, involved in social service (charity) and social action and advocacy. As a result, Orthodox social service developed locally and often informally at the level of dioceses and parishes, which typically act as the key driving engines of social work (Fokas, 2012). It is only recently, in 1992, that a concerted and material effort has been made to coordinate, streamline and expand the Church's social work through the creation of a pan-Orthodox humanitarian organisation (International Orthodox Christian Charities, or IOCC) to provide emergency relief and development programmes worldwide, somewhat in the spirit of Caritas-Diakonia (IOCC, 2009; Molokotos-Liederman, 2011).

In Greece, where civil society and volunteerism are relatively weak (Roumeliotis and Jones, 2010; Clarke et al, 2015), historically there has been a mutual influence and interaction between the welfare provided by the Church and that provided by the state. For instance, the Church's social service is funded by the Church itself, which in turn is funded indirectly by the state, which pays all priests' salaries. The Church also owns an important property portfolio. The Church formally coordinates social welfare services through its consultative Synodical Committee for Social Welfare and Benefits and other central organisations.[20] This committee provides social welfare services at a local and regional level through parishes and dioceses, which are free to respond as they see fit, since bishops and priests have a direct contact with their local communities (Fokas, 2012). The Church's welfare provision is decentralised and flexible and has the advantage of being easily accessed by local communities in local parishes, even in remote parts that are not well served by state welfare. Local parishes and priests have extensive knowledge of local needs and the socioeconomic circumstances of communities, but because of the decentralised nature of the Church's social welfare provision, there is considerable variation in the type and quality of services across the different dioceses. Social welfare consists of material support (food, clothing, medical assistance) and social care institutions and services for elderly people, disabled people, refugees, migrants and others in need, whether Greek or foreign. During the crisis, the Church's soup kitchens became the most visible, and perhaps most mediatised, part of its social welfare work. The role of the OCG is also significant in informal ways in providing material and spiritual need at a local level, as in extreme cases of personal and family problems, illness and death (Kokosalakis and Fokas, 2012).

As in the case of Italy, in addition to Orthodox organisations, other religious communities and associations are also active in the social field. Organisations such as Caritas Hellas,[21] St Paul's (Anglican) Church,[22] the Greek Evangelical Church,[23] in Athens, and the Muslim Association of Greece[24] provide a range of social services to Greeks and/or migrants, refugees and asylum seekers who are in need of social assistance.[25] As Orthodox churches are typically 'national churches' that are deeply connected to ethnic characteristics, they act as vehicles of national and ethnic identity and identify with a nation state. As part of state mechanisms, Orthodox churches are often subordinated to the state, which has implications for their ability, or willingness, or lack thereof, to go beyond charity and engage in social activism or advocacy and adopt a critical social stance, especially with regard to the state and government policy, on social issues such as poverty, human rights, social justice and peace. In Greece, in particular, the interconnection between national and religious identity has increasingly been challenged by the mass influx of immigrants over the past 15 years, as questions arise about the sharing of welfare resources with 'others' (religious and ethnic minorities), who are often perceived as a threat to the Greek national and religious identity (Kokosalakis and Fokas, 2012). For instance, while the Archbishop of Athens, Ieronymos, has publicly stated the need for his Greek compatriots to be generous and caring with all newcomers, other bishops adopt a much more sceptical, if not openly xenophobic, rhetoric. Similarly, the Bishop of Thessaloniki, Anthimos, organised an event entitled We Remain Greeks – We Remain Orthodox in February 2016 at the city's Convention Centre, calling for a fight against the waves of immigration and the Islamisation of Europe to protect the national and religious (Orthodox) identity of Greek people.[26]

The increasing presence of immigrants in the country has challenged traditional values and has also questioned the basis of religion as a pathway towards societal cohesion. The Greek case study by Effie Fokas of the city of Thiva (Fokas, 2012) focused on welfare provisions in the context of immigration policy and its implementation by looking at the interaction and tension points between the majority population (and Church), and male and female economic immigrants. The pitfalls of immigration policy are found in bureaucratic inefficiencies and delays, and the insecure process of the attainment of residence and work permits, which constitute serious obstacles that immigrants must overcome to gain access to welfare services. Fokas' study further demonstrates that, although the local Orthodox Church shows a willingness to care for minorities' physical needs, much less interest is exhibited in catering for their spiritual needs (especially for non-Christian minorities, such as Indians and Pakistanis). Moreover, although the case study revealed no clear links between the role of the Orthodox Church and the position of migrant women in the context of immigration policy and welfare, the local situation in terms of gender seems to have changed significantly owing to the presence of female migrant workers, which is directly related to the ability of Greek women to free themselves from some of their household responsibilities. Gender issues thus emerged over two types of majority–minority interactions in Thiva. The first concerned competition for men among immigrant women and majority women (as a result of the increased number of Greek men choosing to marry immigrant women); the second related to an exclusive understanding of national identity and culture, expressed through a resistance among the majority society, including majority women, to foreign women 'entering' Greek homes through relationships and marriage, in order to preserve Greek culture and identity within the home (Fokas, 2012, p 293).

As in the case of Italy, despite its significant work offering social services during the economic crisis, the Orthodox Church of Greece has been criticised for having too much property, paying too little in taxes, or not contributing enough during the economic crisis. This has put the Church on the defensive and has prompted its hierarchy to make repeated public statements outlining its finances and highlighting its charitable contributions. More recently, the financial situation of the Church, namely its dwindling lack of financial resources, verging on bankruptcy, has come to the forefront of public attention (see Molokotos-Liederman, 2016).

Conclusion

We have focused on two southern European countries, Greece and Italy, which, apart from their geographic proximity, share similar cultural, social, economic and political profiles, as well as distinct differences. This has had consequences for the responses of the majority churches in these countries to the current economic crisis.

Majority churches in both Italy and Greece fill the large social welfare gaps left by the respective states by actively implementing social services in support of the changes and challenges that the Mediterranean family has been facing. In addition, majority religious traditions in the two countries, Catholicism and Orthodoxy, have helped to maintain a traditional, established interconnection between the welfare system, the dominant role of the family, and the gendered divisions of labour, largely at the expense of women.

In Italy, the work of Catholic associations takes place on two levels: providing basic social welfare services that offer expertise and information on local needs, but also engaging in social advocacy work and mobilisation alongside other social anti-austerity movements. This proactive role has been facilitated by the increasing autonomy of Italian associations in relation to their institutional organisation. It also indicates a greater proximity between Catholic organisations and national and transnational secular movements, such as global justice and peace movements, and associations in support of migrants.

In Greece, the social work of the Orthodox Church of Greece and other Orthodox associations tends to operate primarily at the level of charity and philanthropic assistance. Moreover, by refraining from engaging in social advocacy, and by remaining a primarily philanthropic and charitable institution, the Orthodox Church and its associations do not act as a critical voice in social welfare issues or public debates on social justice (Makris and Bekridakis, 2013). The Church's work has been widely recognised but also criticised by certain milieus as being reactive and addressing the symptoms rather than the root cause of social problems (Makris and Bekridakis, 2013). A partial explanation for this may lie in the financial dependence of the Church on the Greek state that acts as a deterrent, limiting the former's potential involvement in social mobilisation or advocacy in the areas of poverty, inequality and social justice.

The examples of Greece and Italy are not diametrically opposed cases but rather variations on the theme of majority churches as social welfare actors and stakeholders. They are part of a general landscape where Christian churches are at the frontline of social welfare provision, alongside the state and third-sector stakeholders. They take on a range of roles using the typology developed by Per Pettersson (2011), acting as primary, complementary and/or supplementary providers. As 'complementary welfare service providers' and 'improvers', they add to, and improve, overall welfare provision, filling in the large gaps left by the state welfare systems. They can, however, assume a vanguard role, highlighting new areas of need and prioritising groups of people in need, as the Italian case has demonstrated. This situation presents both opportunities and challenges for majority churches. It presents opportunities because the churches' knowledge of, and proximity to, local community and welfare needs may open the way to expanding social service work and to running social welfare programmes in cooperation with the state, which in turn can help churches regain social relevance and public trust and perhaps redefine their function and place in society. It presents challenges, because churches find themselves in a position of having to increase their social profile at a time of decreasing financial resources, thus having to strike a balance between self-sufficiency in the fulfilment of their social work and a quest for more resources, with the possible risk of being reduced to welfare agents.

In a climate of economic depression, where the welfare state coexists with different religious traditions, and church–state relations come face to face with growing religious pluralism and social inequalities, religion has re-emerged as an ever more visible social and political actor. This is the context in which the state, the family and the church in Italy and Greece, as in the rest of Europe, are asked to respond to both the opportunities and the challenges that lie ahead, and to play a key role, amongst others actors, in finding the way forward on issues of social welfare provision in relation to minorities and gender.

Notes

[1] On 11 August 1479, the Ottoman conqueror Gedik Ahmed captured the city of Otranto in south-east Italy. While the fall of Otranto was regarded as a first step toward the capture of Rome, the news of the sultan Mehmet the Conqueror's death in 1481 reached Gedik Ahmed with an urgent request for his return to the capital. Otranto was quickly retaken by the Neapolitans and Italy was spared further Ottoman invasions (Hazard and Zacour, 1989).

[2] The 'clean hands' (*mani pulite*) scandal involved investigations into a vast network of bribes between industry and politicians from all four main parties of the Italian parliament. Following the murder of two judges who were investigating links with the Mafia and suicides of politicians, the old governing parties dissolved and a new party system emerged in 1992: the Second Republic. While some researchers consider this to be a turning point in Italian history that has led to the moral regeneration of Italian politics primarily in terms of lowering levels of corruption, others are much more sceptical and emphasise the limited effect of this window of opportunity (Della Porta and Vannucci, 2007).

[3] That is, patchy industrialisation in Italy, as evidenced in the vast socioeconomic gaps between northern and southern Italy (Piattoni, 2001), and more geographically even, but late, industrialisation in Greece.

[4] We here use Simona Piattoni's definitions of clientelism and patronage as related phenomena, broadly defined as 'the trade of votes and other types of partisan support in exchange for public decisions with divisible benefits' (Piattoni. 2001, p 4). In simpler terms, we could conceive of clientelism as reciprocal or transactional relations in public decision making, which ultimately may 'become a token of exchange' (Piattoni, 2001, p 6).

[5] However, decentralisation and devolution seem to have been slower in Greece and more accelerated in Italy (Sotiropulos, 2004), where regions enjoy increasing autonomy.

[6] See also www.huffingtonpost.com/fabrizio-tassinari/north-south-Europe-divide_b_5288252.html. In 2015, the *German Marshall Fund commissioned, as part of its Europe Programme, a study on the north–south governance divide and cleavage in Europe,* exploring the reality of this divide in terms of economics, governance, finances, and public opinion (see www.gmfus.org/initiatives/southern-Europe).

[7] For example, the establishment of the Italian national health service in 1978 and the Greek national health service in 1983.

[8] The basic criteria of the typology are the financing of the social protection systems by the insurance principle, or by taxation and their overall maturity.

[9] Some decentralisation reforms, which seek to bring the decision-making process to the level where decisions are being implemented, have emerged since the second half of the 1990s (OECD, 2001).

[10] See the BBC (2016) 'Why is EU struggling with migrants and asylum?', 3 March, available at www.bbc.com/news/world-europe-24583286

[11] Greece is in fact considered one of the worst destinations in Europe for refugees, partly because of the inadequacies of its welfare system (Kokosalakis and Fokas, 2012).

[12] In September 2015, EU ministers agreed to resettle 120,000 migrants – a small fraction of those seeking asylum in Europe – from Greece and Italy across 23 member states. (Greece and Italy will not be required to resettle more migrants, and Denmark, Ireland, and the UK are exempt from EU asylum policies under provisions laid out in the 2009 Lisbon Treaty) (Park, 2014).

[13] See Politi, 2016: https://next.ft.com/content/664e52c8-fa4e-11e5-8e04-8600cef2ca75.

[14] An encyclical letter by Pope Leo XIII in May 1891, *Rerum Novarum*, marked the beginning of the Catholic Church's involvement in social policy; it is a key foundational text of the Catholic Church's teaching.

[15] The concept of subsidiarity is also one of the founding elements of the European project, and part of the EU's emphasis on, and championing of, decentralisation and devolution (Muehlebach, 2012).

[16] Despite its privileged relationship with the Italian state and increased presence in the welfare sector, the Italian Catholic Church is not officially endorsed by the state to provide social services (Cancellieri and Longo, 2012). The Catholic Church is funded primarily by the *otto per mille* (0.8%) scheme, according to which all taxpaying citizens can choose to allocate 0.8% of their income tax to one of seven bodies, including the Catholic Church, other recognised Christian denominations and the Italian Jewish communities, or, alternatively, to a social assistance scheme run by the Italian State (Cancellieri and Longo, 2012).

[17] *The Economist* (2015) 'Diverse, desperate migrants have divided European Christians', 6 September, available at www.economist.com/blogs/erasmus/2015/09/migrants-christianity-and-Europe

[18] See World Council of Churches (2015) 'Italian churches urge more "humanitarian corridors" for migrants', 12 November, available at www.oikoumene.org/en/press-centre/news/italian-churches-urge-more-201chumanitarian-corridors201d-for-migrants

[19] See Bloomberg et al (2012) 'Debt crisis leaves nothing sacred as Italy church chased on tax', 18 January, available at www.bloomberg.com/news/articles/2012-01-17/italian-church-chased-on-property-tax-as-debt-crisis-leaves-nothing-sacred

[20] The two most notable organisations are Christianiki Allilengyi (Christian Solidarity), an organisation created in 1957 and providing social services throughout the 145 parishes of the Archdiocese of Athens, and Apostoli (Mission), which is the official non-governmental organisation (NGO) of the Archdiocese of Athens and the Church of Greece. It was founded by Archbishop Ieronymos in 2010 after the Church's former NGO was shut down a few years ago because of mismanagement of funds. The work of Apostoli and Christian Solidarity is well known for the mass distribution of charity meals under the programme The Church on the Streets, its social grocery shops, and social clinics for uninsured people.

[21] See http://www.caritas.gr.

[22] See http://anglicanchurchathens.gr/#pastoral_care.

[23] See http://athensproject.org. A further example here is the Christian humanitarian organisation Faros, which serves and supports refugee minors in Greece, with

particular focus on those that are unaccompanied by parents or relatives: http://www.faros.org.gr.

[24] The Muslim Association of Greece was established in 2003 as an official organisation representing Muslim communities, particularly the largest, a Pakistani organisation, and Islamic affairs in Greece. It advocates the religious rights of Muslims, but also offers some social assistance (food and shelter) to immigrants, refugees and asylum seekers (Oikonomakis, 2011).

[25] The social services and philanthropy offered by non-Orthodox religious communities (Christian or other) in Greece was an issue that emerged in some interviews conducted in the context of the European Research Council project, Grassrootsmobilise (http://grassrootsmobilise.eu). The main concern on behalf of these non-Orthodox communities concerns their belief that their services are not publicised as those of the Orthodox communities, and are being overshadowed by the services offered by the Orthodox Church, thus raising important questions about inter-religious dynamics and cooperation in the country.

[26] See www.tanea.gr/news/greece/article/5334686/anthimos-egklhma-an-anakateytoyn-alloi-laoi-sth-thessalonikh

References

Bugra, A. (2012) 'Introduction', in Y. Ozkan and A. Bugra (eds) *Trajectories of Female Employment in the Mediterranean*, London: Palgrave Macmillan, pp 1–15.

Caciagli, M. (2006) 'The long life of clientelism in Southern Italy', in J. Kawata (ed) *Comparing Political Corruption and Clientelism*, Aldershot: Ashgate.

Calzada, I. and Brooks, C. (2013) 'The myth of Mediterranean familism', *European Societies*, 15(4): 514–34.

Cancellieri, A. and Longo, V. (2012) 'Italy: overview of the national situation', in A. Bäckström (ed) *Welfare and Values in Europe: Transitions Related to Religion, Minorities and Gender, Volume 1. Northern Europe: Sweden, Norway, Finland, England*, Studies in Religion and Society 4, Uppsala: Acta Universitatis Upsaliensis, pp 176–204.

Clarke, J., Huliaras, A. and Sotiropoulos, D. (2015) *Austerity and the Third Sector in Greece: Civil Society at the European Frontline*, Aldershot: Ashgate.

Da Roit, B., González Ferrer, A. and Moreno-Fuentes, F.J. (2013) 'The Southern European migrant-based care model', *European Societies*, 15(4): 577–96.

Da Roit, B., González Ferrer, A. and Moreno-Fuentes, F. J. (2015) 'The southern European migrant-based care model. Long-term care and employment trajectories in Italy and Spain', in F. Javier Moreno-Fuentes and P. Mari-Klose (eds) *The Mediterranean Welfare Regime and the Economic Crisis*, London and New York, NY: Routledge, pp 5–22.

Della Porta, D. and Vannucci, A. (2007) 'Corruption and anti-corruption: the political defeat of "clean hands" in Italy', *West European Politics*, 30(4): 830-53.

Diamandouros, N. and Gunther R. (eds) (2001) *Parties, Politics, and Democracy in the New Southern Europe*, Baltimore, MD: Johns Hopkins University Press.

Donovan, M. (2011) 'The invention of bipolar politics in Italy', *The Italianist*, 31: 62-78.

Driessen, M.D. (2014) *Religion and Democratization: Framing Religious and Political Identities in Muslim and Catholic Societies*, New York, NY: Oxford University Press.

Esping-Andersen, G. (1990) *The Three Worlds of Welfare Capitalism*, Princeton, NJ: Polity Press.

Ferrera, M. (2005) 'Welfare states and social safety nets in Southern Europe', in M. Ferrera (ed) *Welfare State Reform in Southern Europe. Fighting Poverty and Social Exclusion in Italy, Spain, Portugal and Greece*, London and New York, NY: Routledge, pp 1-23.

Fokas, E. (2012) 'Thiva case study report', in A. Bäckström (ed) *Welfare and Values in Europe: Transitions Related to Religion, Minorities and Gender. National Overviews and Case Study Reports, Volume 2. Continental Europe: Germany, France, Italy, Greece*, Studies in Religion and Society 5, Uppsala: Acta Universitatis Upsaliensis, pp 262-95, available at https://uu.diva-portal.org/smash/get/diva2:510653/FULLTEXT01.pdf.

Frisina, A. and Cancellieri, A. (2012) 'Padua case study report', in A. Bäckström (ed) *Welfare and Values in Europe: Transitions Related to Religion, Minorities and Gender. National Overviews and Case Study Reports, Volume 2. Continental Europe: Germany, France, Italy, Greece*, Studies in Religion and Society 5, Uppsala: Acta Universitatis Upsaliensis, pp 205-36. https://uu.diva-portal.org/smash/get/diva2:510653/FULLTEXT01.pdf.

Gal, J. (2010) 'Is there an extended family of Mediterranean welfare states?', *Journal of European Social Policy*, 20(4): 283-300.

Hazard, H.W. and Zacour, N.P. (1989) *A History of the Crusades. The Impact of the Crusades on Europe, Volume VI*, Madison, WI and London: University of Wisconsin Press.

IOCC (International Orthodox Christian Charities) (2009) 'Orthodox diaconia worldwide. An initial assessment', IOCC, 19 May, available at http://orthodoxdiakonia.net/

Itçaina, X. (2015) 'The crisis as a constrained opportunity? Catholic organisations and territorial welfare in the Basque Country and Emilia-Romagna', *Religion, State and Society*, 43(2): 118-32.

Katrougalos, G.S. and Lazaridis, G. (2003) *Southern European Welfare States. Problems, Challenges and Prospects*, London: Palgrave Macmillan.

Kokosalakis, N. and Fokas, E. (2012) *Welfare and Values in Europe: Transitions related to Religion, Minorities and Gender (WaVE). State of the art report B2: Greece - overview of the national situation*, Uppsala: Acta Universitatis Upsaliensis, available at: http://uu.diva-portal.org/smash/record.jsf?pid=diva2%3A303134&dswid=-4767.

Makris, G. and Bekridakis, D. (2013) 'The Greek Orthodox Church and the economic crisis since 2009', *International Journal for the Study of the Christian Church*, 13(2): 111–32, available at http://dx.doi.org/10.1080/1474225X.2013.793055.

Mari-Klose, P. and Moreno-Fuentes, F-J. (2015) 'The Southern European welfare model in the post-industrial order', in F.-J. Moreno-Fuentes and P. Mari-Klose (eds) *The Mediterranean Welfare Regime and the Economic Crisis*, London and New York, NY: Routledge.

Matsaganis, M. (2013) 'The crisis and the welfare state in Greece: a complex relationship', in A. Triandafillidou, R. Gropas and H. Kouki (eds) *The Greek Crisis and European Modernity*, Basingstoke and New York, NY: Palgrave Macmillan, pp 152–77.

Molokotos-Liederman, L. (2011) 'Religion as a solution to social problems: a Christian Orthodox approach', in T. Hjelm (ed) *Religion and Social Problems*, London and New York, NY: Routledge, pp 82–97.

Molokotos-Liederman, L. (2016) 'The impact of the crisis on the Orthodox Church of Greece: a moment of challenge and opportunity?', *Religion, State and Society*, 44(1): 32–50.

Moreno, L. (2006) 'The model of social protection in Southern Europe: enduring characteristics?', *Revue française des affaires sociales*, 5: 73–95.

Moreno, L. and Mari-Klose, P. (2013) 'Youth, family change and welfare arrangements: is the South still so different?', *European Societies*, 15(4): 493–513.

Morin, J. (1990) *Underground Economy and Irregular Forms of Employment*, Luxembourg: Commission of the European Communities.

Muehlebach, A. (2012) *The Moral Neoliberal: Welfare and Citizenship in Italy*, Chicago, IL: University of Chicago Press.

OECD (Organisation for Economic Co-operation and Development) (2001) *Territorial Reviews – Greece (Tzoumerka)*, Paris: OECD.

Oikonomakis, L. (2011) 'Faith-based organisations and social exclusion in Greece', in L. Oikonomakis, J. Barou, A. Walliser and S. Villanueva (eds) *Faith-Based Organisations and Social Exclusion in Greece, in France and Portugal*, Cahier 9, Research report of the Faith-Based Organisations and Social Exclusion in European Cities (FACIT) project, Leuven: Uitgeverij Acco.

Ozzano, L. and Giorgi, A. (2016) *European Culture Wars and the Italian Case: Which Side Are You On?*, Oxford: Routledge.

Papademetriou, D.G. and Emke-Poulopoulos, I. (1991) 'Migration and development in Greece: the unfinished story', in D.G. Papademetriou and P.L. Martin (eds) *Labor Migration and Economic Development*, Westport, CN: Greenwood Press.

Papakostas, A. (2012) *Civilizing the Public Sphere: Distrust, Trust and Corruption*, London: Palgrave Macmillan.

Park, J. (2014) 'Europe's migration crisis', Council on Foreign Relations, www.cfr.org/refugees-and-the-displaced/europes-migration-crisis/p32874.

Petmesidou, M. (2013) 'Is the crisis a watershed moment for the Greek welfare state? The chances for modernization amidst an ambivalent EU record on "Social Europe"', in A. Triandafillidou, R. Gropas and H. Kouki (eds) *The Greek Crisis and European Modernity*, Basingstoke and New York, NY: Palgrave Macmillan, pp 178-207.

Petmesidou, M. and Guillen, A. (2014) 'Can the welfare state as we know it survive? A view from the crisis-ridden South European periphery', *South European Society and Politics*, 19(3): 295-307.

Petmesidou, M. and Polyzoidis, P. (2013) 'Religion, values and the welfare state in Greece', in H.R. Reuter, and K. Gabriel (eds) *Religion, Values and the Welfare State* (in German), Münster: Westfälische Universität.

Pettersson, P. (2011) 'Majority churches as agents of European welfare: A sociological approach', in A. Backstrom, G. Davie, N. Edgardh and P. Pettersson (eds) *Welfare and Religion in 21st century Europe: Volume 2. Gendered, Religious and Social Change*, Farnham: Ashgate, pp 15-59.

Piattoni, S. (2001) 'Clientelism, interests, and democratic representation' in S. Piattoni (ed), *Clientelism, Interests, and Democratic Representation: The European Experience in Historical and Comparative Perspective*, Cambridge Studies in Comparative Politics, Cambridge: Cambridge University Press, pp. 193-212.

Politi, J. (2016) 'Italy pleads for Greek-style push to return its migrants', *Financial Times*, 4 April, https://next.ft.com/content/664e52c8-fa4e-11e5-8e04-8600cef2ca75.

Ratzinger, J. (Pope Benedict XVI) (2006) *Deus Caritas Est* (encyclical letter), available at http://w2.vatican.va/content/benedict-xvi/en/encyclicals/documents/hf_ben-xvi_enc_20051225_deus-caritas-est.html.

Reuters (2015) 'European Union approves 2.4 billion Euros funding for migration crisis', 10 August, available at http://uk.reuters.com/article/uk-Europe-migrants-funding-idUKKCN0QF16620150810.

Rose, R. (2011) 'Common goals but different roles. The state's contribution to the welfare mix', in P. Alcock and M. Powell (eds) *Welfare Theory and Development*, London: Sage, pp 61-88.

Roumeliotis, S. and Jones, N. (2010) 'Volunteerism in the context of environmental non governmental organizations in Greece', *International Journal of Interdisciplinary Social Sciences*, 4(12): 27-34.

Sartori, G. (1976) *Parties and Party Systems: A Framework for Analysis*, Cambridge: Cambridge University Press.

Schartau, M.B. (2009) 'The road to welfare pluralism: old age care in Sweden, Germany and Britain', IPSA online paper, available at http://paperroom.ipsa.org/papers/paper_2399.pdf.

Sotiropoulos, D. (2004) 'Southern European public bureaucracies in comparative perspective', *West European Politics*, 27(3): 405-22.

Symeonidou, H. (2013) 'Social protection in contemporary Greece', in M. Rhodes (ed) *Southern European Welfare States. Between Crisis and Reform*, New York, NY: Routledge.

Tassinari, F. (2014) 'The crystal curtain: a postscript on Europe's North–South divide', *The International Spectator: Italian Journal of International Affairs*, 49(3): 118-31.

The Economist (2015) 'Diverse, desperate migrants have divided European Christians', *The Economist*, 6 September, available at www.economist.com/blogs/erasmus/2015/09/migrants-christianity-and-Europe

Therborn, G. (2015) 'Introduction', in F.-J. Moreno-Fuentes and P. Mari-Klose (eds) *The Mediterranean Welfare Regime and the Economic Crisis*, Abingdon: Routledge, pp 1-4.

Trautsch, J.M. (2013) 'Review of the South in postwar Europe: Italy, Greece, Spain, and Portugal', H-Soz-uKult, H-Net Reviews, October, available at www.h-net.org/reviews/showpdf.php?id=40235.

Tsoukalas, K. (1986) *Social Development and State: The Formation of the Greek Public Space*, Athens: Themelio.

Vasarri, C. and Rotondi, F. (2012) 'Debt crisis leaves nothing sacred as Italy church chased on tax', 18 January, www.bloomberg.com/news/articles/2012-01-17/italian-church-chased-on-property-tax-as-debt-crisis-leaves-nothing-sacred.

World Council of Churches (2015) 'Italian churches urge more "humanitarian corridors" for migrants', 12 November, available at www.oikoumene.org/en/press-centre/news/italian-churches-urge-more-201chumanitarian-corridors201d-for-migrants

SEVEN

Religion, welfare and gender: the post-communist experience

Siniša Zrinščak

Introduction

This chapter is about religion, welfare and gender in post-communism, or more precisely about the role of religious organisations in welfare provision and the social position of women in post-communist countries. In order to understand the role of religion, welfare and gender, it is necessary to outline the interplay between a distinctive legacy and a complex, contradictory and markedly uneven social development. In addition, the common features of post-communist countries are identified, alongside the important differences between them, with regard to both past and present social development, and the role of religion in each country.

The discussion is based mainly on theoretical work with regard to social policy changes and socio-religious dynamics in post-communist Europe. In particular, it is inspired by the concept of variegated welfare capitalism, which perceives the modernisation and Europeanisation process as uneven, relational and multi-scalar. Furthermore, it is inspired by the concept of collectivistic religions that are not reducible to their identity-oriented expressions, but are in reality combined with individually shaped religiosity and criticism regarding the social role of a particular religion.

The theories presented frame the reflection on the empirical data gathered as part of the Welfare and Values in Europe: Transitions Related to Religion, Minorities and Gender (WaVE) project in four post-communist countries: Croatia, Poland, Latvia and Romania. Four common factors are of interest, although in slightly different ways: a weak tradition of religious involvement in welfare; controversies about the public position of churches; the dominance of a public welfare system that cannot meet the promises made to citizens; and the ways different stakeholders cooperate in each society. The position of women is taken into account in terms of tensions between traditional gender patterns, 'communist' and 'post-communist', 'Europeanised' gender equality ideals, and the social reality, particularly with regard to the enormous social consequences of post-communist transition. Thus, legacy, opportunities and crisis frame the tensions between a romantic vision of family life, uncertainties about desirable gender relations and the difficulties families and women face in their everyday lives.

Social context I: a path-dependent, variegated welfare patchwork

From a scholarly point of view, insight into the ways of post-communist social development coincided with a seminal work on three worlds of welfare capitalism: the liberal, conservative–corporative and social-democratic welfare models (Esping-Andersen, 1990). As the transformational process in general was progressing towards a western democracy and market economy, it only remained to be seen which direction would prevail in the countries initially classified as having a post-communist welfare model: the liberal, conservative, or social-democratic (Deacon, 1993). However, the complexity of social transformation in the post-communist world and simultaneous global changes, in particular the increasingly prominent and (in many instances) contradictory role of global institutions, such as the European Union, International Monetary Fund and World Bank, contributed to the uncertainty about whether, and which, post-communist countries were on the path towards the European conservative–corporative or the American liberal model, while traces of the Scandinavian or statist social financing were still present (Deacon, 2000). An additional attempt to classify post-communist countries based on an extensive set of criteria has resulted in interesting, though not very illuminating, labels, putting Bulgaria, Croatia, the Czech Republic, Hungary, Poland and Slovakia in the category of countries with a post-communist welfare model; Belarus, Estonia, Latvia, Lithuania, Russia and Ukraine in the category of the former USSR model; and Georgia, Romania and Moldavia in the category of the so-called developing welfare state model (Fenger, 2007). What this proves is that post-communist countries do not fit into any of the models that were originally developed for western countries. Enormous social consequences of transition, including rising unemployment, poverty, inequality, mortality and contagious diseases, have added to an already complex and uncertain situation (Unicef, 1994, 1955, 2001; EBRD, 2007). No less importantly, the different institutional capabilities of states and other social actors to face challenges and implement reforms have been an additional factor in this regard (Guillen and Palier, 2004). Thus, the overall picture is a complex mix of diversity and change (Manning, 2004), or, as argued by János Kornai (2006), a unique combination of exceptionally successful post-communist transformation (from the point of view of comparative historical analysis) and deep economic troubles experienced by considerable segments of the population, coupled with a widespread perception of loss.

Differences in post-communist transformation are also visible through the lens of two approaches which Bohle and Greskovits (2012) used in their analysis: the varieties of capitalism approach of Peter Hall and David Soskice, and the Polanyian 'great transformation' approach. Without neglecting the somewhat peculiar interplay of legacies and initial choices that shaped transformation in different ways, or the impact of uncertainty, the 2008 global financial crisis and the role of international organisations, this combined approach has nevertheless enabled the identification of different regimes of transformation. The Baltic States are characterised by a neoliberal type of capitalism, the Visegrad countries (the Czech Republic, Hungary, Poland and Slovakia) by an embedded neoliberal type, and Slovenia by a neo-corporatist type. Being transformative laggards, and owing to certain particularities, Bulgaria and Romania have adopted many features of the neoliberal model, while Croatia has adopted those of the embedded neoliberal model. Moreover, in the latter three countries, state weakness is another important feature (Bohle and Greskovits, 2012).

This chapter is inspired by another, more radical analysis known as variegated welfare capitalism. It was developed on the basis of dissatisfaction with the dominant functionalist, rationalist and modernist Europeanisation approach, which sees the process of European Union (EU) membership mainly as a linear and rational process, while the problems associated with becoming a modern and developed society are primarily attributed to post-communist countries (Lendvai and Stubbs, 2015). But quite the contrary is true, since social and economic development is in general uneven, relational and multi-scalar. In other words:

> The variegated capitalism approach, therefore, offers to provide a more dynamic analysis able to capture the continual dynamic restructuring of institutional practices. Dynamics of 'Europeanization' are not based on an institutional equilibrium, or a stable institutional fix; rather, they involve constant reforming, reworking and

recalibration. This work is neither fully 'path-dependent' nor random. The 'variegated capitalism' approach traces the different mechanisms of structural accumulation, arguing that these set limits to the range of policy outcomes possible. The systematic dimension of uneven neo-liberalisms can never account fully for the political choices made, however. (Lendvai and Stubbs, 2015, p 450)

Though more difficult to analyse than other 'model approaches', the variegated capitalism perspective captures the exceptionally unstable and contradictory nature of welfare development, as well as the uneven role of actors in the process of social transformation. This becomes more apparent when trying to understand the significant impact of the 2008 global financial crisis and current political affairs on post-communist countries, not only in terms of economic development, but also in terms of overall democratic and social development (Ágh, 2010, 2013). As shown in the Hungarian case, the current economic and political crises additionally contributed to a confused and contradictory welfare development as 'the directions of welfare reforms have been diffuse, embracing opposing ideologies of neo-liberalism, étatism and neo-conservatism' (Szikra, 2014, p 495). This can be termed the 'variegated welfare patchwork', which, in any particular field, inevitably entails the analysis of legacies, no matter how different they may have become, or are becoming. As this chapter demonstrates, the role of churches in welfare provision and the position of women in society can be fully appreciated only when viewed through the combined prisms of legacy and contradictory welfare development.

The capacities of public, profit and non-profit actors to address social problems remain critical in post-communist countries. Figures 7.1 and 7.2 compare welfare indicators in four post-communist countries in 2007 – when research for the Welfare and Values in Europe: Transitions Related to Religion, Minorities and Gender (WaVE) project was conducted – and 2014 (the latest available data). The figures show that Croatia, Latvia, Poland and Romania remain underdeveloped, at least in terms of GDP, in comparison with the EU average. There has been some slow improvement in all countries except for Croatia, which has been particularly badly affected by recession since the 2008 global downturn. At the same time, in all four countries, and in Latvia and Romania in particular, the risk-of-poverty rate[1] is higher than the EU average. Income inequality, as measured by Eurostat using the Gini coefficient, is also a little higher in Latvia and Romania. The indicator of severe material deprivation, measured as the lack of four out of nine items considered as necessary for a decent life, shows the real living conditions of people, and although there has been some improvement in this area, living conditions are still very problematic for large sections of society. Of particular concern are the data on social expenditures, which are consistently lower than the EU average, and significantly lower in comparison with Scandinavian and continental European countries. Yet social expenditure in post–communist countries is still under constant pressure from international financial organisations to remain low, or to be even lower.

Figure 7.1: Main welfare indicators, 2007*

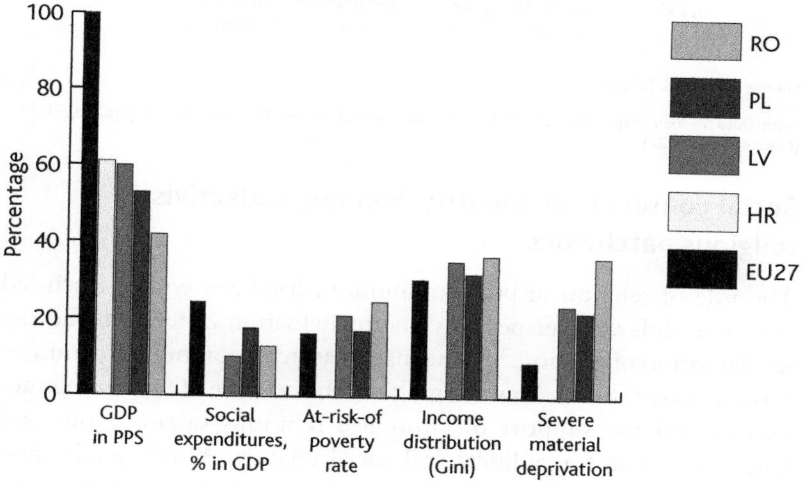

Source: Eurostat database.

Note: Data for Croatia not available. * RO (Romania), PL (Poland), LV (Latvia), HR (Croatia), EU27 (European Union 27).

Figure 7.2: Main welfare indicators, 2014*

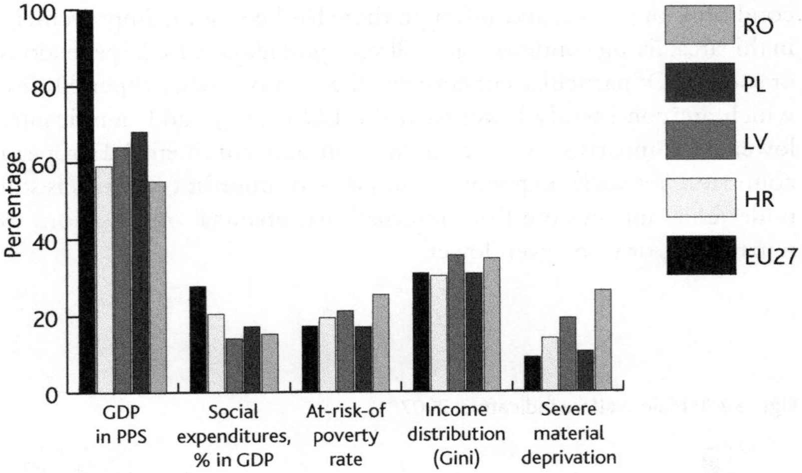

Source: Eurostat database.

Note: Data on social expenditures in 2012. * RO (Romania), PL (Poland), LV (Latvia), HR (Croatia), EU27 (European Union 27).

Social context II: an identity-building collectivistic religious patchwork

The role of religion in post-communism has been widely discussed from two different perspectives: the revitalisation of religion and the secularisation of religion.[2] As the main feature of communist countries was a negative attitude towards religion, the collapse of former regimes encouraged the support of churches, religious organisations and religious people for political and social change. A new public role for religions, particularly those with a long and dominant tradition or presence, became an important part of the new social order. This has been reflected in the reformulation of church–state relations in post-communism. The majority of the post-communist countries opted for a constitutional principle of separation of church and state. However, this was viewed not as a strict separation, but rather as an act of cooperation between (legally recognised) churches and the state – usually very comprehensive cooperation between different social and political fields (Zrinščak, 2011). Similar to many European countries, a multi-tier system was established, according to which the dominant, or a few dominant, and historically present religions received more rights in relation to other minority religions (such as the right to teach religion in public schools, official recognition of church weddings, tax exemptions, and so on).

In countries with a Catholic majority, the multi-tier system was reinforced by agreements with the Holy See on the legal position of the Catholic Church. Similar agreements were also signed with some other religious communities. In addition, the Polish Constitution even contains an *Invocatio Dei*, and stipulates that the relations between the Republic of Poland and the Roman Catholic Church shall be determined by the international treaty concluded with the Holy See; for other churches and religious organisations there are separate agreements between the appropriate representatives and the Council of Ministers (Rynkowski, 2005). In Romania, the 2006 law on the freedom of religion and the general status of denominations underlined the freedom of religious belonging and confirmed that there was no state religion in Romania; nevertheless, it stressed that the state recognised 'the important role of the Romanian Orthodox Church and that of other churches and denominations as recognised by the national history of Romania and in the life of the Romanian society'.[3]

The religious revitalisation thesis was based on individual indicators of religiousness and the visibility of religion and churches in the post-communist public sphere. Although these two categories are highly correlated, the difference between them is important. It is mainly because of individual levels of religiousness that the thesis of rising religiosity has been questioned. In some countries, the rise in religiosity has been negligible given that religiosity levels were already very high under communism. Moreover, the European post-communist world is in fact a region of huge differences and variations. For example, Romania and Poland have the highest religiosity levels in Europe, while the Czech Republic, Estonia and the former East Germany have the lowest.

The new and enhanced legal status of religion, coupled with rather negative attitudes towards minority religions, in particular new religious minority groups (usually framed as new religious movements), has provoked a variety of debates on the (in)appropriate position of religion in democracy, (in)appropriate connections between religion and politics and the (un)equal position of different religious communities. Secularisation has also been discussed and there are arguments about emerging European patterns of secularisation in post-communist Europe, framed as either contextual secularisation, in the sense that the secularisation process depends on different contextual factors that are surprisingly different across countries (Pickel, 2011; Pickel and Sammet, 2012), or differentiated secularisation, in the sense that the pace of secularisation differs across different levels (Pickel et al, 2012, p 252).

As far as the post-communist countries included in the WaVE research are concerned, the concept of collectivistic religions is very relevant (Jakelić, 2010; Zrinščak, 2014). Not denying the usefulness of a refined secularisation approach to enable 'a more accurate analysis of religion in different parts of the world' (Davie, 2007, p 51) and of a fundamental shift from obligation to consumption (Davie, 2007, pp 96–8; Davie, 2015, p 133–54), the concept of collectivistic religions, as argued by Jakelić (2010), appropriately describes many contemporary religions as entities into which people are born, to which they do not choose to belong, and which are ascribed to people as fixed and unchangeable. This underlines the indispensable role of religion in identity building, both collectively and individually. However, the notion of collectivistic religions has two important implications. First, it suggests that there is no dominant trend either towards secularisation or towards a voluntary type of religious belonging, and consequently that collectivistic religions are not outdated, soon to die, conservative, and nationalistically oriented types of religion. Second, it implies that, based on empirical analysis, collectivistic religions, although collectivistic, are nevertheless able to adapt to different social circumstances and accommodate other identities, and thus are not reducible to the image of a powerful church. On the contrary, and as already demonstrated, an identity-oriented collectivistic religion may coexist with an individually shaped religiosity, together with a widespread criticism of the church as an institution (Nikodem and Zrinščak, 2012; Ančić and Zrinščak, 2012). Thus, a powerful church may coexist alongside a religious patchwork of very different ways in which people live their religion. It is about a simultaneous coexistence and tension, which, taken together, can better explain debates on the role of the church and the position of religion in some post-communist societies, thus going beyond a simple and binary revitalisation–secularisation tension thesis.

There is no doubt that the role of religion has been significant in the four post-communist countries in the WaVE research. The respective religions in each case have been very much connected with the protection of a distinct national identity, which, in the Croatian case, was also marked by the dissolution of former Yugoslavia, the war for Croatian independence and a new state-building process. Yet the religious situation varies across the countries on account of different historical and social circumstances, as well as different confessional traditions. As shown in Figures 7.3 and 7.4, there is a dominant religion in three countries: the Catholic Church in Croatia and Poland, and the Orthodox Church in Romania. Only Latvia is clearly mixed in terms of denominational belonging, with almost the same percentage of Lutherans, Catholics and Orthodox, but also with a significant number of people with no religion.

When looking at another set of data on religiosity, the differences between the four countries become rather more marked, mainly in terms of religious practice. The share of those who never attend religious services is considerable in Latvia, but ongoing and rising in Croatia. All the selected variables indicate that Romania is the most religious country, although it is questionable what this means in different social sectors. The European Values Study (EVS) 2008 data, on which Figures 7.3 and 7.4 are based, show that the percentage of those who think that churches can offer adequate answers to social problems is relatively low in all countries, ranging from 18.7% in Latvia, 24.8% in Croatia, and 31% and 31.6%, respectively, in Poland and Romania. This may indicate the weak tradition of the churches' involvement in welfare issues in these countries, as well as dissatisfaction with the churches' current social engagement. On the other hand, it might be argued that this is a sign of perceiving the church primarily as a spiritual institution. Whatever the case, research shows that, at least in central European countries, people expect churches to be socially, but not politically, engaged (Ančić and Zrinščak, 2012). This framework is important for understanding research results.

Figure 7.3: Dominant religions, 2008*

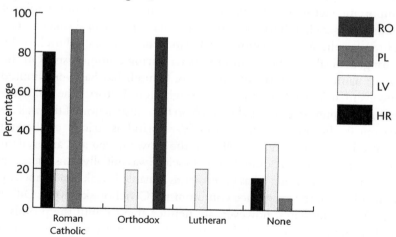

Source: 2008 European Values Study data

Note: Only dominant religions in each country are presented in the graph. * RO (Romania), PL (Poland), LV (Latvia), HR (Croatia).

Figure 7.4: Importance of religion – selected variables, 2008*

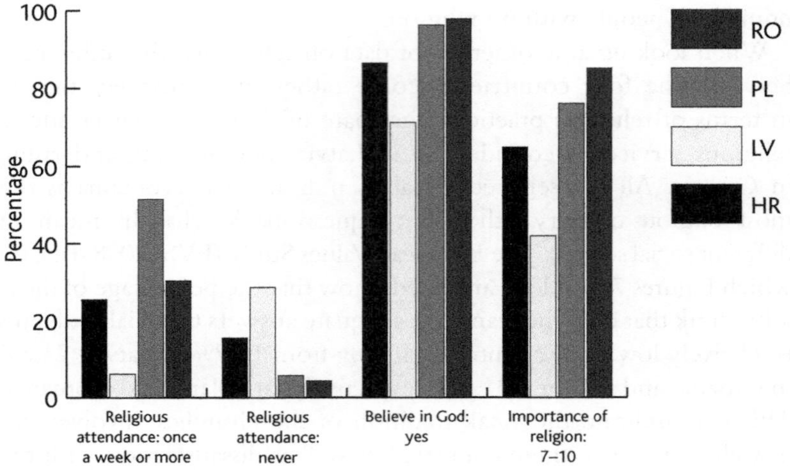

Source: 2008 European Values Study data. * RO (Romania), PL (Poland), LV (Latvia), HR (Croatia).

Which welfare role? Churches as welfare actors in four countries

The role of religion in welfare is inseparable from the general social situation, including the way social policy is constructed and the position of churches in the societies in question. The communist legacy is an important factor, which explains the weak or intermittent role of churches as welfare providers and/or in having a critical social voice. However, there are variations. In Poland, the Catholic Church had a stronger social presence than in Croatia during communism. On the other hand, the Romanian Orthodox Church has had very limited involvement in welfare activities throughout its history. The influence of the communist legacy is also visible in the construction of the welfare system in the post-Second World War period as strictly public and controlled by the state, as well as in the slow, uneven and ambivalent role of civil society. Though the civil society was initially constructed in opposition to the state, it has nevertheless remained weak and financially dependent on the state since communism (Celichowski, 2008; Dill at al, 2012). The states, however, are neither able to fulfil the promises and commitments they made to their citizens, nor effectively able to coordinate different actors to fill in the gaps.

Croatia

Although the history of Croatia's social policy goes as far back as the 19th century, when it was part of the Austro-Hungarian Empire and the first social insurance laws were passed, a specific welfare model did not develop until after the Second World War – that is, during the communist period (Geiger and Zrinščak, 2012; Geiger et al, 2012; Nikodem and Zrinščak, 2012). Therefore, the welfare sector developed as firmly secular and detached from any religious influence. The Catholic Charity of the Zagreb Archdiocese was established in 1935, but was outlawed after the war. However, since the late 1960s and following the partial normalisation of church–state relations, the Catholic Church has launched charitable activities that have been somewhat tolerated by the state, but the extent of these activities has remained very limited.

Post-communist religious freedom and increasing levels of social need have encouraged religious involvement in welfare, in particular the development of the organisation Catholic Charity, to the extent that such involvement is widely accepted and regarded as trustworthy. But underlying tacit questions remain. What is the actual role of Catholic Charity? To what extent should it be further developed? What are its relations with the state? Three partially related answers may be offered to these questions.

First, the development of the Church's social services took place on two levels. At the level of dioceses – albeit in different degrees, depending on the size of each diocese and other contextual factors – Catholic Charity developed as a professional organisation offering many services, such as homes for elderly and disabled people and abandoned children, soup kitchens, shelters for family victims, family counselling, and so on. On the other hand, at the level of parishes, Catholic Charity developed unevenly, relying only on volunteers and focusing mainly on traditional charitable activities, such as the collection and distribution of in-kind donations to the poor.

Second, and irrespective of the fact that the Catholic Church obtained full social recognition, church–state tensions in delivering welfare services are noticeable and are based on different ideas about the position of each actor. The Church itself does not want to assume welfare responsibility, arguing that its role is simply an additional one, which could be understood as a so-called 'complementary' type of service provider, whereby 'the church is offering services which are qualitatively different from what is provided by the public welfare system' (Pettersson, 2011, p 33). Yet, in the context of Croatia, these should be viewed as services not otherwise provided by the state in specific localities or, more often, provided inadequately. At the same time, the state does not want to assume full financial responsibility for the services offered by the Church; rather, it prefers to maintain the difference between fully funded public services and partially funded private/non-profit services. For example, public homes for abandoned children continue to be fully funded, but the same types of homes, owned by Catholic Charity or any other non-profit organisation, are only partially funded depending on the agreements in place between the state and the respective organisation. Such funding is based mainly on the number of children placed in institutions by the public authorities, but the latter place more beneficiaries than agreed and do so without adequate financing. Although there are difficulties in obtaining data and a full picture of the situation, the share of Church-run schools, kindergartens and homes for elderly people has remained below 5%. This indicates a limited scope for such activities, thus suggesting the limited complementary role of the Church in providing these services.

At the same time, the Church's limited complementary role is connected with the so-called 'value-guardian role':

> In its role as value guardian, the church acts as a defender of, and advocate for, various human values. In parenthesis, it is important to note that if the value-guardian role comes in the conflict with the existing political regime and is actively expressed, it will become a directly political role. (Pettersson, 2011, p 33)

In public, the Church argues that the state should be more effective in addressing social issues (poverty, inequality, the position and rights of workers, and so on). But in practice the Church has been much more preoccupied with family issues, particularly in light of Croatia's demographic decline, as well as other ethical issues, such as abortion, homosexuality and the influence of the so-called 'alien', non-traditional values emanating from abroad. As rightly noted by Pettersson, this creates heated public debates and political controversies.

Third, the small-scale charitable activities of other religious communities should also be mentioned; they have remained largely unnoticed by the public, although they may be very important for specific groups and localities. This is particularly true for the Islamic community and various Protestant denominations. Some of these communities were more active during the war in Croatia in the early 1990s when they responded to the severe humanitarian crisis and relied extensively on foreign help. At times, they acted more as simple humanitarian hubs rather than charities with fully developed programmes. A notable exception is the Adventist Development and Relief Agency of the Seventh-Day Adventist Church in Croatia, which implemented programmes aimed at community building and economic reconstruction and development in the war-affected areas.

As mentioned earlier, at the local level, and according to research conducted in the town of Sisak, Catholic Charity relies mainly on the work of volunteers, while cooperation with other stakeholders relies very much on informal connections between the people in charge. As it is very dependent on local conditions, the situation varies across parishes and dioceses, but informal cooperation between Catholic Charity and other stakeholders is very common. Interestingly, while trying to help people in need, volunteers engage with government authorities and other public institutions, such as centres for social welfare, hospitals and schools, thus creating a formal–informal mix that is publicly invisible, but locally very important, albeit very specific and non-transparent. This type of cooperation is neither well structured nor formalised, and there is insufficient knowledge in the public sector about what religious communities or other civil society organisations offer with regard to welfare. Along the lines of the variegated welfare capitalism approach, one might say: 'we argue that welfare state research needs to acknowledge and systematically engage not only with formal social policies and their outcomes, but also with bottom-up forms of welfare that might complement, act as an alternative to or challenge formal social welfare provision' (Polese et al, 2015, p 3).

Poland

Poland is a country with a history of a very strong Catholic Church during the communist period. Today, the Church still maintains an important social position, despite public debates about its role and opposition to some of its activities. It is very visible in the field of welfare and plays a significant role in supplementing public welfare services, in cooperation with the local authorities (Borowik et al, 2012a, 2012b). According to the WaVE research data, Caritas Poland is an organisation of about 60,000 volunteers, 1,000 clergymen and 3,900 employees (Borowik et al, 2012a, 2012b). The services offered include shelters and homes for victims of violence and single mothers, day-care centres, hospices and shelters for the homeless. Religious orders also play a very important role as they run kindergartens, schools and homes for elderly people. The important role of the Church should also be viewed in the context of decentralisation in Poland through which local governments became responsible for a large part of the welfare system, and the rising but still minor role of the private profit and non-profit sectors. Another important fact worth mentioning is that, owing to the lack of funding in general, and of the decentralisation process more particularly, the state has partially withdrawn from social service provision, thus leaving families to take care of their needs alone. At the same time, the family has become enormously burdened by rising poverty, unemployment and emigration, as well as by changes in the family structure itself, such as the increased number of one-parent families.

Research at the local level (in the city of Przemyśl) demonstrates that the strong presence of the Church in supplementing the state has come about because of the weakness of the public sector in the area of welfare. In Przemyśl, the Church offers a shelter for women, a soup kitchen, a house for single mothers and their children, and a number of other programmes (Borowik et al, 2012b). Church provision is open to everyone irrespective of whether or not they are religious, although some outlets are accompanied by religious practices through which the religious character of the service offered is emphasised, thus exerting pressure on the beneficiaries to become (more) religious. Minorities, for example Pentecostals, are also involved in welfare provision through small-scale activities in local children's homes, such as organising holidays for children and helping the poor. However, the majority of small religious communities, except for Greek Catholics on account of their traditional presence, are not visible in public; they are viewed as 'dangerous' or 'suspicious', which results in practically non-existent relations between religious minorities and local authorities.

Latvia

The situation in Latvia seems to be similar to that in Croatia. Researchers have concluded that it was only after the collapse of communism that religious organisations became increasingly active in social services, but they have limited financial resources (Graudiņš, 2012; Graudiņš et al, 2012). The fact that there is no strong tradition of church involvement in welfare provision in Latvia is important. The Catholic Church offers social assistance to families in poverty, supplying food, books, clothing and domestic necessities. In addition, it operates as a unifying actor, offering services to both the Latvian and Russian speaking populations. The Lutheran and Baptist Churches are also active, although not as extensively. For example, the Lutheran Church has set up day-care centres for children, a counselling telephone line and soup kitchens. The Diaconal Centre of the Lutheran Church has helped establish local diaconal centres throughout the country (Graudiņš, 2012). Even though churches offer a range of social services, they are perceived more as a source of moral and spiritual, rather than material, support. As in Croatia, and while keeping a distance from the government, churches in Latvia are nevertheless pressing the government to be more actively involved in welfare issues; moral issues, however, are seen as the priority.

The national situation is replicated at the local level and, according to research in the town of Ogre, the public sector is the main welfare provider. Yet religious organisations have an increasing, but still very limited, role, which varies according to 'the initiative of the individual parishes and priests, financial resources, and the relative development of social theology in the specific religious denomination' (Graudiņš et al, 2012, p 63). The Catholic Church is the most prominent in this respect, while the Lutheran Church in Ogre provides social assistance and organises social events primarily intended for parish members.

Romania

Romania is another post-communist country where the public welfare system developed during the communist era and served ideological purposes. During the post-communist transition period, the welfare system has faced many problems in responding to increasing levels of need among the populace. As in other post-communist countries, the Romanian Orthodox Church has only a complementary, and limited, role in providing social services (Zagura, 2012; Zagura and Hauser, 2012). The Orthodox Church's weak tradition of welfare engagement and its limited financial sources are critical factors that explain the current situation. According to the WaVE research data, the Romanian Orthodox Church runs about 330 welfare institutions nationwide, but the situation varies considerably across communities. More specifically, the Church owned 121 centres for children, 35 centres for elderly people, 106 social canteens and bakeries, 52 diagnosis and treatment centres, 23 support centres for families in difficulties and two centres for victims of human trafficking in the mid-2000s (Zagura and Hauser, 2012). However, bearing in mind the size and needs of the Romanian population, the Orthodox Church is still perceived more as a source of spiritual, rather than material, support. Minority religions are also involved in welfare service provision, the Catholic

Church in particular, but their activities match their limited size and importance in the Romanian society.

At the local level, in the town of Medgidia, the role of churches as welfare providers is very much consistent with the poorly developed public welfare sector. The Romanian Orthodox Church is perceived as an important public actor, but not so much as a service provider because the social services it offers are sporadic and lack coordination. The neo-Protestant Churches, including Pentecostals and Seventh-Day Adventists, are also very visible welfare providers. Muslim organisations offer some social welfare services, which are financed by Muslims and governments or organisations in Turkey or the Arab countries, but they are almost exclusively intended for their own members and are not offered in cooperation with the public sector.

Women in post-communism: torn between competing gender ideals and everyday reality

Post-communist social development has resulted in two processes relating to gender. The so-called gender equality agenda started to influence policy changes, primarily through the Europeanisation process. Although gender issues were publicly discussed and contested, they had very different results on the realities of existing gender patterns. At the same time, the social position of women was affected by complex social changes, bringing opportunities and restrictions alike. Thus, the discussion about the triangular relationship between gender, religion and welfare is framed by the similarities and diversities of post-communist cases, coupled with past legacies and complex social changes.

The communist legacy is connected with the particular way in which communism was affected by the modernisation process. Communism involved forced and rapid industrialisation, strong state/party control and no free market or democracy. Industrialisation (cheap labour) and ideology (liberation of men and women through publicly provided jobs) contributed to the employment of women and in general to higher levels of women's employment in eastern Europe compared with western Europe. In terms of gender regime types, this might be viewed as a dual-earner model, very similar to the one developed in Scandinavian countries (particularly Sweden) after the Second World War (Pascal and Kwak, 2005; Saxonberg, 2014). Yet some important differences have remained. In addition to industrialisation and ideological factors, women had to work because of poor economic circumstances. Furthermore, despite the communist ideology of liberation for both men and women, there was a strong traditional gender pattern and no division of labour, so domestic work had to be performed exclusively by women. There was no mention of the position of women in public discourse, and there were no independent women's organisations. Similarly, while the state invested in public provision for children, the family was still viewed as 'sacred' and not requiring any state involvement.

Needless to say, the post-communist transition process had an adverse impact on women, in particular because of the overall decrease in levels of employment and difficulties with finding new opportunities in the labour market, especially among older and less skilled female workers. As families and women became even more burdened and the influence of religion grew more powerful, this trend could be viewed as a step toward re-traditionalisation (Pascal and Kwak, 2005). Although the influences of economic hardship and religion should not be underestimated, the re-traditionalisation thesis, either explicitly or implicitly, starts from the assumption that the modern family and gender patterns already existed during communism. As already mentioned, modernisation in communism was quite specific, and resulted in a peculiar mix of modern components pertaining to the social position of women, and strong elements of a traditional gender pattern. In addition, not only is the re-traditionalisation thesis only partly accurate, but it also undermines the complexity of the new economic, social and gender situation in post-communist countries. Consequently, the picture is in no way unidimensional, as underlined by Pascal and Kwak (2005, p 67):

> We would argue that the emerging regimes in CEE [Central and Eastern European] countries could be seen as dual earner regimes, with comparatively strong collective support for women's employment and for parents and few characteristics of male breadwinner regimes. But these dual earner regimes have suffered economic blows, leading to some losses of state support for gender equality, low living standards and unemployment as a new risk. Their dual earner status is thus more challenged than in Scandinavian countries, and their support for gender equality more fragile.

At the same time, the Europeanisation process strengthened the gender equality agenda that, in one way or another, influenced the new EU member states. However, the Europeanisation process itself is contested.

It was considered as an important 'window of opportunity' in terms of putting gender equality on the public agenda, in particular issues that had not been addressed during communism, such as domestic violence, lesbian, gay, bisexual, transgender and intersex (LGBTI) rights, and the gendered division of labour. Yet other political and economic reforms were prioritised, and despite the diversity of gender regimes in EU countries and gender equality seemingly being high on the EU public agenda, the Europeanisation process has proved to be a rather weak factor. As summarised elsewhere, the literature on this subject outlines numerous factors that have influenced the implementation of gender equality and the process of Europeanisation, including the communist legacy, the state-building process and dominance of national ideology, the ideologies of political parties, the role of dominant churches, the strength of women's movements and civil society in general, and the capacity for policy learning (Dobrotić et al, 2013). Thus, family policies and emerging gender regimes have included a fascinating mix of continuing path dependence persisting differences among countries, invisible links between overall welfare developments and family–gender patterns in one country, and even some recent convergence trends (Saxonberg and Szelewa, 2007; Formánková and Dobrotić, 2011; Inglot et al, 2012; Saxonberg, 2014).

The concept of familialism, introduced by Leitner (2003), is relevant here. Four ideal types of familialism may be distinguished: explicit familialism (a strong role for the family in caring for children, and disabled and elderly people); optional familialism (the family is responsible for care, but there are available options in terms of services and supportive care policies); implicit familialism (there is no explicit state policy, but as there are no alternatives, responsibility for care rests primarily with the family); and de-familialism (state and market services are available for care of family members). When this model is applied to post-communist countries, we find that both explicit and implicit familialism is particularly strong (Javornik, 2014). Explicit familialism is found in Hungary, the Czech Republic and Slovenia, while implicit familialism is present in Poland, Slovakia and Latvia. Hence, 'explicit familialism in Hungary, the Czech Republic and Estonia supports familial childcare, reinforcing gendered parenting … implicit familialism in Poland, Slovakia and Latvia leaves parents without public support' (Javornik, 2014, p 253). Only in Slovenia and Lithuania is de-familialism found, albeit combined with familialist tendencies.

This typology is very much in line with the qualitative data gathered in the four post-communist countries in the WaVE project, although researchers were unable to find more sensitive indicators with regard to the types of familialism and gender regimes in each country. Gender equality ideas also have to be viewed in the context of the family. Almost all respondents in all the post-communist countries emphasised the central role of family, comprising both a societal point of view (family as social keystone) and an individual point of view (family as the basis for individual value and overall social orientation). In addition, family is an important social service provider to its members (both immediate and extended), especially in countries without much state support. Therefore, it is the family not the state that acts as a basic social safety net, both on a national and local level, as is the case in southern Europe and in the Mediterranean countries of Greece and Italy (see Chapter Six).

'Putting right' families that are unable to function, usually termed 'pathological families', was highlighted by many research interviewees as the main social task to enable the family to function properly. This implies that a 'non-pathological' family is a heterosexual family with children, which is able to be self-sufficient. It is clear, moreover, that the role of the family in welfare is particularly important for national or religious minorities partly for cultural reasons, but mainly because they tend to be excluded from society and thus have difficulty in accessing services. This by no means implies a lack of different views on families and the role of women, noting nonetheless that a traditional, somewhat 'romantic', view very often prevails.

Although gender equality as a value remains for the most part undisputed (albeit unelaborated and vague regarding the exact meaning of the term), the reality of women's positions and roles, torn between family and work responsibilities, limits the possibilities of changing the traditional gender order. The role of the church is of particular importance in this respect, along with some subtle differences among major political parties and their views on families and the role of women. For example, the role of the Catholic Church in Poland in maintaining the traditional gender order is documented in many published papers and underlined by the WaVE research (Borowik et al, 2012a and 2012b). The Church has vehemently opposed any idea that might question the idea of natural differences between men and women including the notion of gender equality. Consequently, 'the role of men is seldom discussed. Usually, they are treated as the primary breadwinners and the official Church opts for a social policy that would allow them to provide their families with sufficient means for living, even if their spouses do not engage in any paid work' (Borowik et al, 2012a, p 107). Yet the Church's role is only a part of the story, as views of younger and older women differ, irrespective of their religiosity. The WaVE research in Croatia, while focusing on the Bosniac minority, has revealed that older women advocate a strong gender division and the subordination of women to men, but younger women opt for more flexible gender relations. Here, the need for a nuanced understanding of the religious influence on gender roles and equality becomes particularly apparent, but with a potential cultural turn. Younger Muslim women in Croatia have openly criticised what they refer to as the western model of gender equality. As the interviewees in the Croatian case study explained, although the Islamic view of gender involves a strict gender division in the private sphere (men as providers, the subordination of women, the home as the woman's domain), this does not undermine the emancipation of women in the public sphere, in particular when it comes to their right to education and work (Geiger et al, 2012). Also, the traditional gender pattern, even if seen as 'natural', does not necessarily mean that women are not aware of difficulties in handling multiple tasks both in and outside the home. Many women across the WaVE research pointed out the numerous challenges they face: lower positions and fewer opportunities in the labour market, uneven division of housework, sexual harassment, and so on. Hence there is a visible tension between gender ideals, their application to everyday life and the social reality.

In lieu of a conclusion

There are two possible theoretical perspectives when examining the relationship between religion and social policy (Jawad, 2012). The macro-institutional approach focuses on how religion influences specific models of social policy. The micro-normative perspective is about the content, that is, how religious values shape the way social policy is defined and practised. Based on this way of conceptualising the religion–welfare nexus, this chapter is more inclined to the first approach, although it also touches on the second, particularly in relation to the position of family and women in the welfare system and in society in general.

Although post-communist countries are systematically excluded from comparative analyses, a re-examination of the decisive role of religion in shaping distinctive social policy arrangements and public expectations is receiving more attention in the social sciences. This chapter is a modest step in that direction. However, it aims not only to highlight new cases, but also to rethink the usual, very static and functionalist, way in which social development is analysed. Hence it is concerned with a variety of concepts: the variegated welfare capitalism approach, the collectivistic religion approach, the formal–informal interplay between individuals, networks and organisations, issues of legacy and complex changes, competing and unrealised ideals, and religion as a cultural resource.

The variegated welfare capitalism approach highlights the very complex and contradictory social context in which the welfare state evolves and which shapes the possibilities for the state and other stakeholders to meet people's needs. The concept of variegation captures the social context of post-communist countries and may also be useful for understanding similar contradictory welfare reforms in other European countries. Religion is an important collectivistic, identity-building force, which, together with the legacy of the welfare state model built during the communist period, helps to explain its prominent public position but at the same time very limited role as a service provider. Yet a collectivistic type of religion is adaptable to social circumstances and may also be inclusive, and not only exclusive of the 'other', thus being able to act as an important cultural reference point. Of particular interest is the way formal institutions function and how alternative strategies are developed when such institutions do not meet people's expectations.

The theory of sociological institutionalism, analysing the social role and impact of institutions, rightly points out that institutions should not be viewed as only formal and impersonal; they are also shaped by people's values, desires and behaviours. However, this also means that informal ways of doing things are not in direct opposition to formal ways. Quite the opposite: the functionality of the social system lies in the structure of a formal–informal interplay, and this is of particular interest in the welfare field, which is by definition structured as a mix of formal and informal actors and their actions: the state, the market, civil society and the family. Of course, the way the formal–informal mix operates in any given society brings different challenges that should be studied and addressed by the society itself. The formal–informal nexus is also a channel through which to study the role of men and women in post-communist Europe. Gender ideals, whether 'traditional' or 'modern', are ideological concepts and in reality are shaped by different social circumstances that in the post-communist case are marked not only by the role of religions favouring traditional gender models, but particularly by economic problems and weak support of the state to women and families.

This chapter indicates that there is a shortage of empirical material. Consequently, its shortcoming is an incomplete insight into the way in which social policy is implemented in everyday life. Thus it demonstrates only a partial understanding of how religion influences welfare provision and how changes in the area of welfare affect the role of religions. As underlined in the literature, 'while in some countries welfare state restructuring creates opportunities for faith-based organisations to expand their role, in others the combination of secularisation and restructuring create unfavourable conditions for these organisations' (Zehavi, 2013, p 561).

Notes

[1] The share of persons with an equivalised disposable income below the risk-of-poverty threshold, which is set at 60% of the national median equivalised disposable income.

[2] This section summarises socio-religious development in post-communist countries presented in Zrinščak, 2004; Zrinščak and Nikodem, 2009; Zrinščak, 2011; Ančić and Zrinščak, 2012.

[3] Law 489/2006 on the freedom of religion and the general status of denominations. Available at www.legirel.cnrs.fr/spip.php?article461&lang=fr

References

Ágh, A. (2010) 'Post-accession crisis in the new member states: progressing or backsliding in the EU?', *Studies on Transition States and Societies*, 2(1): 74–95.

Ágh, A. (2013) *Progress Report on the New Member States: Twenty Years on Social and Political Developments*, Together for Europe Series 13, Budapest: Budapest College of Communication and Business.

Ančić, B. and Zrinščak, S. (2012) 'Religion in Central European societies: its social roles and people's expectations', *Religion and Society in Central and Eastern Europe*, 5(1): 21–38.

Bohle, D. and Greskovits, B. (2012) *Capitalist Diversity on Europe's Periphery*, Ithaca, NY and London: Cornell University Press.

Borowik, I., Dyczewska, A. and Litak, E. (2012a) 'Poland. Overview of the national situation', in A. Bäckström (ed) *Welfare and Values in Europe: Transitions Related to Religion, Minorities and Gender. National Overviews and Case Study Reports, Volume 3. Eastern Europe: Latvia, Poland, Croatia, Romania*, Studies in Religion and Society 6, Uppsala: Acta Universitatis Upsaliensis, pp 91–117.

Borowik, I., Dyczewska, A. and Litak, E. (2012b) 'Poland. Przemyśl case study report', in A. Bäckström (ed) *Welfare and Values in Europe: Transitions Related to Religion, Minorities and Gender. National Overviews and Case Study Reports, Volume 3. Eastern Europe: Latvia, Poland, Croatia, Romania*, Studies in Religion and Society 6, Uppsala: Acta Universitatis Upsaliensis, pp 118–56.

Celichowski, A. (2008) 'Civil society in post-communist Europe: the challenges posed by social isolation', in V. F. Heinrich and L. Fioramonti (eds) *CIVICUS: Global Survey of the State of Civil Society, Volume 2: Comparative Perspectives*, Bloomfield, CT: Kumarian Press, pp 143-61.

Davie, G. (2007) *The Sociology of Religion*, Los Angeles, CA, London, New Delhi and Singapore: Sage.

Davie, G. (2015) *Religion in Britain. A Persistent Paradox*, Malden, MA and Oxford: Wiley Blackwell.

Deacon, B. (1993) 'Developments in East European social policy', in C. Jones (ed) *New Perspectives on the Welfare State in Europe*, London and New York, NY: Routledge, pp 163-83.

Deacon, B. (2000) 'Eastern European welfare states. The impact of the politics of globalization', *Journal of European Social Policy*, 10(2): 146-61.

Dill, A.P., Zrinščak, S. and Coury, J.M. (2012) 'Nonprofit leadership development in the post-socialist context: the case of Croatia', *Administration in Social Work*, 36(3): 314-41.

Dobrotić, I., Matković, T. and Zrinščak, S. (2013) 'Gender equality policies and practices in Croatia: the interplay of transition and late Europeanization', *Social Policy and Administration*, 47(2): 218-40.

EBRD (European Bank for Reconstruction and Development) (2007) *A Life in Transition. A Survey of People's Experience and Attitudes*, London: EBRD.

Esping-Andersen, G. (1990) *The Three Worlds of Welfare Capitalism*, Cambridge: Polity Press.

Fenger, H.J.M. (2007) 'Welfare regimes in Central and Eastern Europe: incorporating post-communist countries in a welfare regime typology', *Contemporary Issues and Ideas in Social Sciences*, August: 1-30.

Formánková, L. and Dobrotić, I. (2011) 'Mothers or institutions? How women work and care in Slovenia and the Czech Republic', *Journal of Contemporary European Studies*, 19(3): 409-27.

Geiger, M. and Zrinščak, S. (2012) 'Croatia. Overview of the national situation', in A. Bäckström (ed) *Welfare and Values in Europe: Transitions Related to Religion, Minorities and Gender. National Overviews and Case Study Reports, Volume 3. Eastern Europe: Latvia, Poland, Croatia, Romania*, Studies in Religion and Society 6, Uppsala: Acta Universitatis Upsaliensis, pp 157-83.

Geiger, M., Zrinščak, S. and Puhovski, T. (2012) 'Sisak case study report', in A. Bäckström (ed) *Welfare and Values in Europe: Transitions Related to Religion, Minorities and Gender. National Overviews and Case Study Reports, Volume 3. Eastern Europe: Latvia, Poland, Croatia, Romania*, Studies in Religion and Society 6, Uppsala: Acta Universitatis Upsaliensis, pp 184-221.

Graudiņš, R. (2012) 'Latvia. Overview of the national situation', in A. Bäckström (ed) *Welfare and Values in Europe: Transitions Related to Religion, Minorities and Gender. National Overviews and Case Study Reports, Volume 3. Eastern Europe: Latvia, Poland, Croatia, Romania*, Studies in Religion and Society 6, Uppsala: Acta Universitatis Upsaliensis, pp 25-57.

Graudiņš, R., Berdņikovs, A. and Mazūra, A. (2012) 'Latvia. Ogre case study report', in A. Bäckström (ed) *Welfare and Values in Europe: Transitions Related to Religion, Minorities and Gender. National Overviews and Case Study Reports, Volume 3. Eastern Europe: Latvia, Poland, Croatia, Romania*, Studies in Religion and Society 6, Uppsala: Acta Universitatis Upsaliensis, pp 58-90.

Guillen, A. and Palier, B. (2004) 'Introduction: does Europe matter? Accession to EU and social policy developments in recent and new member states', *Journal of European Social Policy*, 14(3): 203-9.

Inglot, T., Szikra, D. and Raţ, C. (2012) 'Reforming post-communist welfare states', *Problems of Post-Communism*, 59(6): 27-49.

Jakelić, S. (2010) *Collectivistic Religions. Religion, Choice, and Identity in Late Modernity*, Farnham, Surrey and Burlington, VT: Ashgate.

Javornik, J. (2014) 'Measuring state de-familialism: contesting post-socialist exceptionalism', *Journal of European Social Policy*, 24(3): 240-57.

Jawad, R. (2012) *Religion and Faith-Based Welfare*, Bristol: Policy Press.

Kornai, J. (2006) 'The great transformation of CEE. Success and disappointment', *Economics of Transition*, 14(2): 207-44.

Leitner, S. (2003) 'Varieties of familialism: the caring function of the family in comparative perspective', *European Societies*, 5(4): 353-75.

Lendvai, N. and Stubbs, P. (2015) 'Europeanization, welfare and variegated austerity capitalisms – Hungary and Croatia', *Social Policy and Administration*, 49(4): 445-65.

Manning, N. (2004) 'Diversity and change in pre-accession Central and Eastern Europe', *Journal of European Social Policy*, 14(3): 211-32.

Nikodem, K. and Zrinščak, S. (2012) 'Croatia's religious story: the coexistence of institutionalized and individual religiosity', in D. Pollack, O. Müller and G. Pickel (eds) *The Social Significance of Religion in the Enlarged Europe*, Farnham, Surrey: Ashgate, pp 207-27.

Pascal, G. and Kwak, A. (2005) *Gender Regimes in Central and Eastern Europe*, Bristol: Policy Press.

Pettersson, P. (2011) 'Majority churches as agents of European welfare: a sociological approach', in A. Bäckström, G. Davie, N. Edgardh and P. Pettersson (eds) *Welfare and Religion in 21st century Europe: Volume 2. Gendered, Religious and Social Change*, Farnham: Ashgate, pp 15-59.

Pickel, G. (2011) 'Contextual secularization. Theoretical thoughts and empirical implications', *Religion and Society in Central and Eastern Europe*, 4(1): 3-20.

Pickel, G. and Sammet, K. (2012) 'Introduction: transformation of religiosity in Central and Eastern Europe twenty years after the breakdown of communism', in G. Pickel and K. Sammet (eds) *Transformations of Religiosity. Religion and Religiosity in Eastern Europe 1989–2010*, Wiesbaden: Springer VS Verlag für Sozialwissenschaften, pp 7-20.

Pickel, G., Pollack, D. and Müller, O. (2012) 'Differentiated secularization in Europe: comparative results', in D. Pollack, O. Müller and G. Pickel (eds) *The Social Significance of Religion in the Enlarged Europe. Secularization, Individualization and Pluralization*, Farnham: Ashgate, pp 229-55.

Polese, A., Morris, J. and Kovács, B. (2015) 'Introduction: the failure of the future of the welfare state in post-socialism', *Journal of Eurasian Studies*, 6: 1-5.

Rynkowski, M. (2005) 'State and Church in Poland', in G. Robbers (ed) *State and Church in the European Union*, Baden-Baden: Nomos, pp 419-38.

Saxonberg, S. (2014) *Gendering Family Policies in Post-Communist Europe. A Historical-Institutional Analysis*, Basingstoke: Palgrave Macmillan.

Saxonberg, S. and Szelewa, D. (2007) 'The continuing legacy of the communist legacy? The development of family policies in Poland and the Czech Republic', *Social Politics: International Studies in Gender, State and Societies*, 14(3): 351-79.

Szikra, D. (2014) 'Democracy and welfare in hard times: the social policy of the Orbán government in Hungary between 2010 and 2014', *Journal of European Social Policy*, 24(5): 486-500.

Unicef (United Nations Children's Emergency Fund) (1994) *Crisis in Mortality, Health and Nutrition*, Regional Monitoring Report 2, Florence: International Career Development Center.

Unicef (1995) *Poverty, Children and Policy*, Regional Monitoring Report 3, Florence: International Career Development Center.

Unicef (2001) *A Decade of Transition*, Regional Monitoring Report 8, Florence: Unicef Innocenti Research Centre.

Zagura, N. (2012) 'Romania. Medgidia case study report', in A., Bäckström (ed) *Welfare and Values in Europe: Transitions Related to Religion, Minorities and Gender. National Overviews and Case Study Reports, Volume 3. Eastern Europe: Latvia, Poland, Croatia, Romania*, Studies in Religion and Society 6, Uppsala: Acta Universitatis Upsaliensis, pp 249-76.

Zagura, N. and Hauser, M. (2012) 'Romania. Overview of the national situation', in A. Bäckström (ed) *Welfare and Values in Europe: Transitions Related to Religion, Minorities and Gender. National Overviews and Case Study Reports, Volume 3. Eastern Europe: Latvia, Poland, Croatia, Romania*, Studies in Religion and Society 6, Uppsala: Acta Universitatis Upsaliensis, pp 223-48.

Zehavi, A. (2013) 'Religious supply, welfare state restructuring and faith-based social activities', *Political Studies*, 61(3): 561-79.

Zrinščak, S. (2004) 'Generations and atheism: patterns of response to communist rule among different generations and countries', *Social Compass*, 51(2): 221-34.

Zrinščak, S. (2011) 'Church, state and society in post-communist Europe', in J. Barbalet, A. Possamai and B.S. Turner (eds) *Religion and the State. A Comparative Sociology*, London: Anthem Press, pp 157-82.

Zrinščak, S. (2014) 'Re-thinking religious diversity: diversities and governance of diversity in "post-societies"', in G. Giordan and E. Pace (eds) *Religious Pluralism. Framing Religious Diversity in the Contemporary World*, New York, NY: Springer, pp 115-31.

Zrinščak, S. and Nikodem, K. (2009) 'Why, at all, do we need religion? Religion and morality in post-communist Europe', in G. Pickel and O. Müller (eds) *Church and Religion in Contemporary Europe. Results from Empirical and Comparative Research*, Wiesbaden: Springer VS Verlag für Sozialwissenschaften, pp 13-24.

Part Three:
Gendered and minority perspectives

EIGHT

Understanding religious minority communities as civil society actors

Annette Leis-Peters

Introduction

Is religion part of civil society? Most sociologists of religion would reply in the affirmative, not least since José Casanova questioned the hypothesis that growing modernisation, secularisation, differentiation and individualisation lead to the shrinking importance of religion in the public sphere (Casanova, 1994). However, in social science research on civil society, the religious perspective has remained marginal for a long time. In German and Swedish textbooks on civil society, religion and religious organisations are often covered in a short chapter or in a few pages, even if the authors are experts in the field of religion (see, for example, Adloff, 2005; Wijkström, 2012; Zimmer and Simsa, 2014). At the same time, religious diversity has grown on account of increasing waves of migration, and globalisation has revitalised debates on the role of religion and religious organisations in civil society in Europe. This is mirrored by an increasing number of publications and research projects in the field (De Hart et al, 2013; Baumann, 2014; Nagel, 2015).

It would be interesting to examine changes in the discourses on the role of religion and religious organisations in civil society over the past 10 years and to follow how research questions and arguments have evolved. The aim of this chapter, however, is rather more modest. Using as a starting point the research landscape outlined very briefly in the previous paragraph, this chapter examines what a local case study on the contribution of religious minority communities to social welfare can say about the role of religion and religious organisations in civil society. It draws in particular on the German case study in the Welfare and Values in Europe: Transitions Related to Religion, Minorities and Gender (WaVE) project, which explored relations between minority and majority in European societies through the prism of welfare (Leis-Peters and Albert, 2012).

Against this background, the first part of the chapter introduces recent studies on religion and civil society. The second part explains the setting and background of the German case study. The third part presents a particular example, a Turkish association, within the German WaVE case study, while the fourth and final part discusses the implications of these data against the background of the studies on religion and civil society presented in the first part of the chapter.

Debates on minority religions and civil society: some European perspectives

Current debates on civil society and religion in Europe have a number of important distinguishing features. One of them is the distinction between religious majority and religious minority communities. Often researchers focus on either one or the other. In most European countries, religious majority communities, such as national churches, can easily be identified. Most have close bonds with the state. This is true, even for countries where both the Protestant and the Catholic Church can be perceived as a religious majority community with regional differences, as in Germany, Switzerland or the Netherlands. The close links between large majority churches and the state is a key reason for questioning whether such religious majority communities may even be considered part of civil society. Many of them have been, or are, part of the public administration, or are at least involved in the public domain (such as in the welfare sector and education). This can make it difficult to draw clear lines between majority churches and the public sector. The Nordic countries, where the Lutheran churches, as religious majority communities, were state churches until very recently, are a case in point.[1]

In this respect, there is a basic difference between the role of religious communities in Europe and in the US, where religious organisations have been a natural part of civil society for centuries rather than decades (Adloff, 2010). Frank Adloff, who has compared civil society in the US and Germany, points out that typically in the European context, both external observers (including researchers) and the religious majority communities themselves have not really decided yet if the religious communities, that is the churches, can be considered part of civil society. On the one hand, there are advocates both within and outside the churches who start from a system theory approach that conceives all church activities in terms of their religious function of mediating salvation. On the other hand, there is an increasing number of voices that claim that all religious activities have to be interpreted as actions within society (Adloff, 2005).

Studies focusing on religious majority communities

Most of the studies on religious actors in civil society focus either on religious majority or on religious minority communities. There are three types of studies on religious majority communities.

The first type takes as its main point of departure the observation that the relationship between a religious majority community and the state has changed in European countries during the past few decades, just as relationships between the state, the market and the third sector, where civil society organisations are usually placed, have changed. In this perspective, civil society organisations are increasingly seen as hybrids of different sectors. For example, a former state church could be described as a hybrid between the state and the third sector in terms of its role in, and contribution to, society. In addition, the growing marketisation of the third sector and civil society is receiving an increasing amount of attention. Some researchers have concluded that the task of civil society organisations has changed from representing the interests of specific groups and acting as a critical voice to delivering various social services on behalf of the state (including municipalities) (Wijkström, 2012).

Another way of studying these changes is to track how the idea of New Public Management (NPM)[2] is applied to, or used, in the everyday practice, structure and ideology of religious organisations, seeing these as an example of civil society organisations. A particularly interesting area in this respect can be found in faith-based organisations that act in the field of welfare. These organisations have either been providing welfare services for a long time (such as traditional religious charities or diaconal institutions) and are now experiencing changes in the framework of their welfare work (see Eurich and Maaser, 2013), or they are entering the field for the first time, motivated by their new status as institutions that have become independent from the state (see Wijkström, 2014). As welfare actors, both the more established and the newer religious civil society organisations participate in public service procurements, in which they tender and compete with other, often commercial, providers. Interestingly, studies on the internal structures, procedures and processes of churches have produced similar findings to studies on faith-based welfare actors, showing how the idea of an

NPM is infusing religious communities in various ways (see Linde, 2010 on the Church of Sweden).

The second type of studies is mostly quantitative and tries to establish a connection between religious attendance and civil society, that is, civic engagement or social trust. Such works often include studies from the US that start from the hypothesis that mainline Protestant churches are crucial players in their local communities (Norris, 2013). The data used in this type of research are quantitative, comprehensive value studies, such as the World Value Survey. Comparing the results of such quantitative studies between the US and Europe reveals that active religious affiliation correlates with higher civic engagement in both contexts, even though the numbers of religious attenders are much lower in Europe than in the US (Norris, 2013). There are also national studies in Europe that look for similar connections between religious affiliation and social capital or social trust. For example, in a multilevel analysis of 97 small-scale German regions, Traunmüller (2011) studied the impact of religious identity and religious context on social trust. He found a strong correlation between religious attendance and social trust in Germany, in particular in Protestant regions. However, his results also point to a general weakness among such quantitative studies with regard to religious minority communities. Even though religious minority communities, in particular Muslim communities, were included in the study, their representation was based on such small numbers in relation to the representation of the religious majority communities that it was almost impossible to draw any conclusions (Traunmüller 2011).

A third type of studies concentrates on the organisational level of civil society. A state-of-the-art report on civil society identified the mapping of the new organisational structure of civil society as a key task for future research. The report states that in the context of globalisation there is a growing social and spatial diversity and an increasing differentiation of civil society, in relation to both the ecology of different civil society actors and the growing number of tasks they take on (Lilja and Åberg, 2012). The German political scientist Sigrid Roßteutscher contributed to this area of research by asking what role churches and religion play in civil society and to what extent their role is democratic or promotes democracy. Roßteutscher started from the hypothesis that civil society and social capital at the meso level can be studied only if the social context, that is interactions at the local level, are taken into consideration. She developed a research design that encompasses eight cities in four countries (Demark, Scotland, Switzerland and Germany) with either a clear majority church or two equally strong churches.

In these cities, all civil society associations (both religious and secular) were surveyed through the use of a questionnaire on structure, funding, members, volunteers, paid staff and so on. After the mapping was complete, she found that, compared with their secular equivalents, religious organisations are strong in recruitment, internal mobilisation (of volunteers) and the integration of people with different interests into the organisation. Consequently, religious organisations seem to have a stronger social orientation and motivation to engage with and assist people in need as part of a culture of benevolence (Roßteutscher, 2009). However, one of the shortcomings of this study was that non-Christian communities were not visible in the results of the study because the numbers in the sample were too low.

In short, quantitative studies on the representation of religious organisations in civil society in general seem not to be able to map the representation of religious minority communities as well as that of religious majority organisations. In addition, most of the studies that explore the role of religious organisations at the meso level still aim at religious majority organisations. It follows that religious minority organisations have so far been under-represented in research studies on civil society research.

Studies focusing on religious minority communities

The fact that religious minority organisations have become interesting from a civil society perspective may be explained by the growing religious diversity in Europe, prompting a challenge to traditional perceptions of civil society. Indeed, studies on religious minority communities as civil society organisations are clearly responding to a perceptible uncertainty about what these organisations actually do, particularly with regard to non-Christian associations. It is not surprising therefore that many studies on religious minority communities consist of mapping and categorising their activities. Another feature with regard to such studies is that those conducted within the past five to 10 years often adopt a somewhat apologetic approach, arguing against negative descriptions of minority religious communities operating as parallel societies with the aim of offering a more balanced picture. This might easily be understood as a result of a perceptible Islamophobia, which is also a topic of research (see, for example, Gardell, 2010). One of the most elaborate examples of mapping religious minority communities is the study by the German political scientist Alexander-Kenneth Nagel. His research uses case studies of different minority communities and classifies their activities with the help of a network model based on four categories: contents (*Inhalt*), constellations (*Konstellationen*), arrangements (*Arrangements*) and influencing factors (*Einflußfaktoren*). The project is based on detailed mapping, and each of the four main categories consists of a number of sub-categories. The study aims to shed light on the potential of religious migrant communities in civil society, asking whether this potential can be realised, given the beliefs of these communities, and how they are regarded in local society (Nagel, 2015). Through the network model, Nagel and his research team were able to offer a more nuanced picture on the potential of religious minority communities as civil society actors and on the obstacles they face.

The objectives of Nagel's study can be compared with those of a representative survey of Muslim congregations in Sweden that was conducted by the sociologist Klas Borell and professor of social work Arne Gerdner. Both researchers train social workers. They were inspired to initiate the study by their students, who pointed out that they, as future social workers, had almost no knowledge of religions, and in particular of Islam and Muslim communities in Sweden. Borell and Gerdner (2011) found that Muslim congregations are both religious and social meeting spaces where a great deal of voluntary social work takes place (for example, offering assistance to newly arrived immigrants, children, young people or prisoners). Their findings also revealed that welfare activities offered by Muslim congregations encourage their members to interact and make connections with the majority or host society, and not, as has been presumed in some public debates, exist or live in isolated parallel structures in society.

A similar finding was expressed by the religious studies scholar Martin Baumann, who since 2005 has been researching immigrant religious communities in Switzerland and other European countries from a Swiss perspective. In a recent article, he showed how the growing visibility of religious minority communities in the public sphere (for example, erecting religious buildings such as mosques in prominent public places) can affect their position as civil society organisations in Switzerland and the UK (Baumann, 2014). In his conclusion he highlights the function of immigrant religious communities as 'multifunctional service centres' for individuals and diaspora communities that 'have the means to transform a marginalized situation into one of more visibility and social cohesion' (Baumann, 2014, p 125).

From the research findings mentioned here, we might conclude that although religious minority communities are viewed as operating in isolation compared with the religious majority communities, the variety of services they offer (often responding to the social needs of their members) helps them to interact, to make connections and to work with the majority or host society. Such developments, however, are all too often viewed with suspicion in public discourse (that is, in media or political discourses) in majority societies, and perceived as a risk (namely, of establishing parallel structures or communities). Precisely this is identified by Chantal Munsch (2010) in her study on political participation and civil society among ethnic minority organisations in Germany. She showed how migrant organisations are excluded through a mechanism of normalisation and generalisation that prevails in civil society in an invisible and largely unconscious way. The norms of the majority are not questioned and are thereby generalised. Although civil society organisations of ethnic minorities have different norms, they are compelled to relate to majority norms, while majority civil society organisations do not have to relate to the ethnic minority equivalents. Consequently, organisations representing various parts of the majority society can easily adapt to existing norms and therefore benefit from a better position in civil society. While their demands are better understood and accepted by the majority society, the demands of ethnic minority civil society organisations are often perceived as inappropriate.

Munsch's analysis involves feminist theory and shows that civil society in Germany is biased by norms based on western, middle-class, white, Christian male perspectives. One feature of this theory is the distinction between the public–political and the private–personal. Feminist theorists claim that this is a male power strategy to differentiate between the public–political sphere, where rationality rules, and the private–personal sphere dominated by subjective emotions. Munsch argues that German civil society operates according to the norm that it should abide by the same rationality principles as the public–political sphere, that is, that it should be free from emotions, personal relations, interests and personal experiences. Clearly, the commitment of minority organisations, including religious minority communities, in civil society originates from group interests and personal experiences. If Munsch's understanding of civil society is correct, it follows that religious minority communities must deal with an underlying inequality when participating in society because their motivation is defined as private–personal and therefore dismissed as secondary in the public sphere.

Based on the studies presented here, we can assume that religious minority communities are not automatically treated equally or given equal access in civil society. Initially, the WaVE project, including the German case study, explored such communities to gain a better understanding of their values in relation to welfare, religion and gender. However, the empirical material from the case study may also be used to gain further insight with regard to their role and position in the local civil society. In the following section, the German case study is outlined both in general and in terms of one religious minority organisation in particular in order to reflect further on the observations made above.

German case study

Design of the case study

The aim of the WaVE project was to explore the significance and impact of values and religions in the area of welfare. In designing the national case studies, researchers were given a great deal of freedom to choose both the religious minority communities and the welfare issues they wanted to focus on. An important criterion, however, was that the communities and the issues had to be relevant to the background of the national and local context. In Germany, the area of care for elderly people is both a topical and controversial issue owing to the demographic evolution of the society. Like other European countries, Germany has had low birth rates for decades. This makes it easy to predict that both German society as a whole and German people will face huge challenges with regard to the care of elderly people in the near future. In German public debates, these issues are reflected in several types of conflict: for example, conflicts between generations (intergenerational conflicts), conflicts between the demands of working life and the demands of family-based care (in particular for women), and conflicts between those who are able to pay for their own care when they are old and those who are dependent on public services (Leis–Peters and Albert, 2012).

Most German residents from migrant backgrounds were recruited as guest workers in the 1950s. The German case study used the industrial city of Reutlingen (about 114,000 inhabitants in 2015), which mirrors the German situation quite well. About 15% of the residents in Reutlingen did not have a German passport (which is the only way of measuring immigrant background in the German statistical system). The largest groups among migrants in Reutlingen were Turkish (2.7%) and Greek citizens (2.6%) (Stadt Reutlingen, 2005, p 50). Among the new arrivals, the largest group comprised migrants from the former USSR who either had German ancestors and were considered to be German citizens, or who were Jews allowed to emigrate to Germany because of their religion, based on a law that was passed as a gesture of compensation after the Shoah. These immigrants often came from Asian parts of the former USSR, since many ethnic Germans had been deported to Kazakhstan and Kyrgyzstan during the Stalinist era (see also Albert and Leis-Peters, 2008). The share of residents in Reutlingen holding a foreign passport or having an immigrant background differs from district to district. In the city centre and in the industrial parts of the city, 38% of the residents did not have a German passport in 2005, while in more affluent residential areas (in the villages that were incorporated into the city of Reutlingen after the Second World War) only 3% to 7% of residents had a foreign passport (Stadt Reutlingen, 2005, p 55).

Many residents from migrant backgrounds who came to Germany in the 1950s and 1960s are now growing old, or are the children and grandchildren of ageing working immigrants. Consequently, the care of elderly people is likely to be a prevailing issue for both the majority population and those from migrant backgrounds (for further discussion on this point, see Chapter Nine). In Germany, as in other countries in north-western Europe, there is a general expectation that most families from migrant backgrounds will take care of their elderly relatives themselves, while German families tend to rely more on public services. The reasons for this are various. In the German case study, this expectation was expressed both by representatives of the religious minority communities and by representatives of the public authorities. Swedish studies on informal caregivers among migrant families also show that there is an unspoken rule that care in the family is reciprocal and that elderly people should be protected from anything that is new and unknown (Forsell, 2010).

The case study material consisted of seven individual interviews (ii) and eight (focus) group interviews (gi),[3] complemented by statistics and documents on the religious minority communities, as well as press articles covering topics that were relevant to the study and notes from participant observations of the religious minority communities. The study focused on the three largest ethnic migrant groups: the Turkish community, the Greek community, and German migrants who came from the former USSR. In terms of religion, Muslims, Christians (Orthodox, Catholic and Protestant) and Jews were all represented in the study, which also included non-religious individuals. One of the most interesting examples in the case study was a Turkish association that also functioned as a local mosque. For this organisation, in addition to participant observation, we conducted group interviews with both female members and male leaders, as well as association members, and an individual interview with one of the male leaders. The following section focuses on this association and discusses the findings of the research in relation to the observations on religious minority communities as civil society organisations made at the beginning of this chapter.

Switching the focus from the old to the young

On a general level, the German case study confirmed what was expected: the representatives of religious minority communities were very clear that the family is supposed to take care of the elderly, while the representatives of public authorities claimed that only a few families from migrant backgrounds used public services for elderly care (gi 6).

According to the interviewees from migrant backgrounds, elderly people in Germany cannot expect to receive the same level and quality of care offered by the state that family members offer to the elderly from migrant backgrounds. Many of them said that the living conditions of elderly German people in need of care were dismaying. One of the male Turkish interviewees said: "My father expects me to care for him. In his way of thinking, he cannot imagine anything else.... Of course I will care for him" (gi 1). The interviews revealed that caring for elderly members of the family is central to the values that immigrants have brought with them to Germany; they are also values that are closely related to their religious tradition, whether Muslim or Christian. Specifically, religion and religious education have a crucial function in passing on these values to the next generation. It is therefore expected that the children of Turkish and Greek women and men who came to Germany as guest workers will share the same (family) values as their parents and grandparents (gi 2).

This may explain why the focus of the research shifted during the course of the case study from concern about the elderly to concern about younger generations. The main worry of the people from minority backgrounds that we interviewed was not the care of the elderly people, but rather the situation of the younger generation. Parents felt they could manage the care of elderly family members (for example, grandparents), but could not control the development and future of their children, the younger generation, in Germany. They had two key concerns: first, that the younger generation would not be able to enter the labour market, find a good job and establish a professional career, and, second, that they would not share the same values as the older generations (parents and grandparents), but would instead adapt to, and adopt, the prevailing values of young people in Germany (see also Leis-Peters, 2011)

It is not difficult to understand why the interviewees from migrant backgrounds were concerned about the younger generation in German society. Statistics show that fewer students from migrant backgrounds graduate from school in comparison with their German peers (Flam, 2007). Poor school results, either because of the low expectations of the German school system with regard to such students (often mentioned by migrants from a former USSR background), or the lack of support from the school when children and young people are not able to keep up with academic standards, were brought up in several interviews (gi 1, gi 2, gi 3, gi 8). Young people who do not develop a sense of achievement in school are often hesitant about engaging in extracurricular activities and end up just hanging around in the neighbourhood, which makes matters worse (ii 3). It follows that the young people in question will miss out on entering the labour market and will end up living in adverse socioeconomic conditions, and will therefore be unable to provide for the family in general and, more particularly, take care of the elderly. In other words, there is a direct connection between the problems that young people face in school and in their working life, and their ability to take care of elderly family members. At the same time, the people from migrant backgrounds that we interviewed also stressed that to ensure that elderly people are taken care of by the family it is necessary to preserve and pass on their traditions from one generation to the next. As we have seen, religion is considered a principal source in sustaining these values.

The people we interviewed were also worried that young people might be influenced by individualistic values in Germany, and thus end up giving less priority to family care obligations. For this reason it becomes especially important for first and second generations to teach and pass on family values to young people through religion. The point to note is that the religious traditions and values that parents want to transmit to the younger generations are clearly related to welfare needs and welfare practices. They include respect and care for older generations in general and for parents in particular (gi 1, gi 2, gi 8). There is therefore a direct connection between how young people from migrant backgrounds develop in Germany, the values they espouse, and the care of elderly people in migrant families.

Private interest or common good? The interests of religious minority communities in relation to the majority society

This surprising turn in the German case study, that is from a concern about the elderly to a concern about the younger generations, revealed two crucial points shared by all those we interviewed across all religious minorities represented in the case study (Muslim, Christian and Jewish). First, parents want young people within their community to succeed in German society and in their working lives, and, second, they want them to preserve their religious traditions. Both concerns are directly linked to existential values and welfare needs and practices. The fact that representatives from all religious communities in the case study shared the same concern illustrates that these are issues that are very important to them. However, such concerns are barely understood by the majority society. Indeed, all too often, the worries of religious minorities presented here translate into public debates in which minority communities are viewed as representing and caring only for their own interests. Worse, they may be perceived as advocating concerns or ideas that are in conflict with the majority community and thus threaten the common good and/or social cohesion.[4]

As we have seen, the studies on religious minority communities that map and categorise their activities as civil society organisations seem, in a somewhat apologetic way, to come to the defence of these communities when they are accused of isolating themselves from the rest of society (Borell and Gerdner, 2011; Baumann, 2014). They suggest that minority communities in general, including religious ones, have more difficulties than majority (religious) communities in representing their interests as a legitimate endeavour in civil society. For example, Munsch (2010) concluded that the motivations of minority community associations that come from personal experience and the need to represent their own interests clash with the norm of (German) civil society to act in a way that Munsch describes as public–political, which is seen as more neutral and objective. As a result, minority community associations often have a disadvantaged position and are viewed negatively by the host society in question.

Against the background, and given the interesting turn in the German case study, I argue for a different approach. The role and function of religious minority communities in civil society can only be understood if we focus on the key social concerns and specific goals that they strive for. This is illustrated through the following example of one of the Turkish associations covered in the German case study, in which the need to be supported by the majority society in order to help young people from the Turkish community was expressed very explicitly. In the interviews we conducted with members and representatives of the association, the two key interests mentioned earlier emerged very clearly: the wish for the younger generation to succeed in their working life and in German society and for them to preserve religious traditions and values. To analyse the case of the Turkish association we will use Nagel's four dimensions (contents, constellations, arrangements and influencing factors) (Nagel, 2015).

Forms of cooperation between religious minority communities and the majority society: the case of a Turkish association

Nagel uses a network analysis model to evaluate the potential of religious minority communities in civil society. As we have seen, the model distinguishes between four dimensions or levels: contents; constellations and contexts of relationships; arrangements; and external and internal influencing factors. The Turkish association will be analysed with the help of these four dimensions in relation to the two main concerns that were voiced by the religious minority communities in Reutlingen and reflected the association's main goals: helping young people succeed in school and in their working life, and passing on religious values and traditions to younger generations.

The dimension of content

Nagel's initial question in mapping the content of the activities of religious minority communities is straightforward enough: what do the relationships of such communities consist of? He suggests the following examples of possible content categories: maintaining contact between members of the minority community and the culture they come from; transferring money and goods; transmitting knowledge; providing social services; engaging advocacy; representing the interests of the community; and offering pastoral care and religious healing.

Applying Nagel's content categories to the main activities and goals of the Turkish association and analysing its goals using Nagel's content dimension reveals that the aims of the association are interconnected at a content level. The association's aims relate to several of Nagel's categories.

One of the key goals of the Turkish association was the transfer of money and goods. It wanted more resources from the municipality, such as the use of larger facilities and more financial support, so as to expand its activities in youth work, including homework tutoring programmes. It wanted to help young people from a Turkish background to thrive in society, namely to do well in school and have a good job and a successful working life. To be able to do this, the association stated that it needed more space and money for teaching materials and homework tutoring programmes, because at the time of the interviews the association could only accommodate 60 young people at the same time. With more space, it was hoping to increase its capacity to reach out to more young people.

In so doing, it is clear that the association very largely shared the interests of German society in general. Its desires also reflected its members' aim to offer social services to young people, who often end up on the streets and get into trouble with alcohol, drugs and youth delinquency. As one of the association's representatives said: "We are doing the municipality a favour, when we support young people" (gi 2). They were also hoping to provide a space where young people could meet and be supported in their personal development, thus encouraging their integration into German society. A precondition for this is graduating from school. The idea of offering homework tutoring was a key concern in this respect. Although similar services were offered by the municipality, according to the interviewees these services were neither useful nor helpful since those who ran the programmes were not familiar with dealing with the particular problems that these young people faced. That said, the idea of running homework tutoring programmes within the association might also be understood as a way of representing the interests of the community, that is, of its own young people, rather than German society as a whole.

Since the issue of care for elderly people was so critical, the interviewees were also quite open in saying that they wanted the younger generations to share their religious values and to care for their parents when they were old. From this perspective, another goal of the association was to support the older generations' (the parents') wish to transmit religious values to the younger generations. This reflects Nagel's content category of knowledge transfer.

The dimension of constellations and contexts

Nagel distinguishes between constellations and contexts. Relationships take place in the form of constellations among individuals within the religious community, between individuals and the religious community, and between different communities, groups and institutions. Consequently, he defines four contexts: inner-religious, intra-religious, inter-religious or extra-religious.

All of Nagel's constellations are reflected in the main goals of the Turkish association. Helping young people from Turkish backgrounds succeed in German society while also sharing Muslim values relates to relationships between individuals within the association (such as parents and their children), as well as to the relationships between individuals (young people) and the association. To support young people and pass on religious values, the Turkish association also had to interact with other/different groups, organisations and institutions in society, such as the municipality. A key element in the association's interaction with the municipality was the issue of space. The association is housed in the first floor of an apartment building, which is bursting at the seams due to shortage of space when running its activities and programmes. One of the interviewees put the situation like this:

> 'We teach 231 young people and children at the moment and have about 130 square metres…. The association does more than [name of] Secondary School. Perhaps [name of] Secondary School helps young people read well, and they may receive a good certificate from the school, but when it comes to learning for life, how to become a human being, the school does not impart anything like this, we do.' (gi 1)

As an ordinary registered voluntary organisation, the Turkish association did not have access to larger space through the municipality. As the interviewees saw it, they had to find a better location with almost no money. Applying Nagel's context dimension to the Turkish association and its need for more space and larger facilities, we observe that its interactions took place at the inner–religious level (that is, with members of the association), and at the extra–religious level (in its discussions with public authorities). Interactions with other Muslim organisations or with other religious communities were not mentioned by the interviewees.

The dimension of arrangements

Nagel's arrangements dimension is a tool used to identify the spectrum of relationships of religious minority communities with other actors in terms of intensity, complexity, time span (long or short term), value and purpose. By combining these categories, Nagel identified four ideal types of arrangements: strategic alliances, partnerships, projects and ad hoc activities. These ideal types work like indicators on a scale from very formal to very loose. At one end of the scale are strategic alliances based on contracts and common plans for the future. At the other end, ad hoc activities represent loose and random forms of cooperation.

Focusing on arrangements relating to the two main concerns expressed by religious minorities, the case study showed that only loose and random ad hoc activities took place between the association and the municipality. Clearly, the municipality did not invest time in engaging in more formal arrangements, which also suggested that the association was rather isolated from the city as a whole. There was no stable cooperation between the association and the municipality. One of the complaints voiced by the association representatives was that the politicians and representatives of the municipality never visited the Turkish association (even though they had been regularly invited). Only the police had paid a visit to the association to discuss the increasing dangers of criminal gangs in the city. Even though the police's visit had been viewed positively, it had not led to more support for the association and its work. Other relationships with public external stakeholders were not mentioned in the interviews.

The dimension of influencing factors

To understand the network mechanisms of religious minority communities, Nagel introduces the idea of internal and external influencing factors. Among internal factors, he includes theological self-understanding, migration history, social structure and demographic change. External factors comprise legal frameworks, incentives and opportunity structures, the structure of civil society and public discourses.

All of Nagel's internal factors could be directly applied to the Turkish association and its two main goals. The association's theological self-understanding is based on the view that religious values and traditions are to be passed on to the next generation. On account of their migration history, the association comprises young people from the second or third generation (which inevitably affects their views). The association's social structure is determined by the fact that it consists mainly of migrants who have a more peripheral position in relation to the general norms of the majority society. Recently it has also been influenced by the difficulties that its young members have faced in school and in building professional careers. The association has been affected by broader demographic changes in Germany, including difficulties in finding jobs and weakening commitments regarding religious and family values, which in turn threaten the model of family-based care for the elderly.

In terms of external factors and influences, the legal framework and public discourse were frequently mentioned in the interviews. The legal framework in Germany has an impact on the activities and scope of the Turkish association, and can limit its resources. It is an ordinary civil society organisation with no additional benefits or rights. At the same time, the association representatives we interviewed felt that their association was not like any other. Public debates that pre-judged them meant that they did not have an equal opportunity to contribute to society. One of the interviewees said, "They think still, 'An Islamic association, oh, they are terrorists', they should come and see" (gi 1). The interviewees faced such attitudes quite often, not least in the media. They felt that this was constraining not only their participation in, and contribution to, society, but also their overall motivation to continue their work.

Applying Nagel's categories mentioned above to the Turkish association reveals the breadth and importance of its two main goals: to support the educational and professional success of young people and transmit religious and traditional values, including family values. To represent and realise its goals, the association has to cooperate both internally and with external partners, in particular with the public authorities/the municipality. However, the level of cooperation with the municipality is precarious, consisting of mainly ad hoc activities and projects on account of the lack of interest on behalf of the municipality. A glance at external influencing factors, such as the German legal framework and public and media discourses, reveals the challenges that the association faces. The end result is a paradox. On the one hand, the Turkish association is an ordinary organisation – one among many others; but on the other hand, it is singled out as a Muslim association, and has therefore to struggle against pervasive negative stereotypes concerning Islam in both Germany and Europe as a whole.

Conclusion

This chapter started by examining existing research with regard to religious majority and minority communities, and civil society in Europe. It was observed that researchers are often not able either to grasp or to map adequately the contributions of religious minority communities. It is therefore difficult for such communities to attract attention or to have the same visibility as their majority equivalents. This means that they are inherently disadvantaged, even in academic research. That said, studies that do focus solely on religious minorities and civil society tend to adopt an apologetic approach as if to prove the argument that religious minority communities are important contributors to civil society. The starting point for the latter is an awareness that the frequently negative representations of minority religious communities as parallel societies in the majority society do not offer a balanced picture of the situation. Specifically, they fail to take into consideration the perspectives of the religious minority communities themselves. This raises the question of what would be the best way to research and study such communities in civil society. I have argued that researchers studying religious minority communities and civil society must focus on the key social concerns, goals and perspectives that are specific to the communities themselves.

The German case study in the WaVE project provides an interesting starting point for this approach. The issue of elderly care revealed two main goals that all religious minority communities shared: offering support to young people in school and in their professional life, and passing on religious values and traditions to the next generations. The analysis of a Turkish association in the German case study using Nagel's network model shows that the community's main goals are closely connected to the very purpose and mission of the association, but also to broad interests in the majority society. The study also reveals that the association has no stable external partnerships in general or with public authorities in particular, which hinders its ability to represent its purpose in the public sphere and thus fulfil its goals. This position of invisibility and marginalisation of a significant civil society actor is furthermore complicated by public discourses presenting Islam as a threat to society.

Based on these findings, I argue that when studying religious minority communities in civil society, researchers should take into account not only the perspectives of the majority society, but also the religious minorities' own needs and circumstances. Studies that start from the specific needs of a religious minority in relation to the majority society must complement existing studies that start from the concerns of the majority society. Only if the perspectives of the minority communities themselves are taken into account, and are built into the research design of studies on religion and civil society, will a more in-depth and accurate picture of the new ecology of religion in civil society emerge.

Notes

[1] For example, the Church of Sweden was not disestablished until 2000.
[2] NPM is a political strategy that emerged in the 1990s and aims to make public services more effective. To achieve this aim, NPM applies methods and tools from market-orientated management, including measuring the efficiency of different public services.
[3] Individual interviews (ii) versus group interviews (gi).

4   Using an idea of social cohesion that refers to an inclusive society founded on a sense of communality and responsibility of members towards each other (for example, Helly, 2003).

References

Adloff, F. (2005) *Zivilgesellschaft. Theorie und politische Praxis (Civil Society. Theory and Political Practice)*, New York, NY and Frankfurt: Campus.

Adloff, F. (2010) 'Dichotomizing religion and civil society? Catholicism in Germany and the USA before the Second Vatican Council', *Journal of Civil Society*, 2(3): 193-293.

Albert, A. and Leis-Peters, A. (2008) 'Dem Kind das Beste zu geben, das bedeutet, die beste Bildung, die möglich ist. Bildung und Bildungsverständnis in interkultureller Perspektive. Ein russlanddeutsches Beispiel' ('Giving children the best means possible in education. Education and understanding of education in an intercultural perspective. A Russian–German example'), in J. Eurich and C. Oelschlägel (eds) *Diakonie und Bildung. Heinz Schmidt zum 65. Geburtstag (Diakonia and Education. A Publication on the Occasion of Heinz Schmidt's 65th birthday)*, Stuttgart: Kohlhammer, pp 171-85.

Baumann, M. (2014) 'Becoming a civil society organisation? Dynamics of immigrant religious communities in civil society and public space', *Nordic Journal of Religion and Society*, 27(2): 113-30.

Borell, K. and Gerdner, A. (2011) 'Hidden voluntary social work. A nationally representative survey of Muslims in Sweden', *British Journal of Social Work*, 42: 968-79.

Casanova, J. (1994) *Public Religions in the Modern World*, Chicago, IL: University of Chicago Press.

De Hart, J., Dekker, P. and Halman, L. (eds) (2013) *Religion and Civil Society in Europe*, Dordrecht, Heidelberg, New York, NY and London: Springer.

Eurich, J. and Maaser, W. (2013) *Diakonie in der Sozialökonomie. Studien zu Folgen der neuen Wohlfahrtspolitik (Diakonia in the Social Economy. Studies on the Consequences of the New Welfare Policy)*, Leipzig: Evangelische Verlagsanstalt.

Flam, H. (ed) (2007) *Migranten in Deutschland: Statistiken – Fakten – Diskurs (Migrants in Germany: Statistics – Facts – Discourses)*, Konstanz: UVK Verlag.

Forsell, E. (2010) 'Anhörigomsorg i migrantfamiljer' ('Caring for family members in migrant families'), in S. Torres and F. Magnusson (eds) *Invandrarskap, äldrevård och omsorg (Immigration, Elderly Care and Welfare)*, Malmö: Gleerups, pp 93-108.

Gardell, M. (2010) *Islamofobi (Islamophobia)*, Stockholm: Leopard.

Helly, D. (2003) 'Social cohesion and cultural plurality', *Canadian Journal of Sociology*, 28(1): 19-42.

Leis-Peters, A. (2011) 'Family, values and social commitment through the prism of welfare: reflections based on a German case study in a European project about welfare and values', *Beliefs and Values*, 3(1): 27-40.

Leis-Peters, A. and Albert, A. (2012) 'Reutlingen case study report', in A. Bäckström (ed) *Welfare and Values in Europe: Transitions Related to Religion, Minorities and Gender. National Overviews and Case Study Reports, Volume 2. Continental Europe: Germany, France, Italy, Greece,* Uppsala: Acta Universitatis Upsaliensis, pp 55-84.

Lilja, E. and Åberg, M. (2012) *Var står forskningen om civilsamhället? En internationell översikt (Research on Civil Society? An International Survey)*, Stockholm: Vetenskapsrådet.

Linde, S. (2010) *Församlingen i granskningssamhälle (The Parish in the Audit Society)*, Lund: Lunds universitet, Socialhögskolan.

Munsch, C. (2010) *Engagement und Diversity. Der Kontext von Dominanz und sozialer Ungleichheit am Beispiel Migration (Commitment and Diversity. The Context of Dominance and Social Inequality Through the Example of Migration)*, Weinheim and München: Juventa.

Nagel, A.-K. (ed) (2015) *Religiöse Netzwerke. Die zivilgesellschaftlichen Potentiale religiöser Migrantengemeinden (Religious Networks. The Civil Society Potential of Religious Migrant Communities)*, Bielefeld: Transcript.

Norris, P. (2013) 'Does praying together mean staying together? Religion and civic engagement in Europe and the United States', in J. De Hart, P. Dekkerl and L. Halman (eds) *Religion and Civil Society in Europe,* Dodrecht: Springer, pp 285-303.

Roßteutscher, S. (2009) *Religion, Zivilgesellschaft, Demokratie. Eine international vergleichende Studie zur Natur religiöser Märkte und der demokratischen Rolle religiöser Zivilgesellschaften (Religion, Civil Society, Democracy. An Internationally Comparative Study on the Nature of Religious Markets and the Democratic Role of Religious Civil Societies)*, Baden-Baden: Nomos.

Stadt Reutlingen (2005) *Reutlingen im Spiegel der Statistik (Reutlingen Through the Mirror of Statistics)*, Reutlingen: Amt für Wirtschaft und Immobilien.

Traunmüller, R. (2011) 'Moral communities? Religion as a source of social trust in a multilevel analysis of 97 German regions', *European Sociological Review*, 27(3): 346-63.

Wijkström, F. (ed) (2012) *Civilsamhället i samhällskontraktet. En antologi om vad som står på spel* (*Civil Society in the Social Contract. An Anthology About What is at Stake*), Stockholm: European Civil Society Press.

Wijkström, F. (2014) 'Svenska kyrkan i ett omförhandlat samhällskontrakt' ('The Church of Sweden in a renegotiated contract with society') in A. Bäckström (ed) *Välfärdsinsatser på religiös grund. Förväntningar och problem* (*Welfare Achievements on Religious Grounds. Expectations and Problems*), Skellefteå: Artos and Norma, pp 221–57.

Zimmer, A. and Simsa, R. (2014) 'Quo vadis?', in A. Zimmer and R. Simsa (eds) *Forschung zu Zivilgesellschaft, NPOs und Engagement. Quo vadis?* (*Research on Civil Society, NPOs and Engagement. Quo Vadis?*), Wiesbaden: Springer, pp 11–37.

NINE

Striving to live the good life: the tension between self-fulfilment and family obligations for women in northern England

Martha Middlemiss Lé Mon

Valuing the good life

Overarching quantitative studies, such as the World Values Survey, consistently show that for a majority of men and women in the advanced industrialised societies of the western world, values that are upheld as important are focused not merely on survival, or even on improvement of material living conditions, but on living the 'good life'. However, as Ronald Inglehart and Christian Welzel's cultural map of the world (formed from data from the World Values Survey) shows, there is considerable international variation in the priority given to particular values (Inglehart and Welzel, 2005). By extension, it is reasonable to assume that variations in conceptions of what the good life is also appear within national contexts and have to be negotiated by individuals in the day-to-day decisions that they make.

Also using data from the World Values Survey, Thorleif Pettersson and Yilmaz Esmer analysed the case of Sweden, considering the implications (both for individual migrants and for the development of Swedish culture) of the differences between the dominant values in Sweden and those that prevail in the countries from which many migrants come. They note not only that there are clear differences, but also that these differences may have a significant impact on how migrants adapt to the new culture (Pettersson and Esmer, 2005). Following an analysis of the extent to which international migration from Islamic countries to western Europe influences the values systems of the migrants, Pettersson and Esmer conclude that such migration has different consequences for different aspects of the migrants' value systems. Therefore, it is an oversimplification to say that migrants either completely hold fast to the values of their old culture or adopt entirely those of the new (Pettersson and Esmer, 2005, p 35). With this in mind, it is interesting to investigate further which elements of value systems might be particularly difficult for members of minority communities to negotiate in relation to living the 'good life'. In this chapter, however, the focus is on Britain rather than Sweden.[1]

Susan Pickard has identified two competing discourses of the 'good life' evident in contemporary Britain that, she argues, the individual has to negotiate (Pickard, 2010, p 472). One is associated with a focus on individualised society, which emphasises choice and 'pure' authentic relationships, and the other, prevalent in current social policy, underscores the role of the family in caregiving. Furthermore, Pickard, who identified these two discourses in her analysis of the moral narratives of informal carers, argues that the socioeconomic resources at the disposal of the individual seeking to balance these two discourses are crucial to the impact they may have on an individual's situation. For those without such resources the two discourses may be experienced as 'givens' that impose on the individual, whereas for those with resources 'ethical discourse can be utilized inventively in the construction of a good life associated with a chosen and valued identity' (Pickard, 2010, p 483).

This chapter takes as its starting point the UK context, and in particular the experiences of women who are members of 'minority communities' in the town of Darlington in the north-east of England. The chapter focuses on value conflicts that arise in the lives of these women in relation to notions of the 'good life', in order to explore values that underpin the arguably gender-mediated tension between self-fulfilment and family obligations highlighted by Pickard. These issues are explored through the narratives of women in Darlington who are not members of the ethnic or religious majority. The chapter also discusses not only value clashes but the impact of lack of resources, and therefore the clashes between practical and symbolic domains in the arena of welfare that are particularly evident in, and pertinent to, the lives of women.

Defining and studying basic values

Before embarking on a presentation and discussion of the empirical material from the case study in Darlington, however, it is important to address the question of what the values under review are and how it is possible to study them.

The Welfare and Values in Europe: Transitions Related to Religion, Minorities and Gender (WaVE) project as a whole used the arena of welfare as a prism through which to observe and assess basic values that otherwise remain elusive. It followed a line of thought similar to that of Arthur Kleinman, who has argued that the complexity of moral choices can best be observed at the level of concrete reality (Kleinman, 1998). The project was not, however, founded on a single definition of basic values, so for the purposes of this chapter it is necessary to introduce such a definition to underpin the analysis. Here I have utilised the definition formulated by Henk Vinken and colleagues (2004), who write that basic values can be defined as:

> the ultimate, most frugal, and yet most meaningful basic set of axes with which to explain the broad range of attitudes, beliefs, life styles and the diversity of practices among large populations and/or organizations across societies … a unifying, universal pattern that regardless of social differentiation, displays homogeneity, is broadly shared and has the power to shape people's identities, attitudes and all other aspects of their culture. (Vinken et al, 2004, p 8)

Such a definition, while a helpful starting point, needs further development before it can act as a tool in the study of the lives of women in a medium-sized town in contemporary Britain. Here I turn for help to the work of Linda Woodhead, who has sought to widen the discussion, definition and study of values beyond the notion of abstract cognition and take account of embodiment and emotion. Values, she argues:

> have to do with the good life in a good society. We have personal and collective notions of what this is not because we have consciously elaborated sets of abstract norms to direct our action from the 'outside', but because our lives are shaped and saturated with emotively charged myths, symbols, and narratives which propel us and repel us from the 'inside'. They exist in dialectical relationship with our unfolding experience, both being shaped by and shaping that experience. They help us make basic sense of our world not first by thinking about it, but by reacting immediately and *viscerally* to it. (Woodhead, 2009, p 9; emphasis in original)

Some elements of the basic values to which individuals relate can be studied through the use of quantitative surveys, such as the World Values Survey, that produce statistical pictures of national and cross-national patterns. Qualitative research can, however, complement such pictures by illustrating the differences within societies and the conflicts that appear around values through the use of narrative embedded in the cultural context. In other words, qualitative methods may be useful in highlighting the ambiguities and tensions that are an integral part of human opinions and attitudes. Here I follow Bernice Martin's application of the thought of Charles Taylor in arguing that qualitative work is required to access the 'powerful, but semi-articulate dimensions of our moral and religious being' (Martin, 2003, p 3). The opinions and attitudes that one could hope to access though a qualitative approach to a study of values related to welfare do not, however, exist independently of the context in which those who profess them live and act. To study opinions and attitudes, therefore, necessitates research through interviews, supported by various other materials, including data on the national welfare system, religious composition, gender regime and minority presence, which can illuminate and contextualise the interviews. It is important, though, to bear in mind Douglas Davies' reminder to the researcher that 'life lived is not as life documented' (Davies, 2002, p 20), by which he means to warn against imposing artificial order on human existence in the intellectual quest to systematise thoughts and actions so as to be able to study them.

A case study of Darlington

The data presented here are the result of fieldwork in the town of Darlington, a medium-sized town in the north-east of England, undertaken between September 2006 and September 2007. Darlington, like the north-east region as a whole, does not have a particularly diverse population in terms of either ethnicity or faith. According to the 2001 UK Census, nearly 98% of the population of the town were of white ethnic origin and 80% identified themselves as Christian.[2] However, given that most of the minority ethnic and religious communities in the UK as a whole are concentrated in large urban conurbations, the situation for minority communities in Darlington is similar to that of many others in medium-sized towns throughout the country (see Middlemiss Lé Mon, 2009 for further details).

Statistics that break down the town into its 25 wards also show that the town mirrors the national situation as regards inequalities in health and wealth. Figures from the national index of multiple deprivation from the time of the fieldwork clearly show that while some in Darlington live in comfortable circumstances, 44% of the town's residents live in wards that are in the 25% most deprived in the country (Middlemiss Lé Mon, 2009, p 5). Most of the individuals who ascribe to an ethnic identity other than white British live in two of the most deprived wards in central Darlington (Soni, 2002, p 55). In addition, statistically more deprived wards on the east side of town have experienced dramatically larger increases in rates of immigration than the more prosperous west side (BBC News, 2005). It therefore seems reasonable to suggest that – in line with other research that has identified similar trends in other areas and on a national level (Gough and Adami, 2013) – minority communities in Darlington are over-represented among those who have significant welfare needs.

A decade on from the data collection, a number of changes have taken place, not least in the welfare system in the UK, as austerity measures have resulted in widespread cuts often focused on the most vulnerable (Hill, 2015). This, following more general cutbacks designed to curb long-term challenges to the health and social systems, has had a significant impact on those relying most heavily on benefits, especially women and families on low incomes (Taylor Gooby, 2013). Similarly, the growth in anti-immigration sentiments being aired in public, spurring more restrictive immigration policies and encouraging restrictions in welfare provision for recent immigrants, has had a negative impact on the lives of all those in minority groups in the country (Wilkinson and Craig, 2012; Ford et al, 2015). A further point is important: these policy developments clearly reflect the significant role played by emotions and beliefs in the current formation of welfare policy (Carmel and Cerami, 2012, p 10).

The important role of values and preferences in the structuring and function of welfare is discussed further in this chapter. At this stage, suffice it to say that if the data collection were to be replicated today, the noticeably harsher climate for those living as part of a minority group in Darlington would be visible in the material. Themes identified in the research 10 years ago would continue to surface, but in light of the new austerity in social policy (Farnsworth and Irving, 2015) issues relating to lack of resources would be even more prevalent.

In the WaVE study, data collection focused in particular on three very different minority groups:

- the established Bangladeshi/Bengali community, which is also a Muslim community, concentrated in one area of the town;
- the Traveller/Gypsy community, which has been a presence in the area for many generations, but is a moderately invisible minority; and
- the very new and fast-growing Polish community.

In addition, the study highlighted issues concerning children, elderly people and women's roles. These three themes were chosen because in all groups in society, including the majority population, they represent areas where welfare services are in particular demand and where debates and conflicts around issues of welfare are explicitly value-laden.

The study took place in two stages. In the first mapping stage, a considerable amount of documentary material was collected and complemented by short, fact-finding interviews, mainly held over the telephone. The second, in-depth phase of the study focused primarily on open-ended interviews with members of the minority communities and with people who work with these communities in a professional or voluntary capacity. I carried out 17 semi-structured interviews of between 45 minutes and two hours long. These were supplemented by participant observation in three groups, followed by shorter interviews with staff and participants.

Hierarchies of values

In approaching this material and following Linda Woodhead's definition of values, I wanted to ascertain what values the informants in my study referred to as important, but also to discover where tensions existed and how these values were expressed in relation to one another in concrete decisions and actions in the welfare sphere.

The analysis of the material as a whole revealed many interesting lines for further enquiry. At a general level, my observation of the ways in which members of the minority groups studied interact with welfare services, coupled with the relevant interviews, show that while many are happy with the services on offer there are important areas and difficulties connected to their minority status that need to be overcome. In actions and attitudes expressed in relation to welfare issues, basic values can be identified. These values have their roots in cultural traditions and religion and, while by no means exclusive to the minority communities in the town, they seem to be particularly strong motivators within these groups. Over and above this, while many underlying values, such as that of self-sufficiency, appear to be the same in both majority and minority communities, they seem to be 'stronger' in the minority communities where the 'threshold' for seeking help is higher. It is possible that this is an indication of different hierarchies of values in the majority and minority communities, but a more detailed analysis of more specific themes in the material is needed if this question is to be explored further.

Gender-specific tensions

This chapter focuses specifically on the value tensions as experienced by women. Research into value systems has indicated that while age, ethnicity and education have a significant impact on an individual's value system and priorities, gender is a less significant, or even nominal, factor in identifying differences in value priorities (Prince–Gibson and Schwartz, 1998). Furthermore, the impact of a person's values on his/her attitudes is moderated by his/her age, race and gender (Sawyerr et al, 2005). However, there is also evidence that women in most cultures bear the primary responsibility for welfare work and, not least in western European societies, that they often bear a double burden of responsibility for the home along with paid work (see, for example, Bratberg et al, 2002). This has led researchers who have developed the notion of a feminist ethics of care to argue that a focus on the particular situation for women in relation to family responsibility and caregiving is crucial to an understanding of welfare systems and their inherent values.

In arguing for the introduction of such an ethic to studies of the implications of social policy at local level, Amanda Gouws has articulated the key issues in a helpful manner. Using a feminist ethic of care as an analytical starting point, she reasons, puts the caregiving role of women at the heart of the analysis of care and explains the relational context of caregiving. The ethic of care, she continues, 'recognizes that women are vulnerable because of the way society deals with caring responsibilities' (Gouws, 2009, p 62). Thus, following Gouws' approach, this chapter takes as a starting point the idea that in the area of welfare it is particularly relevant to study the hierarchies of values as expressed by women. More specifically, it focuses on which values are emphasised when practical and more existential concerns clash, recognising that tensions between care roles and individual self-fulfilment are particularly evident in, and pertinent to, the lives of women.

Practical and symbolic domains in the welfare arena

Within social psychology studies of minority–majority relations, a model has been developed that is used to distinguish between two domains of threat as perceived in minority–majority relations (Stephan and Stephan, 1996; Ward and Masgoret, 2008, p 229; Fokas, 2009). This model distinguishes between realistic and symbolic threats. In the context of this study of tensions and values in relation to welfare provision, this conceptualisation is a helpful model for assessing minority groups and their relations to, and perceptions of, welfare provision. In applying the model to this study I have, however, chosen to use the term 'practical' rather than 'realistic'. In this context, the term 'realistic' is not helpful given the assumptions that can be read into the terms used – namely that the one domain (realistic) is superior to the other (symbolic). The use of the term 'practical' also adapts the model for use in an analysis of different levels of practical resources available to different individuals and groups. In the welfare arena, therefore, we can speak of two domains, the practical, which concerns resources of different kinds, and the symbolic, where beliefs and values related to welfare are situated.

Tensions between practical and symbolic domains in welfare

In the case of Darlington, tensions appear at different levels when these two dimensions collide. In many instances, what has been found to be important is not the possible differences in values between groups, but how those differences are highlighted when a lack of resources force individuals to seek help that they would prefer to avoid. This is illustrated in a number of examples, such as when financial constraints force people to seek help, or when language issues cause difficulties. However, differences in values and tensions between the practical and symbolic domains in welfare are also evident in other areas. These include important factors such as time and space, as well as issues of food and clothing, noting that both have a particularly strong gender dimension. The shift in seasonal work patterns for the men in some families, for example, affects women at many levels. Space is a factor both for communities as a whole, as seen in tensions over community halls and religious buildings, and for individuals, as seen in the social implications of living as a member of a small minority community in a small town.

Money

Many would prefer to care for their elderly relatives within the immediate family circle and without support from public welfare services, but lack of financial resources means that they feel forced to seek help. This can create conflict within the family and in particular among the women who bear the main burden of care as they struggle with feelings of guilt. Similar tensions appear when women who think they have to work because of the family's economic situation feel caught in a tension between the need to earn money and the feeling that they are abandoning their family duties. Here external and internal dimensions are often evident as, while a woman may be happy with the situation herself, she may face disapproval from others in the community.

Language

Lack of competence in English can both hinder people seeking help outside the community where they might otherwise be willing to do so, and lead individuals to compromise on principles that they would otherwise be reluctant to concede: for example, where mothers have to use husbands or children as interpreters in healthcare situations. One member of a basic English class fought hard with her limited English to convey the frustrations of having to rely on members of her family as interpreters. In particular, she wanted to stress her inadequacy as a mother when having to rely on one's own child for translation in situations where the maternal figure should be able to shield her child – for example, during negotiations with the local school, or at the doctor's surgery.

This study is by no means the first time that issues of language competence within minority communities, and the impact that this has on other areas of life, has been highlighted. A study in 2002 of educational and employment needs among black and minority ethnic (BME) communities in Darlington drew out many of the same issues addressed here (Thandi, 2002). Using questionnaires translated into a number of community languages, this survey reached people I could not reach with interviews and found that although residents in Darlington from minority communities are generally satisfied with services provided by the council (Thandi, 2002, pp 107-9), language was identified by both professionals and members of the different communities as the most common barrier for members of BME communities to services and education and employment prospects

(Thandi, 2002, p 134). A number of the recommendations that Mandeep Kaur Thandi makes, such as increasing the availability of interpretation services and information leaflets translated into a variety of languages, have been implemented. However, language remained one of the major concerns to which interviewees referred, and not least with regard to problems in communicating with doctors and the associated complications of needing to involve family members in visits to healthcare services.

Time

In the Bangladeshi community, it is the working hours of the men (often 'antisocial', with nights on shift work, in the catering/hotel business, or as taxi drivers) that define the pattern for the whole family. Many women structure their day around the man's shift pattern in order to be able to spend time with their husband and also to be able to prepare traditional food. In that they have responsibility for childcare, however, in addition to adapting to these hours, the women are also required to get up and get children ready for school and so on. Once the children have gone to school, a mother may then be able to rest for an hour or two, but as it is during school hours that crèches and activities for mothers with small children are available, these women are not able to make use of such provision and are cut off from the wider community. A language class for women that runs during school hours, and also provides a crèche for very young children who are too young to go to school, is an example of a service that has been adapted to fit the needs of the intended target audience.

For the Traveller community, time constraints are seasonal as many families travel during the summer months, following the work of the father, a situation which affects the entire family. One of the consequences is that families often return to the town too late to register their children for their preferred school for the following academic year. This is a choice closely connected to faith–based values, as Traveller families tend to prefer the local Roman Catholic schools because of their Christian ethos. But since such schools are also popular with other parents because of their academic record, they fill rapidly. Families also experience significant difficulties in accessing healthcare as a consequence of adhering to their travelling lifestyle. One healthcare worker has witnessed the priority that members of the Traveller community place on healthcare, particularly where children are concerned, despite practical problems with registration and the relay of information while they are on the move. They are frequently, she noted, "labelled very much as poor attenders/non-attenders, but in actual fact that is not the case, they weren't receiving the appointments ... but I can ring and say little Johnny has an appointment next Wednesday and nine times out of 10 they will move mountains to get back for it".

Space

One issue of space concerns the town itself. For members of the minority communities, the contrast between living in a town the size of Darlington and living in an urban conurbation seems to be particularly acute and affects individual and community life in both positive and negative ways. Several Bangladeshi women, all members of a basic English class, commented that living in Darlington, rather than in one of the larger urban conurbations, which have larger minority communities, meant sacrificing social opportunities and access to ethnic food and clothing stores as well as to community centres. In line with Thandi's (2002, p 110) findings, however, while there was an element of regret in these comments, they were not uttered as a critique of Darlington, which in most respects was seen as a place in which people enjoyed living. It is possible that this sense of contentment among the established minority communities, despite the fact that Darlington lacks the advantages of larger communities in terms of cultural resources, is connected to the tightly knit nature of the communities in a small town.

Food

Food plays an important role in the family lives of minority communities in Darlington. The relationship to food and food preparation is a helpful illustration of the family obligations for many of the women. In the various Asian communities in particular, including the Bangladeshi, the women have responsibility for the children, and, as one interviewee put it:

'For the food, you have to cook fresh every day and you have to cook so many dishes, it is a big thing really, you can't just get things out of the oven.... It is a big thing in our lives really, the focus on the family meal and the kind of meal.'

This illustrates the ties that continue to bind women in these communities to the domestic sphere. The same woman continued, commenting on the difficulties for women who want to work:

'In our Asian culture, the home is the priority still. There isn't, you would not get so much help from your partner, they have to be looked after, so it is only the little bit of spare time which you can have when you are not supposed to do something else that you can do. I suppose once the children are in school that is the time when you get those six hours to start working.'

In the Traveller community too, providing well-cooked food for the family is a matter of importance and pride. A year or so before this study, a suggestion had been made to arrange lessons in cooking healthy food on one of the sites as a service to the community. This proposal never made it as far as the community itself, given one health worker's horror at the suggestion, which resulted in its rejection. The idea, clearly a product of good intentions, had failed to take into account not only the absence of need for such a service in this group, but also the insult that would be implied by its provision, in that the women of the community would take it as a sign that the food they were providing for their families was not good enough.

Identity, entrepreneurship and social interaction

The fact that Asian women in Darlington find it hard to find the type of clothing that they want to wear prompted one woman to request, and then attend, sewing classes, with the aim not only of making clothes for herself, but also of setting up a business for making and selling them. The sewing classes in Darlington, funded by community grants, have led to women setting up their own businesses, but have also had a confidence-building function. In addition, they have become a point of contact for meeting women from other cultures and for some this has been a way into other services. One reason why this has functioned so well, and the same is true of language classes organised through the government's Sure Start programme, seems to lie in the fact that they are for women only. This feels less threatening to some women; indeed, for some it enables them to take part. If there were men present in the classrooms, the male members of their family would not allow participation. For many of the Muslim women this is also true for women's only swimming and aerobics sessions, also arranged through Sure Start. Religious and cultural modesty norms mean that these women are not able to swim or exercise in a mixed-gender environment.

Motherhood

As the previous examples have indicated, motherhood is, within the dynamics of the communities studied, an important factor that can both draw women closer to mainstream society and push them away. Three further examples from the interview material elaborate this more clearly. Both women themselves and workers in the health sector comment that many women readily seek healthcare or assistance from social services when pregnant. They will also make use of such services for their children, but not otherwise for themselves. A woman may, for example, consult a doctor on behalf of her child, but then once at the health centre mention in passing issues with her own health. In a similar vein, the study has also demonstrated that midwives have been an important first point of contact for many, opening doors to other areas. For one Polish woman with little English and no contact network in Darlington, the midwife she consulted during a well-advanced pregnancy was the person who introduced and helped her to join an English language class. Here she was able not only to learn the language but also to meet other women in a similar situation, some of whom shared her mother tongue. Finally, on a less positive note, as some of the earlier examples have already shown, motherhood can also be a turning point confining women to the home, despite the fact that they have been able to lead a more independent life before having children. The expectation that responsibility for childcare belongs to the woman, combined with other practical constraints such as lack of time and the need to prepare food, means that for many women motherhood is experienced as a clash between values of self-fulfilment and family obligations.

Self versus family as a value clash

Interestingly, the focus on the particular value clash between self-fulfilment and family obligations in women's lives in the material also reveals two separate findings that may be of interest, not just in relation to the gender issue but also in furthering theoretical work in the connection between value formation and individual identity construction in contemporary societies.

The first finding is that 'the self versus the family' clash can be seen as a value clash at two levels for the women concerned. At one level, it appears as what may be termed 'external tension', that is to say, a clash between the woman's own priorities and those expressed by other members of the family. There is a difference, in other words, between the hierarchy of values of the individual woman and those of the family unit. However, it can also appear as 'internal tension' when the individual's own hierarchy of values is unclear, or when an individual has formed two separate hierarchies of values that come into conflict when the roles of carer and working woman collide.

The second finding relates to the clash between self-fulfilment and family obligations, noting that the clash is not only between different values, or even between different hierarchies of values, but between different interpretations and applications of one and the same value. In both the external and internal conflicts described here, for example, the value of self-sufficiency can be shown to be the basic value at play on both sides of the divide. Here, the value of the self-sufficiency of the family unit in welfare terms clashes with the value of the self-sufficiency of the independent woman who can care for herself and, through her paid employment, provide for her own long-term care. I find support for this reasoning in the work of Linda Woodhead (2009), who, in her study of conflict around the issue of the veil in European societies, has argued that:

> If we look closely at how public, policy and political debates about the veil are actually being framed, we find not a clash of cultures, civilisations or discourses, but a clash of values. But if we look even more closely, we see that both parties are, in many cases, invoking the *same* values (like 'freedom' and 'equality'). (Woodhead, 2009, p 2; emphasis in original)

Similarly, Geert Hofstede has argued at an individual level that:

> Our values are mutually related and form value systems or hierarchies, but these systems need not be in a state of harmony: most people simultaneously hold several conflicting values, such as 'freedom' and 'equality'. (Hofstede, 1984, p 8)

The issue of whether these observations could equally well apply to the majority community remains pertinent. Indeed, many other studies of religious communities have made similar observations about the particular value clash of caring tasks and career when looking at religious communities with a strong emphasis on tradition. For example, Chia Longman's findings on the impact of strong adherence to tradition combined with tight-knit community or extended family on the lives of Orthodox Jewish women finds parallels in the material from Darlington (Longman, 2008). Self-sufficiency becomes a value in the expression of the ideal family unit, as indeed does self-subjugation, given that it is the taming of possibly contradictory individual desires that enables the family as a collective to flourish.

This issue becomes particularly obvious in the roles of women and in particular in tensions between contradictory sets of values held by younger women. In the choice between career and caring for elderly relatives within the family home, values of independence, self-determination and personal fulfilment collide with those of duty to the family and the self-sufficiency of the family unit. Here there are clear similarities with the conclusions of Susan Pickard, who, as noted earlier, found in her research on carers two competing discourses of the 'good life' that the individual has to negotiate (Pickard, 2010, p 472). Pickard's focus is on the 'good life', as it is for the women of minority communities in Darlington. More specifically, however, the focus here has been on the construction not just of the good life for oneself, but also of the 'good family'. In the value conflict surrounding the notion of the 'good family', women who have caring responsibilities and their families can get caught up in what can be termed 'vicious cycles of care'. This is best demonstrated with an example. In situations where care for an elderly family member, for instance, cannot be supplied by women within the immediate family circle, the next best option that would uphold the notion of the 'good family' is care provided by members of the extended community family (members of the same ethnic, religious or cultural community). In the Darlington case, the council sought to meet such requests by attempting to recruit members of various minority communities, including from the Bangladeshi community, to act as home care helpers in such situations. This proved virtually impossible, however, and although a few people applied they later withdrew their applications. Investigations into the cause soon ascertained that the reasons given for the reluctance to apply for, or take on, such a post lay in the fact that it was deemed unsuitable for women to undertake such care work outside of the immediate family circle. So here too the value of self-sufficiency of the immediate family unit is pitted against the value of self-sufficiency of the larger family or 'community'.

Thus, we can see that for both Pickard's informants and for the women from minority communities interviewed in Darlington, value conflicts between self-fulfilment and family obligation serve to illuminate broader value conflicts in late-modern society. Tensions exist at the individual level as individuals try to construct a coherent worldview while seeking to form a coherent identity, which they struggle to combine with contrasting value hierarchies.

Problems on the horizon

Based on her study in Antwerp, Longman argues that the younger generation in particular faces restrictions in negotiating different religious and secular expectation of gender roles. She focuses on structural factors, arguing that 'their prospects depend on the dynamic between global fundamentalist tendencies and local liberal state policies of multicultural accommodation' (Longman, 2008, p 223). The results of the Darlington study, however, show that over and above such dynamics, which affect the gender role negotiations of women within religious communities, other factors are at play in the lives of women from minority communities, whether or not religious. It is evident within all the minority communities focused on in Darlington that conflicts within the domain of welfare are being stored up for the future when the next generation become the very elderly and a new generation of children are born whose grandmothers work.

For women in all communities there is a question of whether or not those who have made a career for themselves will leave work or work part time in order to care for elderly parents. Several women I interviewed felt that they could see such a conflict on the horizon, which would involve both internal conflict, as they struggle with their own conflicting priorities, and external conflict, as family members exert pressure. This is best illustrated with two examples from the Darlington material.

One Sikh woman, interviewed in the study on account of her professional position in the social services in Darlington, acknowledges that she now benefits from the availability of childcare in the family structure, but (interestingly in this respect) also assumes that this support is to enable her 'as a woman' to work while her husband's role as breadwinner is taken for granted. Regarding the future, she comments:

> 'Now for my kind of generation there are a lot more women who are going out to work, professional qualifications, and actually career is a big thing to them and I actually say to my mum. It is going to be difficult when she gets older and if she wants the support that she gave to my grandma, it may not be readily available by me because of my working commitments and circumstances. So there will be a generational shift, but it has not happened as of yet.

So to be honest it is twofold. I wouldn't move out of the area because of the support they provide to me, but vice versa I would always want to be here for my mum and dad as well and I think despite me saying yes there will be a clash of priorities later on. I very much imagine we would end up working either part time to accommodate what was needed between the family that was there.'

There is a further dimension for more recent immigrants who add a new question to the mix: whether to bring over elderly relatives and care for them in the UK, or to return 'home' for this reason when the time comes. In the words of one Polish immigrant:

'The generation of our parents they expect from us support when they get ill and can't manage on their own.... But still in Poland you can find three generations in one house so this is natural.... The grandparents they take care of the small grandchild and then it is natural that when they are getting old they get care from their children. I think about this very, very often, what will be if I learn that my mother is very ill for instance ... and that she needs care. I think a lot of Polish staying here that are our age, they have to think about this ... this could be a reason for moving back because there is not enough state support for old or seriously ill people. They are mostly, they need to be based on the family.'

In other words, the value conflict these women experience is not necessarily related to gender role negotiations that fit easily into a clash between secular feminist ideals and traditional cultural or religious gender norms. The relationship is considerably more complex and more research is needed to understand what it is to live the 'good life', taking into account the subtle relationships between basic values related to welfare and caring, the value basis of gender norms, and the role of both in women's identity construction. Such decisions, moreover, will become all the more difficult in 'post-Brexit' Britain,[3] where the as yet unclear future relationship of the UK to the EU and the corresponding impact on welfare and immigration policies in the UK are already having an effect. There can be no doubt that the ensuing uncertainty will continue to be a significant factor in the lives of many members of minority groups in the UK, not least recent immigrants from the EU.

The results of this study pose questions as to how social change on a larger scale is influenced by the value negotiations detailed here and enacted by individuals in their everyday lives. Welzel and Inglehart have argued that people 'can and do change their strategies to maximize happiness and that changes in value priorities are an inherent part of this process' (Welzel and Inglehart, 2010, p 43). Furthermore, they claim that the individual's value priorities and choices must be understood within an evolutionary model of social change. Therefore, people adapt their strategies in response to their needs, duties and resources, and 'when these needs and opportunities shift in the same way for many people, this nurtures similar adaptation strategies. Similar strategies accumulate to collective trends, which is social change' (Welzel and Inglehart, 2010, p 44). In the risk society described by Ulrich Beck and Elisabeth Beck-Gernsheim, however, individualisation has resulted in a society where 'Life, death, gender, corporeality, identity, religion, marriage, parenthood, social ties – all are becoming decidable down to the small print; once fragmented into options everything must be decided' (Beck and Beck-Gernsheim, 1996, p 29). For Beck and Beck-Gernsheim, the result of this overload of choices can be both autonomy and anomie, and 'as modernity gains ground, God, nature and the social systems are being progressively replaced, in greater and lesser steps, by the individual – confused, astray, helpless and at a loss' (Beck and Beck-Gernsheim, 1996, p 32).

In the face of this 'precarious freedom', Beck and Beck-Gernsheim pose the following questions: whether there is a remaining social unit; how welfare policy, for example, should react to this diversification; and most importantly is it possible to integrate highly individualised societies? (Beck and Beck-Gernsheim, 1996: 42). Or to phrase the question another way, is it possible in contemporary society to balance the equation of a 'good life' for individuals with a 'common good' for society at large? If Welzel and Inglehart's evolutionary perspective is accepted, this may well be the case, as individualism becomes a value that can have an integrating function. Pål Repstad, for example, has warned against over-exaggerating the tendency towards privatisation, since collective cultural frameworks will always exist, even if they do so in new ways (Repstad, 2002a, 2002b). Individual women from minority communities, striving to achieve the good life for themselves and their families, and in so doing negotiating the value clash between self-fulfilment and family obligation – itself intensified by issues of cultural or religious norms and (lack of) resources – stand at the forefront of social development. For anyone who wants to understand or predict social change, it is important to take their negotiations seriously and seek to understand the complex mesh of value priorities that they reveal.

Notes

[1] A number of the issues addressed in this chapter were first raised in an article I wrote in 2011, 'Care and career: a value conflict with a woman's face', *Beliefs and Values: Understanding the Global Implications of Human Nature*: 3(1). I am grateful to the editors and anonymous reviewers of that publication whose feedback on that article was helpful in developing the analysis further.

[2] Interestingly, by 2011 the percentage identifying as Christian had decreased quite sharply: specifically, 96% of the population of the town was of white ethnic origin and 67% was Christian. See UK Census 2011, www.darlington.gov.uk/your-council/communities/equality-information

[3] Shorthand for the UK's withdrawal from the European Union, following a referendum on the UK's membership of the EU held in June 2016.

References

BBC News (2005) 'Born abroad: an immigration map of Great Britain, North East', available at http://news.bbc.co.uk/2/shared/spl/hi/uk/05/born_abroad/around_britain/html/north_east.stm.

Beck, U. and Beck-Gernsheim, E. (1996) 'Individualization and "precarious freedoms": perspectives and controversies of a subject-oriented sociology', in P. Heelas, S. Lash and P. Morris (eds) *Detraditionalization: Critical Reflections on Authority and Identity*, Cambridge, MA: Blackwell, pp 23–48.

Bratberg, E., Dahl, S.-Å. and Risa, A.E. (2002) '"The double burden": do combinations of career and family obligations increase sickness absence among women?' *European Sociological Review*, 18(2): 233–49.

Carmel, E. and Cerami, A. (2012) 'Governing migration and welfare: institutions and emotions in the production of differential inclusion', in E. Carmel, A. Cerami and T. Papadopoulos (eds) *Migration and Welfare in the New Europe: Social Protection and the Challenges of Integration*, Bristol: Policy Press, pp 1–22.

Davies, D.J. (2002) *Anthropology and Theology*, Oxford: Berg.

Farnsworth, K. and Irving, Z. (2015) 'Introduction: social policy in the age of austerity', in K. Farnsworth and Z. Irving (eds) *Social Policy in Times of Austerity: Global Economic Crisis and the New Politics of Welfare*, Bristol: Policy Press, pp 1–8.

Fokas, E. (2009) *Welfare and Values in Europe: A Comparative Cross-Country Analysis*, Report for the European Commission funded Framework 6 Project on Welfare and Values in Europe: Transitions Related to Religion, Minorities and Gender, Brussels: European Commission.

Ford, R., Jennings, W. and Somerville, W. (2015) 'Public opinion, responsiveness and constraint: Britain's three immigration policy regimes', *Journal of Ethnic and Migration Studies*, 41(9): 1391-411.

Gough, O. and Adami, R. (2013) 'Saving for retirement: a review of ethnic minorities in the UK', *Social Policy and Society*, 12(1): 147-61.

Gouws, A. (2009) 'A gender perspective in social welfare and religion in Paarl through the lens of a feminist ethics of care', *Journal of Theology for Southern Africa*, 133: 59-73.

Hill, M. (2015) 'Conventional wisdom on government austerity: UK politics since the 1920s', in K. Farnsworth and Z. Irving (eds) *Social Policy in Times of Austerity: Global Economic Crisis and the New Politics of Welfare*, Bristol: Policy Press, pp 43-66.

Hofstede, G. (1984) *Culture's Consequences: International Differences in Work Related Values* (abridged edn), Newbury Park, CA: Sage.

Inglehart, R. and Welzel, C. (2005) *Modernization, Cultural Change and Democracy*, New York, NY and Cambridge: Cambridge University Press.

Kleinman, A. (1998) 'Experience and its moral modes: culture, human conditions and disorder', Tanner Lectures on Human Values, Stanford University, 12-16 April.

Longman, C. (2008) 'Sacrificing the career or the family? Orthodox Jewish women between secular work and the sacred home', *European Journal of Women's Studies*, 15(3): 223-39.

Martin, B. (2003) 'Beyond measurement: the non-quantifiable religious dimension in social life', in P. Avis (ed) *Public Faith: The State of Religious Belief and Practice in Britain*, London: SPCK, pp 1-18.

Middlemiss Lé Mon, M. (2009) 'Darlington case study report', in A. Bäckström (ed) *Welfare and Values in Europe: Transitions Related to Religion, Minorities and Gender, Volume 1. Northern Europe: Sweden, Norway, Finland, England*, Studies in Religion and Society 4, Uppsala: Acta Universitatis Upsaliensis, pp 249-84.

Pettersson, T. and Esmer, Y. (2005) *Vilka är annorlunda? Om invandrares möte med svensk kultur* (*Who is Different? On Immigrants' Encounters with Swedish Culture*), Integrationsverkets rapportserie 3, Norrköping: Integrationsverket.

Pickard, S. (2010) 'The good carer: moral practices in late modernity', *Sociology*, 44: 471-87.

Prince-Gibson, E. and Schwartz, S.H. (1998) 'Value priorities and gender', *Social Psychology Quarterly*, 61(1): 49-67.

Repstad, P. (2002a) *Dype, stille, sterke, milde: Religiøsmakt i dagens Norge* (*Deep, Calm, Strong, Mild: Religious Power in Contemporary Norway*), Oslo: Gyldendal.

Repstad, P. (2002b) 'Has the pendulum swung too far? The construction of religious individualism in today's sociology of religion', *Temenos*, 37-8: 181-90.

Sawyerr, O.O., Strauss, J. and Yan, J. (2005) 'Individual value structure and diversity attitudes: the moderating effects of age, gender, race, and religiosity', *Journal of Managerial Psychology*, 20(6): 498-521.

Soni, V. (2002) *Ethnicity in the North East: An Overview* (second edn), Government Office for the North East.

Stephan, W.G. and Stephan, C.W. (1996) *Intergroup Relations*, Boulder, CO: Westview Press.

Taylor Gooby, P. (2013) *The Double Crisis of the Welfare State and What We Can Do About It*, Basingstoke: Palgrave Macmillan.

Thandi, M. (2002) *Researching Black and Minority Ethnic Communities in Darlington: Education, Training and Employment*, Darlington: Darlington Borough Council.

Vinken, H., Soeters, J. and Ester, P. (2004) *Comparing Cultures. Dimensions of Culture in a Comparative Perspective*, Leiden: Brill.

Ward, C. and Masgoret, A. (2008) 'Attitudes toward immigrants, immigration, and multiculturalism in New Zealand: a social psychological analysis', *International Migration Review*, 42(1): 227-48.

Welzel, C. and Inglehart, R. (2010) 'Values, agency, and well-being: a human development model', *Social Indicators Research*, 97: 43-63.

Wilkinson, M. and Craig, G. (2012) 'Wilful negligence: migration policy, migrants' work and the absence of social protection in the UK', in E. Carmel, A. Cerami and T. Papadopoulos (eds) *Migration and Welfare in the New Europe: Social Protection and the Challenges of Integration*, Bristol: Policy Press, pp 177-96.

Woodhead, L. (2009) 'The Muslim veil controversy and European values', *Swedish Missiological Themes*, 97(1): 89-105.

TEN

Religion as a resource or as a source of exclusion? The case of Muslim women's shelters

Pia Karlsson Minganti

Introduction

As part of the European Commission's 6th Framework programme, the Welfare and Values in Europe: Transition Related to Religion, Minorities and Gender (WaVE) project offers insights into the interaction of diverse value systems in local European settings and welfare regimes. In this context, this chapter[1] presents an in–depth case study of a women's shelter[2] in Sweden with a particular focus on Muslim women (including some references to Italy).[3] The chapter also offers further insight into the complex relations between welfare, religion, gender, minorities and majorities.

As highlighted by the WaVE research on European welfare regimes, welfare systems quite clearly exist in various religious contexts, but there is nevertheless an enduring idea of the state as ultimately responsible for the provision of human care. This assumption, however, is increasingly matched by an expectation that both profit and non–profit actors within civil society will assume a complementary role to public care provision, not least for vulnerable groups such as asylum seekers, new immigrants and victims of human trafficking (Bäckström, 2011, 2012a, 2012b, 2014; Frisina and Cancellieri, 2012, p 233). Churches and religious organisations are among these actors, some of which engage in the care of female victims of domestic violence. For instance, the Catholic Church and its social arm Caritas provide support and shelter in both Italy (Frisina and Cancellieri, 2012, p 208) and Sweden. Another example is the Church of Sweden's diaconia institution Ersta Fristad.

In addition to religious organisations engaging in the care of abused women, there are secular organisations that are active within the field. Several such organisations have developed their own feminist theory and practice, together with expertise on violence against women at the intersection of gender, ethnicity and religion. Prominent examples are Trama di Terre, established in Italy in 1999, and Terrafem, established in Sweden in 2000. These organisations have a long experience in dealing with multiple forms of oppression of minoritised women[4] and the difficulties of building alliances within a minefield of identity and migration politics (Patel, 1999, 2013). Common to these organisations is the fact that they offer counselling and protected housing to women from a variety of backgrounds, while also promoting their particular expertise in offering care to those who are categorised as 'ethnic', 'immigrant' or 'minority' women. For instance, on its internet homepage, Terrafem targets women and girls of 'foreign' backgrounds, while Trama di Terre claims to support ethnic and religious diversity among both its activists and clients.

Another common trait of these organisations is that they promote themselves as 'secular places', interpreting this as a guarantee of offering a 'neutral' environment for women seeking help who may have various attitudes and attachments to religion. This position is, for instance, reflected in the organisation of Trama di Terre, which includes self-identifying 'practising Muslim' women among its employees and board members, but does not take religion as a point of departure for its feminist theorisation and practice (Trama di Terre, 2016; see also Pojmann, 2010, p 245). The reasons behind such a stance include an element of doubt that religion can act as a resource in the struggle against gendered violence. There are concerns that religion can be used by shelter clients to create hierarchies and exclusion among themselves (compare Schmidt, 2011, p 1,227). There are also concerns that religious communities may end up 'favouring social relationships between people who are "alike"' (Frisina and Cancellieri, 2012, p 234), hence setting aside the assumed secular ideal of universalism. Such a view on religion as a source of conflict and exclusion, rather than a basic resource in the work of women's shelters, echoes parts of Susan Moller Okin's (1997) seminal essay 'Is multiculturalism bad for women?'. Okin promotes individual rights for women in new immigrant communities on an equal footing with women belonging to the majority populations of western countries. But she also questions the granting of group-specific rights to cultural and religious minorities, given the complexity of patriarchal domination and the right of any individual either to join or exit from a community.

The scepticism toward religion as a resource shown by secular-oriented women's shelter activists also includes doubts about the competence and experience of domestic religious actors when it comes to theorising and practising the complex, intersectional struggles against gendered violence. For instance, how do Catholic actors justify the conservative patriarchal position that prioritises continuity of family ties at all costs other than by framing this position as a specifically 'Muslim problem'? Annalisa Frisina emphasises that this issue cannot be reduced to a simple question of secular versus religious actors, considering the variety of transgressive collaborations and the involvement of progressive religious groups (Frisina, 2010; see also Chapter Eleven in this book). Yet, Muslim congregations that offer social welfare services are viewed with great scepticism by religious and non-religious governmental and non-governmental actors: 'the dominant discourse on Islam in Europe has claimed that Muslim social work is part of an attempt to create self-sufficient enclaves that impede the integration of Muslim immigrants into the wider society' (Borell and Gerdner, 2011, p 968).

The case studies in the WaVE project highlight the fact that Christian churches and Muslim organisations may be strengthened internally (bonding), but also externally (bridging), through collaboration with other religious and non-religious governmental and non-governmental actors (Bäckström, 2014, pp 210-11; see also Borell and Gerdner, 2011). Congregations, including mosques, have been described by immigrant and minority women as inclusive sites for cohesion and empowerment in Italy (Frisina and Cancellieri, 2012, p 234; Pepicelli, 2012) as well as in Sweden (Karlsson Minganti, 2011, 2014 [2007]). Among confessional Muslim organisations and congregations, relationship counselling and family dispute mediation play an important role. There are spin-offs that represent Muslim women and their rights, such as Associazione Donne Musulmane d'Italia in Italy and Muslimska Kvinnoföreningen in Sweden. However, none of these publicly states that it offers expertise on gendered violence or shelter facilities to abused women. New initiatives by devout Muslim women, such as the Milan-based initiative Aisha (a project denouncing violence and discrimination against women – see also Chapter Eleven), disseminate knowledge and guidelines against gender-based violence, but do not organise shelters.

Somaya: a women's shelter run by and for Muslim women

So far I have provided examples of various initiatives to support Muslim women in Italy and Sweden. I have chosen these two countries because they were the national contexts of an ethnological fieldwork study (see later in this section). Furthermore, Sweden and Italy represent and illustrate the north–south dimension of the WaVE project, which investigates both similarities and differences across diverse religious traditions, welfare state regimes, gender regimes and migration regimes. However, when examining welfare across the dimensions of religion, minorities and gender from the starting point of Muslim women's shelters, used here as a thematic case study, it is not divergence between European nations that stands out, but conflictual notions of secularity and religiosity, in particular of Islam.

To illustrate these complex dynamics, this chapter focuses on an almost unique example in the European context: an organisation in Sweden called the Sisters' Shelter Somaya,[5] which was created on the initiative of Muslim women who officially claimed that their activities were Islamic. Founded in 1998, it originally presented itself as a 'Muslim women's shelter *by* and *for* Muslim women' (Lindberg, 1999; emphasis added). However, drawing on Somaya's public self-presentations from the time of its opening to the present, a shift from its original emphasis on the organisation's Muslim profile towards a gradual fading of any public references to Islam and Muslim identity among its activists is revealed in this chapter. This analytical focus on an ambivalent process of self-definition leads in turn to further reflections on the relationship between welfare, religious diversity and feminism.

I analyse the shift in relation to four strands that influenced the process. While briefly introducing them here, I elaborate further on the theoretical concepts involved as they appear in the analysis.

The first strand concerns Somaya's emic introduction of intersectionality[6] as a cross-boundary approach to its activists,[7] clients and partners. I look into the emic expressions of motivations behind this shift, but also analyse it in terms of a critical review of intersectionality as a 'consensus-creating signifier' that has enabled an 'all-inclusive feminism' that 'conceals fruitful and necessary conflicts within feminism' (Carbin and Edenheim, 2013, pp 233-4).

The second strand concerns growing anti-Muslim intolerance in Europe and the construction of Islam as a politicised and dangerous field (Hervik, 2011; Cancellieri and Longo, 2012; Berglund, 2013). In this context, religion and gender are intertwined so that 'equality agendas of feminisms are projected onto the Nordic nation states as if these are inherently gender-equal in their character' (Stoltz and Hvenegård-Lassen, 2013, p 245; see also Hübinette and Lundström, 2011). At the same time, Muslim women are represented as victims in need of help to become 'liberated' from their particular familial, cultural and religious attachments (Bracke and Fadil, 2012, p 54). This dichotomous construction between 'emancipated' western women and 'subordinated' Muslim women is also valid in other European national contexts, for example in Italy: 'Public debates and discussions on gender and religion often make reference to Islam. In general, the question is centred on whether or not Islam is compatible with women's rights' (Cancellieri and Longo, 2012, p 190; see also Salih, 2009).

To cast further light on this assimilationist imaginary of 'liberating Muslim women' from their religion, something that is confronting Somaya very acutely, the third strand concerns the development of 'normative secularism' (Braidotti, 2006, p 80) that is based on a 'sacred narrative of (European) secular progress' (Woodhead, 2009, p 12) and results in a polarised construction of 'good' (secular) and 'bad' (religious) Muslims (Maira, 2009). I take inspiration from the processual intersectional concepts of 'dissolution' and 'saturation', as developed by Staunæs (2003, p 103) and Zhao (2013, p 206), to argue that the category of religion has subsequently become dissolved from Somaya's agenda, and has instead become saturated by matters of secularity. Again, I look into emic expressions of this process in Somaya's self-presentations, and relate it to feminist interactions in the wider society, arguing that the secular needs to engage self-critically with the religious, and not only vice versa (Woodhead, 2009, p 18). This is particularly important, as the feminist philosopher Rosi Braidotti points out, since 'an automatic and unreflective brand of normative secularism runs the risk of becoming complicitous with xenophobia and racism' (Braidotti, 2006, p 80).

Finally, I emphasise the fact that by dissolving Somaya's Muslim profile, religion is being publicly dissociated and prevented from acting as a resource for the organisation and its activists, while continuously reinforcing it as an identity marker for the women seeking help. With the help of Miriam Cooke's concept of the 'Muslimwoman' (2008), I illustrate how this situation can be viewed in terms of the minoritisation and victimisation of Muslim women (Nyhagen Predelli and Halsaa, 2012), with consequences for their recognition as future initiative takers and leaders of women's shelters.

These four strands of research have a close bearing on mainstream western feminism, which is generally known as secular but is increasingly becoming involved in the rethinking of its standpoints on religion (Reilly, 2011; Midden, 2012). It is my wish that this investigation into the ambivalent transformation of Somaya's self-presentation will generate reflection, within Somaya and beyond, on what is at stake when both Islam as a religion and Muslim identity are dissolved and weakened from acting as potential resources in the feminist struggle.

The material used in this study is intended to outline the transformation process of the organisation's profile to prompt a rethinking of the relationship between welfare, religious diversity and feminism. My analysis is based on Somaya's self-presentations, which are examined as social practices that are informed by, and constitutive of, power relations. The organisation's self-presentations have been retrieved from its official website (Somaya.se) and Facebook page, as well as from the writings and presentations on television and radio by some of its activists, including both former and more recent managers. Furthermore, Somaya is presented through the reports of governmental and non-governmental organisations, press articles and undergraduate theses (there are as yet no high-level academic publications on the Sisters' Shelter Somaya).

My own background is in ethnology, particularly in research conducted among activists in Muslim youth organisations (Karlsson Minganti, 2011, 2014 [2007]). During my fieldwork, I came across information on Somaya and occasionally met with Somaya activists, although formal observations and interviews were beyond the scope of the projects I was involved in at the time. However, there are fieldwork notes dating back to the organisation's early years by the organisations' co-founders: Irina Widin, who presented the work of Somaya at the 18th conference of the Islamic Association in Sweden (Stockholm, 3 April, 1999), and Karima Lindberg, who gave a presentation during a weekend course for Muslim youth (Stockholm, 7–8 October, 2000). Additional material includes a telephone interview (4 April, 2013) that I conducted with Susanne Namaani, Somaya's manager from September 2007 to July 2013, and email correspondence with the organisation's manager from August 2013 to February 2016, Anna-Karin Rybeck (September 2013).

A Muslim profile combining Islamic and secular feminisms

The Sisters' Shelter Somaya was established in 1998 by a group of women in a suburb of Stockholm that had many inhabitants from Muslim and foreign backgrounds. The founders were themselves Muslims: some immigrants, some converts to Islam. Already involved in assisting female victims of domestic violence at a grassroots level, they saw a need to establish a formal organisation that acknowledged their experiences of linguistic and cultural misunderstandings, as well as discrimination at 'conventional' women's centres (both Christian and secular). Many resented being met with the presumption that they needed to leave their religion and assimilate into the non-Muslim majority population (Lindberg, 1999; Sonnius, 2002; Ücler, 2007; Somaya, 2016a).

When it was formed, Somaya was promoted as having the capacity to help its clients navigate the Swedish legal and welfare system, and to offer help with various languages. Moreover, members of the organisation affirmed that they provided shelter to women in a way that avoided the stigma of domestic violence as a particularly 'Muslim problem' rooted in Islam. For instance, co-founder Karima Lindberg presented the newly established Somaya in the then important Swedish Islamic periodical *Salaam* (Otterbeck, 2000) in the following way:

> Acts such as wife-beating, honour killing, genital mutilation etc. are *not* compatible with Islam. It is sad that knowledge about Islam is so scant, both among Muslims and non-Muslims, and that this fact needs to be pointed out at all. (Lindberg, 1999, p 6; emphasis in original)[8]

Somaya presented itself as an organisation that offered women the possibility of preserving their faith while challenging gender-based violence: 'A woman who comes to us does not want to get rid of God; she wants to get rid of her husband' (Namaani, cited in Alakangas, 2012). This quotation represents a clear challenge to the assimilationist discourse, widespread in Europe today, that Muslim women need help to free themselves from their particular cultural and religious attachments (Bracke and Fadil, 2012, p 54).

In challenging such assimilationist discourse, Somaya has engaged in both Islamic and secular forms of feminism. The term 'Islamic feminism' is highly contested (Bahi, 2011; Midden, 2012), but refers broadly to a discourse on women's rights that is constructed within an Islamic paradigm (Badran, 2002). Various contemporary Islamic revivalist movements present women with the opportunity to re-read Islamic texts and choose reflexively which interpretations to adhere to and disseminate to others (Bano and Kalmbach, 2011; Karlsson Minganti, 2011). Many women, including Somaya activists, are critical of some interpretations that result from androcentric (male-dominated) readings of Islamic texts. To counteract such bias, they circulate texts and narratives that reflect women's interests and evoke women as role models. In fact, the Sisters' Shelter Somaya is named after Somaya Bint Khayat, a woman who is considered to be one of the original followers of the prophet Muhammad, the seventh person to embrace Islam and its very first martyr.

Using *ijtihad* (independent analysis of religious sources) and *tafsir* (interpretation of the Qur'an), Muslim women (and men) challenge patriarchal cultural patterns as well as traditionalist interpretations that both produce and legitimise these patterns. The methodology is discernible, for instance, in Lindberg's early presentation of Somaya (mentioned earlier) for the predominantly Muslim readers of *Salaam*:

> Of all the excuses used by abusers in order to disclaim responsibility, probably the worst is using Islam to legitimise one's criminal behaviour. By focusing on rituals and disregarding the content and spirit of Islam, they even use Qur'anic verses to justify their sick need for control and power. If the wife has courage enough to oppose such un-Islamic living, the man often misinterprets another Qur'anic verse and uses it as an excuse to abuse her. Abusive men completely disregard Islam's teaching on goodness, love, mercy and respect for others. Also they do not care about the good example of the prophet Muhammad (peace be upon him), who never beat a woman and was extremely kind and goodhearted to his family. (Lindberg, 1999, p 6)

The following is another example of how an original co-founder of Somaya, Monjia Sonnius, confirms the re-reading of Islamic sources as a valid strategy against gender-based violence:

> A Muslim women's shelter is actually an absurdity since violence against women is forbidden in Islam. If someone uses the Qur'an as a means of oppression, the staff of Somaya can refute this behaviour by reading what is written in the Qur'an and how the prophet Muhammad explains the word of God. They can also clarify to the women their rights according to Islam. (Sonnius, 2002; see also Forum Syd et al, 2002, p 21)

In Somaya's early self-presentations from the end of the 1990s and beginning of the 2000s, I identify the ambition of its members for the organisation to be appreciated as a place where Islam stands as an ethos and frame of reference, where women do not have to worry about breaking with dietary habits or dress codes. The organisation presented itself as a shelter where pork was not served and wearing hijabs was the norm, and also where the Qur'an was confirmed to be compatible with feminism. According to the former manager, Susanne

Namaani, the organisation's Islamic profile was also prevalent during her tenure from September 2007 to July 2013.

'We listen to women, affirm that they have experienced violence, and confirm that it is not because of their religion. ... It is common knowledge that when people are in crisis, they need something to hold on to. For many of these women it is their faith, but it now only remains as a narrow thread. Somaya helps them to hold on to this narrow thread.' (Namaani, 4 April 2013)

Although openly problematising the perceived lack of cultural and religious sensitivity in 'conventional' shelters, Somaya teamed up with various Swedish governmental and non-governmental organisations. As early as 1999, Somaya became a member of the secular feminist Swedish Association of Women's Shelters and Young Women's Empowerment Centres (Sveriges Kvinnojourers Riksförbund, or SKR). SKR (now known as Unizon) is one of two major umbrella organisations in Sweden that offer protection and guidance to female victims of domestic violence and work for the prevention of violence against women.

Somaya and SKR worked together and this collaboration enabled Somaya activists to try out combinations of Islamic and secular feminist ideas. At first this was not at all self-evident, given the initial suspicion towards Somaya that was harboured by a variety of women's organisations in Sweden (Larsson, 2007; Ücler, 2007; Namaani, 4 April 2013). In their study of majority–minority relations in contemporary women's movements in Norway, Spain and the United Kingdom, Line Nyhagen Predelli and Beatrice Halsaa point out two typical representations of minoritised women by majoritised actors. The first is the perception that 'minoritised women's problems are mainly rooted in "culture", and minoritised women are regarded as being in need of help from majoritised women, rather than being seen as equal partners in women's movements' (Nyhagen Predelli and Halsaa, 2012, p 262). Such a representation does not leave much potential for strategic alliance or collaboration on an equal footing between the two groups.

The second type of perception presented by Nyhagen Predelli and Halsaa is that 'minoritised women's problems are rooted mostly in racist and discriminatory practices within majority (and minoritised) society, and also that minoritised *and* majoritised women's problems are caused by gender-based inequalities which cut across different cultures' (2012, p 262; emphasis in original). This approach contains a potential for cooperation and alliance, and was adopted early on by Somaya and SKR. In the next section, this cross-boundary approach is further explored as part of a gradual shift in Somaya's self-presentations from a women's shelter run by and for Muslim women to an emphasis on intersectionality.

Toning down the Muslim profile by emphasising intersectionality

Since its foundation, Somaya has defined itself as a religiously and politically independent organisation, open to women of all backgrounds and faiths. However, the debate over Somaya as a mainly 'Muslim women's shelter' is a common thread throughout the organisation's history. The organisation's original statute, dating from 1999, stated that activists 'should as far as possible be of different ethnic origins and thereby competent in several languages, and Muslims'. In 2007 this was changed to: 'preferably Muslims or sharing the values of the Sisters' Shelter Somaya' (Ücler, 2007, pp 35-6). This decision was taken after discussions about excluding women of other faiths from working as Somaya activists: could this be perceived as a deterrent and discriminatory, both for those seeking help and for those who aspire to work for the organisation as activists (Ücler, 2007, pp 35-6)? By acknowledging the diversity of both its clients and activists, Somaya's public self-presentations have become more articulate in the vocabulary of intersectionality, as, for instance, in the following two statements obtained from Somaya's website in 2012 that remain at the time of writing:

> Today the Sisters' Shelter Somaya is open to all women regardless of religion, ethnicity or background. We believe that we, by being a part of the sisterhood, can counteract men's violence against women and honour-related violence. (Somaya, 2016a)

> One must explain and understand honour-related oppression from an intersectional perspective; where gender, class, ethnicity and socio-economic conditions, among other things, are included. (Somaya, 2016b)

From this self-declared intersectional perspective, Somaya collaborates with both secular and religious actors. While some *imams* (Islamic leaders) offer practical initiatives to prevent violence against women, for instance, recognising women's divorces from abusive husbands and reporting abuse to the police, Somaya is overtly critical of the fact that some Muslim actors, including some *imams*, do not take such a stance (Karlsson Minganti, 2012, 2014 [2007], p 224). Even in its early stages, Somaya took a clear position that women and their children need to be taken out of violent situations, that is, out of their families and homes in cases where their lives or health are at stake:

> Sometimes it is enough for a frustrated man to talk with an *imam*. But if he systematically controls and abuses a woman, her situation is desperate and her children's too. Then they urgently need to get away from him. It could happen that they live together again one day, but this cannot be a prioritised issue for us at Somaya. (Field notes from co-founder Irina Widin's presentation of Somaya at the 18th conference of the Islamic Association in Sweden, Stockholm, 3 April 1999)

Declaring itself as a shelter for women who seek refuge from violent family members means challenging the conservative patriarchal position that prioritises the continuity of family ties at all costs. By threatening such patriarchal positions, Somaya has become a target of anti-feminist resistance from certain leaders and members of Muslim congregations and families: 'Just as as the Swedish women's shelters were initially met with distrust, the Sisters' Shelter Somaya has been accused of splitting up Muslim families and inciting divorce' (Sonnius, 2002).

However, yet another reason for Somaya to shift its self-presentation is that the development of an intersectional agenda, with its emphasis on *all* women's subjection under cross-boundary patriarchal oppressions, has simultaneously smoothed Somaya's interactions with Muslim communities. It dismantles the culturalised/racialised view of women's oppression as a particularly 'Muslim problem', and eases the fear among many Muslims that openly talking about violence within their communities might 'put wind in the sails of racists' (Lindberg, 1999, p 8). Such concern is not without foundation: the impact of the rhetoric on Muslim women's oppression as part of pro-assimilation or anti-Muslim/anti-immigration discourse is well documented in academic publications, both in Sweden and abroad (Salih, 2009; Cato and Otterbeck, 2011; Hervik, 2011; Hübinette and Lundström, 2011; Cancellieri and Longo, 2012; Chakraborti and Zempi, 2012; Keskinen, 2012).

In analysing Somaya's public self-presentations, I claim that the profile of a women's shelter with an intersectional agenda has been implicitly there from the start and has gradually developed into an explicit standpoint. This has happened both out of consideration for the diverse backgrounds of the organisation's clients and as a cross-boundary strategy to aid interaction with various Muslim and non-Muslim actors. However, since the growing emphasis of intersectionality has coincided with a de-emphasising of its initial Muslim profile, I now further examine the influence of religion, and particularly Islam, in Swedish society on Somaya's self-presentations.

A normative secularism by dissolving religion as a resource

De-emphasising Islamic references has become even more evident in Somaya's statutes since 2012, according to which it is apparently no longer necessary to be Muslim to become a staff member of the organisation (Somaya, 2016c). *In* August 2013, Somaya employed its first non-Muslim manager *and* the word 'Islam' is now decidedly absent from Somaya's official website. The organisation defines itself as 'the first women's shelter in the Nordic countries that has both a gender and ethnicity perspective' (Somaya, 2016a). There is no mention of the unique religious perspective that was there at the beginning. Taken together, these actions can be read as signs not only of de-emphasising, but also of *dissolving* (Zhao, 2013, p 206) references to Islam and 'Muslimness' – a process worth highlighting and reflecting on.

The Sisters' Shelter Somaya emerged during a time of broad social and political initiatives tackling gender-based violence in Sweden at the end of the 1990s. At that time, the then government had adopted a critical feminist perspective that defined men's violence against women as an expression of structural inequality between men and women; it had also acknowledged battered women as victims of crime. Various educational and public campaigns were launched and funding for national women's organisations was increased. Somaya was born out of, and incorporated into, this wave of social action and knowledge production, and became further strengthened by increasing drives against the so-called honour-related violence at the beginning of the 2000s (Government Offices of Sweden, 2007; Modée and Bohlin, 2009; Modée and Larsson-Thörnberg, 2009).

Over the years, Somaya has gone from being seen as an obscure Muslim/immigrant women's organisation to a widely celebrated contributor to Swedish society. This increased recognition is evident in several awards, such as the prestigious Anna Lindh Memorial Prize. In 2008, the state agency Myndigheten för ungdoms-och civilsamhällesfrågor (Swedish Agency for Youth and Civil Society), formerly known as Ungdomsstyrelsen (Swedish National Board for Youth Affairs), was commissioned by the government to survey the prevalence of arranged marriages against the will of one party. Somaya was invited to participate. In 2010, the government commissioned an official report on increased protection measures against forced marriages (SOU, 2012). Somaya was invited to comment on this report and subsequently recommended the criminalisation of forced marriages (Somaya, 2016d).

Sweden has a tradition of cooperation between women's organisations and the welfare state. The political scientist Helga Hernes has introduced the notion of 'feminism from below and above' (1987), 'denoting the political mobilisation of women and women's organisations on the one hand, and an active strategy by the state to invite women's organisations to take part in policy formation and implementation processes on the other' (Nyhagen Predelli and Halsaa, 2012, p 81). The Swedish state has supported Somaya's mobilisation from below as a valuable part of initiatives against gender-based violence. Moreover, as we have seen, the state has invited Somaya to comment on arranged marriages, that is, in the active implementation of policies from above. However, as stressed by Lina Nyhagen Predelli and Beatrice Halsaa, 'state or institutional feminism [is] an arena where "boundary-making processes" in recognition struggles take place' (2012, pp 84-5), and such struggles, they claim, have tended to result in the marginalisation of minoritised women. Thus, a crucial question is: under what conditions is Somaya considered to be an acceptable partner to work with in the area of preventing violence against women?

It is pertinent to question how the position of religion in Somaya's official agenda might be seen by potential partners and financial supporters. In 2006, the Stockholm County Administrative Board (Länsstyrelsen i Stockholms län) evaluated Somaya as an organisation and gave its assurance that its 'activities are not missionary, hence its particular expertise is suitable also for non-practising Muslims as well as women of other religious backgrounds' (Jemteborn and Pilar Reyes, 2006, p 110). The demand for a 'non-missionary' approach appears to be a sensible requirement, given the wide range of women looking for support from a women's shelter, but let us articulate this question further: how would Somaya be perceived if its approach were deemed to be 'missionary'? Or if it persistently defined its work (indeed itself) as carried out primarily by, and for, Muslim women?

Presenting oneself, or one's organisation, as religious is not a neutral act in contemporary Sweden. Public discourse very largely associates religion with values fundamentally opposed to modernity, equality, freedom and democracy (Lövheim and Axner, 2011). In particular, religion expressed in public is seen as a threat to modern society. As immigration has led to a growing visibility of religion, most notably Islam, Muslims have become stigmatised as the ultimate threat to 'secular Europe', including in countries less secularised than Sweden in terms of the importance of religion in the public sphere, such as Italy (Salih, 2009).

As part of the construction of Muslims as a threat to secular society, Islam is portrayed as an unchangeable monolith and the variety of practices within the religion is largely overlooked. Similarly, 'secularism remains an unmarked term – like "male" or "white" – the taken for granted, the unquestioned standpoint of truth' (Woodhead, 2009, pp 17-18). Linda Woodhead relates this common-sense position to an influential 'European narrative of secular progress' (Woodhead, 2009, pp 12-13; Reilly, 2011). According to this narrative, Europe has moved from a pre-modern state of oppression connected with religion to a more enlightened state of modernity characterised by freedom and other secular values. The feminist philosopher Rosi Braidotti warns that a failure to recognise the historical specificity of this narrative runs the risk of turning it into a form of 'normative secularism' that brings 'European feminism close to that "cultural racism" that Stuart Hall and black migrant women so eloquently denounce' (Braidotti, 2006, p 81).

In fact, the political situation, particularly after the terrorist acts of 11 September 2001, has triggered a wave of anti-Muslim intolerance across Europe and the world. In this context, constructions of religion have been intertwined with constructions of gender in the global discourse about 'the war on terror' and 'bringing "democracy" and "human rights", particularly "women's rights", to regions that presumably need to catch up with Western modernity' (Maira, 2009, p 631). This rhetoric produces two dichotomous modes of expressing cultural citizenship for Muslims in the West that anthropologist Sunaina Maira calls 'good' and 'bad' Muslim citizenship (Maira, 2009, p 632). While 'bad' Muslims are denoted as religious fanatics, 'good' Muslim citizens are distinguished as secular.

In this context, many Muslims feel it is hazardous to use Islamic terminology and symbols publicly, regardless of how their personal attitudes to Islam would be defined on a spectrum between the religious and the secular (Jonker and Amiraux, 2006, p 11; Aspling and Djärv, 2013, pp 55-9; Berglund, 2013). For instance, when asked to explain her faith in a journal interview, the former manager of Somaya, Susanne Namaani, chose to respond with the Islamic term 'jihad', but only after hesitation, making clear that her answer, which could easily be misunderstood, 'means "for the sake of God" and not "holy war". For me every day and every hour here at Somaya means *jihad*' (Namaani, cited in Alakangas, 2012; see also, Karlsson Minganti, 2011, p 381). Namaani's hesitation to use the term 'jihad' is shared by many, since individual explanations offered by Muslims are often drowned by the 'Islam-equals-violence' rhetoric.

The self-presentations of the members of the Sisters' Shelter Somaya have been altered so as to avoid, and perhaps ultimately 'dissolve', explicit references to Islam. As discussed earlier, this move can be understood as an act of inclusion and solidarity that opens up the organisation to women of all kinds of backgrounds – as clients, activists and partners. Yet it can also be read as a sign of anti-Muslim/Islam pressures and the 'saturation' (Staunæs, 2003, p 103) of Somaya's Muslim feminist position with regard to normative secularism.

In the following section I argue that this process involves both a simultaneous fading of religion as a resource in Somaya's public self-presentations, with particular regard to its activists, and a reinforcement of religion as an identity marker for the women who turn to Somaya for help. I also discuss how this development implies the risk of presenting Muslim women as victims and the failure to recognise the staff at Somaya as a unique example of Muslim women managers, namely people in positions of leadership and responsibility.

Reproducing representations of Muslim women as victims

Miriam Cooke, Professor of Asian and Middle Eastern Studies at Duke University in Durham, NC, has introduced the neologism 'Muslimwoman' to explain how Muslim women, particularly Islamic feminists, work to change conditions that justify the persistent image of Muslim women as passive victims (Cooke, 2008). In fusing the words 'Muslim' and 'woman', she draws attention to the contemporary practice of collapsing religion and gender into a singular identity: 'So extreme is the concern with Muslim women today that veiled, and even unveiled, women are no longer thought of as individuals: collectively they have become the Muslimwoman' (Cooke, 2008, p 91).

The identification of women as passive victims is tied to growing Islamophobia that triggers the construction of boundaries between 'us' and 'them', 'insider' and 'outsider'. The 'Muslimwoman' represents such a boundary between two main forces (presented as ideal types in a Weberian sense). On the one hand, gender-conservative political 'Islamists' deprive women of individuality and agency by naming them cultural custodians and standard bearers for the Muslim *ummah* (community, nation, worldwide society). On the other hand, 'neo-Orientalists' ascribe the term 'Muslimwoman' to Muslim women by erasing their diversity and taking them to represent 'Islamic oppression' and everything negative associated with the religion and its followers. These two dominant forces share the goal of controlling Muslim women: 'At the same time that Islamists vie for control of women's bodies, neo-Orientalists bleat their compassion for the "poor" Muslimwoman' (Cooke, 2008, p 93). Consequently, Muslim women are unlikely to be associated with agency, such as being managers of women's shelters.

Recent public representations of Somaya provide suitable examples of how unreflective normative secularism results in a 'neo-Oriental' reproduction of the image of Muslim women as passive victims. For instance, in a PowerPoint presentation, initially produced by Somaya for an interdisciplinary event on psychotrauma, now available online (Somaya, 2013), the concept of religion appears only once: in the expression 'religious views', under the headline 'vulnerability', and in connection with images of two dark-haired, dark-eyed women. One has her mouth covered by a plaster, the other woman's cheek is wet with tears. Matching a typical representation of the Oriental/ Muslimwoman victim (Abu-Lughod, 2013), the images are juxtaposed with a picture of young, smiling women and men[9] of different skin colour who are dressed in short-sleeved and sleeveless tops under the headline '11 persons work at Somaya'. Displayed like this, Somaya activists become associated with the emblematic dress code of free and happy secular individuals, and are distanced from the enveloping clothes of many Muslim women, who instead are linked to 'vulnerability' on account of their 'religious views'.

A further example of a recent public representation of Somaya reflecting the influence of normative secularism and the minoritisation of Muslim women within the organisation is taken from early 2014, when various actors, both inside and outside Somaya, expressed criticism of the organisation's choice to work with the well-known human rights activist Sara Mohammad. Mohammad is widely praised for her work directed against honour-related violence, but she is also criticised for equating this violence with Islam. During this crisis of confidence, the then president of the board of Somaya, Sara Saadouni, participated in a programme broadcast by the internet-based television channel Budskapet.tv (Budskapet.tv, 2014). She announced that she had been replaced after expressing concern about developments that might lead to Muslim women becoming a minority on both the board and in the organisation's personnel and target group. She also expressed worries that Somaya, known for its sensibility to religious women's needs, is changing into a space that allows the breaking of taboos, such as serving pork and coming into contact with dogs, out of consideration for other people involved with the organisation (Budskapet.tv, 2014).

Taken together, these representations of Somaya may be interpreted as a reinforcement of the minoritisation and victimisation of Muslim women, even from within the organisation. At the same time, these representations bring into public view the ongoing tensions within Somaya and show that the fading of Islam as an explicit resource for feminist work is proving to be a subject of criticism and disagreement.

Religion as a resource and as a source of exclusion: an issue at the intersection of women's rights and freedom of religion

This chapter draws attention to the increasingly important issue of the relationship between welfare, religion and feminism. Some feminists are progressively challenging both the 'religious' versus the 'secular' binary and the underlying assumptions of 'secular feminism'. Secularisation, as an inevitable and uniform process, is no longer tenable. As the WaVE project has highlighted, many women believe religion to be an important part of their lives (Bäckström, 2011, 2012a, 2012b), and, as I have shown in this chapter, an increasing number of women strive to combine their religious beliefs with feminist ideas.

The organisation Sisters' Shelter Somaya is a good example of a cross-boundary feminist approach. In fact, it offers a distinctive example in that it is presented as having been established both by and for Muslim women while being open to clients and staff members from various religious backgrounds. However, an analysis of Somaya's public self-presentations reveals a gradual dissolution of a specific Muslim profile in favour of a secular framework with an emphasis on intersectionality.

In examining the motivations behind this shift, I have found evidence of a perceived need to deal with the diversity of the people involved in Somaya (clients, activists and partners). In line with the findings of the WaVE project (Fokas, 2012; see also Chapters Nine and Eleven in this volume), the Somaya case study highlights women of diverse ethnic and religious backgrounds who work across 'conflicting' values to combat gendered violence and protect female victims from such violence. The Muslim women's shelter Somaya declared from the start its openness to clients, activists and partners with different attitudes towards religion, including its secular governmental and non-governmental partner organisations such as the SKR. The values of solidarity and sisterhood were asserted through the conceptual framework of intersectionality. Somaya demonstrated through concrete actions how religion can function as a resource for a women's shelter in ways that correspond with secular feminism.

A major contribution of the WaVE project lay in the fact that it highlighted factors that increase social cohesion (Fokas, 2012). Somaya is a clear example of how a minority social welfare network may play an important role in drawing attention to interests that are shared between minorities and majorities, and thus form a basis for asserting the values of inclusion and cooperation. At the same time, however, there was a perceived need to deal with the normative notions of a secular or Christian society as woman-friendly, positioned in contrast to Islam, which is seen as an inherently oppressive and violent religion. Such external labelling and stereotyping is an example of factors leading to tension and reducing religion to a source of conflict that the WaVE project highlighted (Fokas, 2012).

Given this ambiguity, intersectionality can be seen as a common language that promises to overcome division. Yet the aim to create consensus runs the risk of the majority dictating the agenda and divergent views being ignored. Hence, it is important to reflect critically on what values might be lost in the related process of dissolving Somaya's Muslim profile. The fading of religion as a resource and the minoritisation of observant Muslim women, even within the organisation, mean that women seeking help may lose the opportunity to find and trust an 'Islamic' environment. The norm of freedom from religion in common spaces (Pettersson and Edgardh, 2011, p 98), which is prevalent in contemporary Sweden, as well as the notion of secularity as a guarantee of neutrality, which is widespread not only among women's shelters in Sweden but also in a country such as Italy, needs to be further problematised. This becomes evident in the case of those women who are looking for a shelter that is free from features they view as *haram* (forbidden), such as serving pork and coming into contact with dogs, but also feel the need to normalise issues they consider *halal* (permissible), such as wearing a *hijab* and taking inspiration from the Qur'an.

A factor leading to the marginalisation of Islam and Muslim women in the case of Somaya is a tendency among its governmental and non-governmental partners to acknowledge religion as a potential resource for this specific shelter, but only on account of its expertise with regard to violence against immigrant/minority/Muslim women. 'Minoritised women's organisations are almost exclusively being consulted on "ethnic minority women's issues" related to gender violence (forced marriage, female genital mutilation and honour-based violence) and are rarely consulted on other issues' (Nyhagen Predelli and Halsaa, 2012, p 16). This finding is relevant to the wider European context that has also been highlighted in the WaVE project, in the sense that minority communities and networks very often tend to their own needs and create their own spaces for welfare activities (Fokas, 2012, pp 293-4). But, as shown in this study on Somaya, such efforts need not be limited to internal communities; they can be relevant and socially cohesive across religious and ethnic boundaries.

Dissolving Somaya's Muslim profile may undermine its position as a potential partner of Muslim communities and lead to breaking ties with Muslim organisations, including conservative male-dominated Muslim organisations. In their work against gender-related violence, Muslim organisations may lose a partner with an Islamic frame of reference that does not equate Islam with violence. Muslim organisations in Sweden are currently under pressure to present themselves according to very high and explicit standards vis-à-vis gender equality, but at the same time there is a lack of understanding of the complex conditions under which they operate. Muslim organisations and congregations comprise members from a broad range of different ethnic, social, economic and denominational backgrounds. For example, some are third-generation citizens; others came to Sweden just days ago. Serving such a diverse community is more than a matter of religious sermons; it involves voluntary social work (Borell and Gerdner, 2011), including in the area of gender violence. Somaya activists are involved in operationalising feminism and acting against violence in such a context.[10] Therefore, dissolving any links with mosques and other Muslim organisations, and neglecting these platforms in ongoing negotiations on Islamophobia, gender and violence, is a loss for these Muslim organisations, for Somaya itself, and for society at large.

I have demonstrated that de-emphasising, and even dissolving, Somaya's Muslim profile is taking place in tandem with maintaining its clients as specifically Muslim women. This move carries the risk of reproducing the image of Muslim women as passive victims, while obscuring Somaya as a unique example of Muslim women who act as managers in positions of leadership and responsibility. Failing to see Muslim women as capable activists implies the loss of alternative feminist voices. This is particularly troublesome for Muslim women, who need space to take control of the passive 'Muslimwoman' stereotype. The more Muslim women are able to represent themselves, the more control they will have over deconstructing and transforming this stereotype. Among these are feminist-oriented Muslim women who are extending the space for reinterpreting gender and religion across the alleged Islam–secular divide.

In their unique organisation and over a period of more than 15 years of (internal and external) struggles, activists in Somaya have gained cutting-edge expertise in two of the most complex human rights issues today: that of 'women's rights' and 'freedom of religion'. This in-depth study adds to the broader European dimensions of the WaVE findings that religion can act as both a productive resource and a source of exclusion. Added to this tension is the ambivalent relationship between religion and values that runs not only between but also within religious and secular views. Most importantly it should be recognised that, 'most majority–minority interaction in the domain of welfare lies somewhere between categories of "conflict" and "cohesion", in a large grey area which requires careful navigation' (Fokas, 2012, p 279). This is why the expertise of the Somaya activists and the shelter they offer should be recognised as a valuable and unique space that is both a specific and more broadly applicable social initiative.

Notes

[1]   This chapter has been made possible by support from the Swedish Research Council (grant numbers 2009-867; 2009-1345). Parts of the chapter have been previously published in *NORA – Nordic Journal of Feminist and Gender Research* (Karlsson Minganti, 2015).

[2]   The term 'women's shelter' refers to a place of temporary refuge and support for women escaping violent and abusive situations. The activities are usually divided into two parts: providing shelter to victims of abuse and providing state and non-state actors with information that helps to influence public opinion. Most shelters are run by politically and religiously independent non-profit associations.

[3]   As suggested by Brubaker (2012, p 2), 'the category "Muslim", is both a category of analysis and a category of social, political and religious practice'. Hence, it is an identity category under heavy scrutiny, not only by Muslims themselves, but also by researchers who are involved in the production of public representation and knowledge about Muslims. A critical and self-reflective approach to this analytic endeavour is essential.

[4]   The term 'minoritised' indicates the positioning of minority women as inferior and marginalised, both in relation to minority men and to majority women and men (Nyhagen Predelli and Halsaa, 2012, p 106).

[5]   In Swedish: *Systerjouren Somaya*. On 29 April 2012, the official name changed to *Somaya kvinno- och tjejjour* (Somaya – a women's and girls' shelter), but the previous label is still used in English presentations. Somaya currently presents itself as an organisation with 15 employees from different backgrounds (for example, social work, behavioural science and psychology). Together with a large number

of volunteers, the group represents many languages. Somaya provides telephone guidance and protected housing (for 72 women and children in 2014). Children are recognised as victims of crime and included in the programme with special attention to their needs. A section for young women covers issues that are relevant to their age, such as pressures around sexuality and marriage. In addition, guidance by Somaya activists is offered to relatives, colleagues and friends of battered women. Additionally, Somaya activists are frequently interviewed by the media and they offer lectures and courses to staff members of state institutions and non-governmental organisations to share their specific knowledge and experience (Somaya.se; Somaya, 2016e).

6   The concept of intersectionality, introduced by Kimberlé Crenshaw (1991), has developed into an analytical tool for the study of how different discriminating power orders, and culturally and socially constructed identity categories (such as gender, ethnicity, religion, age and class), interact and contribute to social inequalities. For a critical examination of the expansion of the scope of intersectionality, see Carbin and Edenheim (2013).

7   The term 'activist' is here intended to include both employees and volunteers.

8   All translations from Swedish into English in this chapter have been made by the author.

9   In 2009, the statutes of Somaya were revised so that men could become full members of the organisation and its board.

10 The crucial issue of lesbian, gay, bisexual, transgender and intersex (LGBTI) rights is continuously contested within Muslim organisations, including Somaya. As of today, Somaya's homepage includes the following statements: 'violence occurs in all forms of couple relations, regardless of the partners' sexuality and gender identity'; 'the norm of heterosexuality is central to the logic of honour, which means that LGBT persons run a greater risk of being subjected to threat and violence if they live their sexuality openly. Hence they are a particularly vulnerable group considering honour-related oppression and violence'; 'in 1944 homosexual relations were decriminalised [in Sweden]'; 'in 1979 the Swedish National Board of Health and Welfare abolished the notion of homosexuality as a malady' (www. somaya.se).

References

Abu-Lughod, L. (2013) *Do Muslim Women Need Saving?*, Cambridge, MA: Harvard University Press.

Alakangas, A.-M. (2012) 'De vill inte bli av med Gud utan sin man' ('They do not want to get rid of God but of their husband'), *Tro & Politik (Faith and Politics)*, 3 September.

Aspling, F. and Djärv, C. (2013) *Hatbrott 2012. Statistik över självrapporterad utsatthet för hatbrott och polisanmälningar med identifierade hatbrottsmotiv (Hate Crimes 2012. Statistics on Self-Reported Exposure to Hate Crimes and Police Reports with Identified Hate Crime Motives)*, Report No. 2013:16, Stockholm: Brottsförebyggande rådet.

Bäckström, A. (ed) (2011) *Welfare and Values in Europe: Transitions Related to Religion, Minorities and Gender. National Overviews and Case Study Report, Volume 1. Northern Europe: Sweden, Norway, Finland and England*, Studies in Religion and Society 4, Uppsala: Acta Universitatis Upsaliensis.

Bäckström, A. (ed) (2012a) *Welfare and Values in Europe: Transitions Related to Religion, Minorities and Gender, Volume 2. Continental Europe: Germany, France, Italy, Greece*, Uppsala: Acta Universitatis Upsaliensis.

Bäckström, A. (ed) (2012b) *Welfare and Values in Europe: Transitions Related to Religion, Minorities and Gender, Volume 3. Eastern Europe: Latvia, Poland, Croatia, Romania*, Uppsala: Acta Universitatis Upsaliensis.

Bäckström, A. (2014) 'Religion i de nordiska länderna. Mellan det privata och det offentliga' ('Religion in the Nordic countries: between private and public'), in P. Pettersson, Martha Axner, Annette Leis-Peters, Martha Middlemiss Lé Mon and Anders Sjöborg (eds) *Religiös och social förändring i det glokala samhället. Samtida religionssociologiska perspektiv (Religious and Social Change in the Glocal Community)*, Uppsala: Acta Universitatis Upsaliensis, pp 195-238.

Badran, M. (2002) 'Islamic feminism. What's in a name?', *Al-Ahram Weekly Online*, 569: 17-23.

Bahi, R. (2011) *Islamic and Secular Feminisms. Two Discourses Mobilized for Gender Justice*, EUI Working Papers RSCAS 2011/25, San Domenico di Fiesole: European University Institute. Available at: http://cadmus.eui.eu/bitstream/handle/1814/17294/RSCAS_2011_25_rev.pdf.

Bano, M. and Kalmbach, H. (eds) (2011) *Women, Leadership, and Mosques: Changes in Contemporary Islamic Authority*, Leiden: Brill.

Berglund, J. (2013) 'Islamic identity and its role in the lives of young Swedish Muslims', *Contemporary Islam*, 7(2): 207-27.

Borell, K. and Gerdner, A. (2011) 'Hidden voluntary social work: a nationally representative survey of Muslim congregations in Sweden', *British Journal of Social Work*, 41: 968-79.

Bracke, S. and Fadil, N. (2012) 'Is the headscarf oppressive or emancipatory? Field notes from the multicultural debate', *Religion and Gender*, 2(1): 35-56.

Braidotti, R. (2006) *Transpositions. On Nomadic Ethics*, Cambridge: Polity Press.

Brubaker, R. (2012) 'Categories of analysis and categories of practice: a note on the study of Muslims in European countries of immigration', *Ethnic and Racial Studies*, 13(1): 1-8.

Budskapet.tv (2014) 'Kvinnojouren Somaya och dess samarbete med Sara Mohammad' ('The Sisters' Shelter Somaya and its collaboration with Sara Mohammad'), Broadcast 12 February, available at www.youtube.com/watch?v=NAF6fBIGcYk.

Cancellieri, A. and Longo, V. (2012) 'Italy: overview of the national situation', in A. Bäckström (ed) *Welfare and Values in Europe: Transitions Related to Religion, Minorities and Gender, Volume 1. Northern Europe: Sweden, Norway, Finland, England*, Uppsala: Acta Universitatis Upsaliensis, pp 176-204.

Carbin, M. and Edenheim, S. (2013) 'The intersectional turn in feminist theory: a dream of a common language?', *Nordic Journal of Feminist and Gender Research (NORA)*, 20(3): 233-48.

Cato, J. and Otterbeck, J. (2011) 'Aktivt medborgarskap bland muslimer' ('Active citizenship among Muslims'), in P. Bevelander, C. Fernández and A. Hellström, (eds) *Vägar till medborgarskap (Paths to Citizenship)*, Lund: Arkiv.

Chakraborti, N. and Zempi, I. (2012) 'The veil under attack: gendered dimensions of Islamophobic victimization', *International Review of Victimology*, 18(3): 269-84.

Cooke, M. (2008) 'Deploying the Muslimwoman', *Journal of Feminist Studies in Religion*, 24(1): 91-9.

Crenshaw, K. (1991) 'Mapping the margins: intersectionality, identity politics, and violence against women of color', *Stanford Law Review*, 43(6): 1,241-99.

Fokas, E. (2012) 'Welfare and values in Europe: a comparative cross-country analysis', in A. Bäckström (ed) *Welfare and Values in Europe: Transitions related to Religion, Minorities and Gender, Volume 3. Eastern Europe: Latvia, Poland, Croatia, Romania*, Uppsala: Acta Universitatis Upsaliensis, pp 277-312.

Forum Syd (in cooperation with Föreningen för Utvecklingsfrågor (FUF), Kvinnoforum, Frivilligorganisationernas fond för mänskliga rättigheter, Svenska UMIFEM-kommittén, Riksförbundet för Sexuell Upplysning (RFSU) and Rädda Barnen (2002) *Våld i hederns namn. Rapport från en seminarieserie (Violence in the Name of Honour. Report from a Seminar Series)*, Stockholm.

Frisina, A. (2010) 'What church for what welfare? Conflicting points of view within the Italian case-study', in G. Davie (ed) *Welfare and Church in Europe*, Aldershot: Ashgate, pp 147-66.

Frisina, A. and Cancellieri, A. (2012) 'Padua case study report', in A. Bäckström (ed) *Welfare and Values in Europe: Transitions related to Religion, Minorities and Gender, Volume 1. Northern Europe: Sweden, Norway, Finland, England*, Uppsala: Acta Universitatis Upsaliensis, pp 205–36.

Government Offices of Sweden (2007) *Action Plan for Combating Men's Violence Against Women, Violence and Oppression in the Name of Honour and Violence in Same-Sex Relationships*, Stockholm: Riksdagen.

Hernes, H. (1987) *Welfare State and Woman Power: Essays in State Feminism*, Oslo: Norwegian University Press.

Hervik, P. (2011) *The Annoying Difference. The Emergence of Danish Neonationalism, Neoracism and Populism in the Post-1989 World*, Oxford: Berghahn Books.

Hübinette, T. and Lundström, C. (2011) 'Sweden after the recent election: the double-binding power of Swedish whiteness through the mourning of loss of "Old Sweden" and the passing of "Good Sweden"', *Nordic Journal of Feminist and Gender Research (NORA)*, 19(1): 42–52.

Jemteborn, A. and Pilar Reyes, M. (2006) *Insatser mot hedersrelaterat våld: En utvärdering av projekten 2005 (Actions Against Honour-Related Violence: A Project Evaluation 2005)*, Stockholm: Länsstyrelsen in Stockholms län.

Jonker, G. and Amiraux, V. (eds) (2006) *Politics of Visibility. Young Muslims in European Public Spaces*, Bielefeld: Transcript Verlag.

Karlsson Minganti, P. (2011) 'Challenging from within: youth associations and female leadership in Swedish mosques', in M. Bano, and H. Kalmbach (eds) *Women, Leadership and Mosques: Changes in Contemporary Islamic Authority*, Leiden: Brill.

Karlsson Minganti, P. (2012) 'Ibland ger moskén skydd till slagna kvinnor när samhället svikit' ('Sometimes, when society fails, the mosque offers protection'), *SVT Debatt*, 16 May.

Karlsson Minganti, P. (2014 [2007]) *Muslima: Islamisk väckelse och unga kvinnors förhandlingar om genus i det samtida Sverige (Islamic Revival and Young Women's Negotiations on Gender in Contemporary Sweden)* (2nd edn), Stockholm: Carlsson.

Karlsson Minganti, P. (2015) 'Muslim women managing women's shelters: Somaya, the Muslimwoman and religion as a resource', *Nordic Journal of Feminist and Gender Research (NORA)*, 23(2): 93–108.

Keskinen, S. (2012) 'Limits to speech? The racialised politics of gendered violence in Denmark and Finland', *Journal of Intercultural Studies*, 33(3): 261–73.

Larsson, G. (2007) *Muslims in the EU: City Report. Sweden – Preliminary Research Report and Literature Survey*, New York, NY: Open Society Institute.

Lindberg, K. (1999) 'Kvinnomisshandel och Systerjouren Somaya – en muslimsk kvinnojour' ('Gender violence and the Sister's Shelter Somaya – A Muslim women's shelter'), *Salaam*, 5: 5-8.

Lövheim, M. and Axner, M. (2011) 'Halal-TV: negotiating the place of religion in Swedish public discourse', *Nordic Journal of Religion and Society*, 24(1): 57-74.

Maira, S. (2009) '"Good" and "bad" Muslim citizens: feminists, terrorists, and U.S. orientalisms', *Feminist Studies*, 35(3): 631-56.

Midden, E. (2012) 'Feminism and cultural and religious diversity in *Opzij*. An analysis of the discourse of a Dutch feminist magazine', *European Journal of Women's Studies*, 19(2): 219-35.

Modée, L. and Bohlin, I. (2009) *Gift mot sin vilja (Married Against Her Will)*, Stockholm: Ungdomsstyrelsen.

Modée, L. and Larsson-Thörnberg, J. (2009) *Tjejjourerna – en växande kraft: Insatser mot hedersrelaterat våld och förtryck (Girls' Shelters – A Growing Force: Actions against Honour-Related Violence and Oppression)*, Stockholm: Ungdomsstyrelsen.

Nyhagen Predelli, L. and Halsaa, B. (2012) *Majority–Minority Relations in Contemporary Women's Movements: Strategic Sisterhood*, Basingstoke: Palgrave Macmillan.

Okin, S. M. (1997) *Is Multiculturalism Bad for Women?*, Princeton, NJ: Princeton University Press.

Otterbeck, J. (2000) *Islam på svenska. Tidskriften* Salaam *och islams globalisering Islam (Islam in Swedish. The* Salaam *Periodical and the Globalisation of Islam)*, Lund: Lund University.

Patel, P. (1999) 'Difficult alliances: treading the minefield of identity and solidarity politics', *Soundings*, 12: 115-26.

Patel, P. (2013) 'Multi-faithism and the gender question: implications of government policy on the struggle for equality and rights for minority women in the UK', in Y. Rehman, L. Kelly and H. Siddiqui (eds) *Moving in the Shadows: Violence and the Lives of Minority Women and Children*, Farnham: Ashgate.

Pepicelli, R. (2012) 'Donne migrant e revival religioso in una periferia romana. Islam e cristianesimo a Centocelle' ('Migrant women and religious revival in a Roman neighbourhood. Islam and Christianity in Centocelle'), *La critica sociologica*, XLVI, 182: 45-58.

Pettersson, P. and Edgardh, N. (2011) 'Gävle case study report', in A. Bäckström (ed) *Welfare and Values in Europe: Transitions related to Religion, Minorities and Gender, Volume 1. Northern Europe: Sweden, Norway, Finland, England,* Studies in Religion and Society 4, Uppsala: Acta Universitatis Upsaliensis, pp 72-100.

Pojmann, W. (2010) 'Muslim women's organizing in France and Italy: political culture, activism, and performance in the public sphere', *Feminist Formations,* 22(3): 229-51.

Reilly, N. (2011) 'Rethinking the interplay of feminism and secularism in a neo-secular age', *Feminist Review,* 97: 5-31.

Salih, R. (2009) 'Muslim women, fragmented secularism and the construction of interconnected "publics" in Italy', *Social Anthropology,* 17(4): 409-23.

Schmidt, G. (2011) 'Understanding and approaching Muslim visibilities: lessons learned from a fieldwork-based study of Muslims in Copenhagen', *Ethnic and Racial Studies,* 34(7): 216-29.

Somaya (2013) 'Våra värderingar – påverkar de vårt möte?' ('Our values – Do they influence our encounters?'), PowerPoint presentation, Traumadagen, Stockholm, 5 September, available at http://slidegur.com/doc/4917407/v%C3%A5ra-v%C3%A4rderingar--%E2%80%90-p%C3%A5verkar-de-v%C3%A5rt-m%C3%B6te%3F-traumadagen-2013.

Somaya (2016a) 'Somayas historia' ('The history of Somaya'), available at www.somaya.se/om-oss/somayas-historia-5936115.

Somaya (2016b) 'Tjejjour' ('Girls' shelter'), available at www.somaya.se/start/kvinno-tjejjour/tjejjour-5816997.

Somaya (2016c) 'Somaya stadgar' ('Somaya statutes'), available at www.somaya.se/om-oss/om-f%C3%B6reningen-5936119.

Somaya (2016d) 'Kriminalisera barn- och tvångsäktenskap' ('Criminalise child marriage and forced marriage'), available at www.somaya.se/start/om-v%C3%A5ld/hedersrelaterat-v%C3%A5ld-14002923.

Somaya (2016e) 'Verksamhetsberättelse 2014' ('Annual Report 2014'), available at www.somaya.se/om-oss/om-f%C3%B6reningen-5936119.

Sonnius, M.M. (2002) 'Andakt' ('Worship'), 21 January, available at http://hem.passagen.se/mson/Islam/texter/Andakter.htm.

SOU (Statens offentliga utredningar) (2012) *Stärkt skydd mot tvångsäktenskap och barnäktenskap (Enhanced Protection against Forced Marriage and Child Marriage),* SOU 2012:35, Stockholm: Fritzes.

Staunæs, D. (2003) 'Where have all the subjects gone? Bringing together the concepts of intersectionality and subjectification', *Nordic Journal of Feminist and Gender Research (NORA),* 11(2): 101-10.

Stoltz, P. and Hvenegård-Lassen, K. (2013) 'NORA 20th anniversary (1993-2013). Special issue on "feminist resistance – resistance to feminism"', *Nordic Journal of Feminist and Gender Research (NORA)*, 21(4): 245-48.

Trama di Terre (2016) 'Chi siamo' ('Who we are'), available at www.tramaditerre.org/tdt/indices/index_39.html.

Ücler, H.E. (2007) *Du skall väl vara hemma och föda barn? En fallstudie av systerjouren Somaya, en kvinno- och tjejjoursverksamhet som drivs av största delen muslimska kvinnor* (*Shouldn't You be at Home Giving Birth to Children? A Case Study of the Sisters' Shelter Somaya, a Women and Girls' Shelter run by Muslim Women*), Gothenburg: Gothenburg University, Department of Social Work.

Woodhead, L. (2009) 'The Muslim veil controversy and European values', *Swedish Missiological Themes*, 97(1): 89-105, available at www.eprints.lancs.ac.uk/39909/1/Veil_and_Values_-SMT.doc.

Zhao, Y. (2013) 'Intersectionality, the production of difference and Norwegian transnational adoptees' identity work', *Nordic Journal of Feminist and Gender Research (NORA)*, 21(3): 201-17.

ELEVEN

The moral and gendered crisis of the Italian welfare system seen through the prism of migrant women's reproductive health

Annalisa Frisina

The first part of this chapter[1] reflects on the Padua case study of the Welfare and Values in Europe: Transition Related to Religion, Minorities and Gender (WaVE) project, which focused on reproductive health and on access to local welfare for migrant women (Frisina and Cancellieri, 2012). Using participant observation and in-depth interviews, we compared the discourses and practices of migrants and welfare workers, and identified three sets of values: universalism versus differentialism/particularism; gender equality versus traditional gender roles; and secularism versus religious values in the field of reproductive health. The research reveals the failures of universalism, the conservative nature of the Italian welfare system in practice, and the difficulties of secularism in the field of reproductive health.

The second part of the chapter revisits the video that was produced in order to communicate the WaVE research results to a wider audience. We worked together with intercultural mediators and welfare workers to organise focus group discussions with migrant women from Nigeria and Romania. As the title of the video suggests (As Human Beings and Citizens), it is a 'double' invitation from migrant women, who are asking welfare workers to treat them fairly ('as human beings'), but who are also calling on other women in similar social conditions to act as people with rights ('as citizens'). They refuse to be viewed (by the dominant and disempowering charity framework) as above all needy and destitute people.

The third part of the chapter focuses on how the worsening welfare crisis in Italy has had negative effects on the social rights of women, above all migrants. I argue that this crisis is not simply due to the 2008 global financial crisis and ensuing recession, but to a moral crisis of the European social model that reinforces the traditional conservatism of the Italian welfare system. The moral crisis of the Italian welfare system is a gendered crisis, because growing health inequalities concern primarily migrant women. In response, the new public activism of the Catholic Church contributes to tensions relating to the values of the Italian welfare system and society. In this context, forging connections between migrant and Italian women seems even more difficult because of the rise of racism and Islamophobia. Nevertheless, a recent example of young Muslim activism against gender-based violence has opened the way for exploring new alliances.

Reproductive health and access to local welfare services among migrant women

This chapter starts with the case study of Padua (Frisina and Cancellieri, 2012) in the WaVE research. Padua is one of the major cities of the Veneto region (about 210,000 inhabitants in 2015).[2] It is located in the north-eastern part of Italy, a wealthy area of the country known for its growth in small businesses and low rates of unemployment.[3] The largest migrant groups living in the city are Romanians (8,655), followed by Moldavians (4,865) and Nigerians (2,658).[4]

Padua is characterised by a Christian Democratic political orientation and conservative sub-culture, underlining the existence of family-based and individualistic interests, and a resulting mistrust of state institutions and political parties. Over the past few years, the town administration has seen the centre-left and centre-right coalitions taking turns in power. The city has a mixed welfare system (a particular blend of state, market and third sector) and a massive presence of non-profit organisations (NPOs) rooted in Catholicism[5] as well as a highly developed culture of volunteering.

Using participant observation and in-depth interviews, the Italian WaVE research team investigated the accessibility and availability of local welfare services to immigrants, with particular focus on reproductive health,[6] which is the main motivation for migrants in Italy to use the welfare services. This explains why immigrant women use healthcare services more than men (Tognetti Bordogna, 2004; Lombardi, 2005). The scope of the research also included social practices related to the voluntary interruption of pregnancy (abortions),[7] which revealed the 'moral crisis' experienced by many Italian welfare providers. With Law 194/1978 (on the safeguarding of maternity and regulation of abortion), Italian legislators aimed to eliminate clandestine abortions by increasing public awareness about responsible procreation to prevent the use of abortion as a birth control system. According to the data from the Ministry of Health (Ministero della Salute, 2015), in areas better equipped with family advice bureaux, abortion rates between 1982 and 2013 fell by 54.9%. This law, however, has been constantly criticised by conservative Catholics and doctors, who use their right to conscientious objection in order not to perform abortions (80.5% of doctors in Veneto and 95% in Padua refuse to perform abortions).[8] Moreover, many welfare providers are reluctant to work with migrant women (especially young women, among whom the number of abortions is highest); their discourses sometimes 'naturalise' and essentialise cultural and religious differences, thus reproducing a social process of racialisation.[9] Our fieldwork helped us to identify three sets of values that are critical in welfare practices: universalism versus differentialism/particularism; gender equality versus traditional gender roles; and secularism versus religious values in the field of reproductive health. Some definitions and explanations of these concepts are in order.

- **Universalism:** social rights must be granted to everyone, without distinction.
- **Particularism:** social rights must primarily be granted to certain groups.
- **Differentialism:** social rights must be granted variously to different social groups.
- **Gender equality:** men and women have equal opportunities, that is, they enjoy equal rights and share equal responsibilities.
- **Traditional gender roles:** men and women have different opportunities, rights and responsibilities, depending on their roles.

This framework of values can be broken down further in other ways.

- **Caregiving work is everybody's responsibility:** taking care of non-self-sufficient individuals (first and foremost children and the elderly) is a duty of society as a whole, men included.
- **Caregiving work is a women's responsibility:** taking care of non-self-sufficient individuals (first and foremost children and the elderly) is a woman's task and duty.
- **Secular values in the field of reproductive health:** scientifically based secularised morals of international organisations, such as the World Health Organization (WHO),[10] should guide choices in matters of reproductive health (sex education, birth control, pregnancy and childbirth).
- **Religious values in the field of reproductive health:** religious morals, based on the prescriptions of the Church (for the Catholic

standpoint, see, for example, www.academiavita.org) and of religious leaders and movements, should guide choices in matters of reproductive health (sex education, birth control, pregnancy and childbirth).

The results of the Padua case study revealed the failures of universalism, the conservative nature of the Italian welfare in practice, and the challenges of secularism in the field of reproductive health.

The failures of universalism

The extension of the right of healthcare to 'irregular' (Mezzandra, 2010) immigrants exists at a theoretical level only, given the extreme ambiguity with regard to the rights of immigrants, which prevents them from having concrete access to welfare services. According to one welfare worker from a service dedicated to irregular migrants, the main problem is that immigrants lack a basic knowledge of laws, regulations and their rights. This means that irregular immigrants must first overcome fear, second obtain information on the required bureaucratic procedures, and finally have the ability and patience to follow these through. For this reason, a number of immigrants choose not to use welfare services that are slow and inefficient (characterised, for example, by long waiting lists and the requirement to book an appointment far in advance), which they view as incompatible with their needs. This is particularly clear among immigrants who work in the elderly care sector; these women (so-called *badanti*)[11] are often undocumented migrants who face particularly hard and precarious working conditions.[12]

Providing health services that are specifically targeted towards irregular migrants[13] is a challenge, particularly because they are usually portrayed in the mass media as 'undesirables' that should be expelled (Maneri, 2009). Compared with other family advice bureaux observed during the research,[14] where the staff includes a doctor, a nurse, an obstetrician, a social worker and a psychologist, the health centre for irregular immigrants has only one nurse and two doctors. This service takes on characteristics similar to those of third sector organisations working with irregular migrants, which do not offer a service to people with 'rights', but rather operate on the basis of 'doing a favour' to destitute people. In practice, there is a clear demarcation between irregular immigrants who have difficulties accessing a reduced level of service (that is, with limited opening hours), and legal immigrants and autochthonous citizens who can access family advice bureaux, which offer services with higher standards despite the area's economic hardships.

The conservatism of Italian welfare in practice[15]

Our research revealed a certain degree of frustration among many immigrant women, who feel trapped in traditional caregiving roles while also facing, on a daily basis, a lack of public support, specifically a lack of access to childcare services.[16] This is confirmed by our interviews with welfare operators, in particular those working in information bureaux for immigrant women. Both immigrant and Italian working mothers without family networks face similar problems regarding childcare. According to a European study, Italian fathers are among the least involved in caregiving activities, on account of the low levels of female participation in the labour market, and cultural and ideological reasons (Di Giulio and Carrozza, 2003). Nevertheless, recent studies show that the amount of time spent by fathers with their children is increasing, thus reducing the asymmetry within the couple (Zajczyk, et al., 2007; Magaraggia, 2013). Family advice bureaux play a key role during this socio-cultural transition by promoting 'active paternity' and greater equality within the couple. Our fieldwork revealed a commitment to promoting the value of gender equality, especially in the work of one of the advice bureaux. It is true that women often arrived at the centre on their own, but when their partners were present, the doctors and nurses made a visible effort to make the fathers feel responsible, in an effort to promote gender equality. The men's reactions ranged from amazement to annoyance.

On the flip side, when interviewing a doctor in another family advice bureau, it emerged that some doctors believe that encouraging family responsibilities among fathers should be limited to prevent a 'total redefinition of fatherly and motherly roles' and 'sexual identity problems in children'.[17] Based on her experience at a family advice bureau, a welfare worker expressed her views on the cultural differences in both gender roles and child rearing between different groups of immigrants in Italy.

> 'Immigrant families are a completely different story. Immigrant women often go through pregnancy alone.... Some husbands come here and show interest in the pregnancy, but some, like the ones from Bangladesh, for example, do it only to check how things are going and what their wives are doing.... Moroccan fathers, however,

are very committed and this has to do with their culture....
In Morocco maternity only concerns women, but not in
Italy: in Morocco there are extended families and female
networks of women helping women; here in Italy they have
a nuclear family, thus husbands participate a lot.' (Italian
female doctor, 45 years old)

This doctor said that dealing with 'gender issues' with migrants was
a 'completely different story'. She made generalisations based on the
'ethnic'[18] origin of migrants, setting symbolic and cultural borders and
rendering some groups as inferior, based on the view that people from
certain cultures are prisoners of patriarchal cultures. At the same time,
her discourse allows us to deconstruct the elements of the common
stereotypical image of Muslims as victims of tradition and incompatible
with modern and western values (see also Chapter Ten). The local
welfare providers in Padua therefore have different views, not only
with regard to gender roles among different groups of immigrants,
but also with regard to the promotion of gender equality and health.

The challenges of secularism in the field of reproductive health

Family planning, that is, pregnancy prevention and contraception in
the field of reproductive health in Italy, is a particularly sensitive area:
conflicts are based on the intersection of financial interests with values
(conservative religious versus secular values). This is evident in the case
of sex education. Since there is no national law on sex education, not
every family advisory centre can teach contraception and the prevention
of sexually transmitted diseases (STDs) among young people. During
our observation of a sex education course (organised by a family advice
bureau), it became evident that the workshop leaders were relying
on secular values in the field of reproductive health, but this was in
conflict (often implicitly) with traditional Catholic doctrine. During
a sex education course at a technology and business secondary school,
the gynaecologist decided to make a clear distinction between effective
contraceptive methods and 'pseudo-methods', including 'natural
methods' prescribed by the Catholic Church. The clash of secular
and religious values became even more explicit during a discussion
on the 'morning-after pill'. According to the gynaecologist, quoting
the World Health Organization, this is an emergency contraceptive
method. However, other doctors, guided by the prescriptions of the
Catholic Church, consider this method to be an abortive drug.

The promotion of contraceptives among immigrants, which is very important in preventing abortions and reducing STDs prevalent among immigrants in Italy today, also raises difficult challenges. The problem arises not only from a shortage of resources, but also from conflicts of values, which cut across both native Italians and immigrants, and cannot be reduced to the binary of secular versus religious actors. For instance, the presence in the Italian welfare system of progressive Catholics (Frisina, 2010) must be seen against the role of institutional Catholicism, specifically a number of conservative organisations (for example, advocates of the pro-life movement) that continue to create tensions in the field of reproductive health.

Indeed by the end of our research, we had become so aware of the extent of the challenge that we tried to develop a tool to foster a public conversation: first on how to achieve greater solidarity in the relationship between Italian social workers and migrant women, but more particularly on how to recognise the migrant newcomer as 'a human being and a citizen'.

'As human beings and citizens': discussing the WaVE research findings through a video

We presented the results of our case study to a number of workshops and in a public conference at the University of Padua.[19] But we were also interested in reaching a wider audience (Burawoy, 2005). With this in mind, we decided to work together with intercultural mediators (from Nigeria and Romania) and welfare workers (a gynaecologist and a psychologist from a family advisory centre) to produce a video featuring two groups of migrant women. We saw this as a creative communication tool for the WaVE research findings.

We organised four focus group sessions. In the first, we discussed what to do with the camera, that is, to avoid using the video either in a didactic way (that is, as a sociological film with instructive or prescriptive purpose) or as a form of 'fiction with pragmatic aims' (people acting and following a script with an explicit goal) as we had done when we presented the material at the university. In the focus groups, we opted for a participatory video (Milne et al, 2012) so that we could learn something new.[20] The video did not follow a script or set in advance any specific or pre-determined topics of discussion. Rather the goal was to listen to women talking about their everyday experiences, thus generating reflexive knowledge during the process of communication. This was more important than the final product (the video). We visited a Romanian association and a Nigerian beauty shop in order to recruit people to take part in the focus groups, who were Romanian and Nigerian women, both regular and irregular migrants.[21] The three sessions, all of which were filmed, consisted of a discussion of the findings from the Padua case study that the participants considered most relevant to themselves and their experiences.[22]

The inspiration for the title of the video (As Human Beings and Citizens) came from the words of Endurance and Ureoma, two young Nigerian women whom we talked to during the focus group discussions. Speaking about her difficult experiences with welfare in Italy, Endurance said: "They [welfare workers] have to treat us as human beings. Whites and blacks are the same", while Ureoma reacted to a black social worker asking her to 'participate, come out, speak out', by saying, "We have to feel as citizens, because we don't feel like that."

The video includes a number of discussions on the limits of universalism and the gender conservatism of the local welfare system in Padua, as illustrated in everyday life and personal stories about reproductive health. It starts with the participants sharing their feelings about discrimination, commonly experienced by migrants in Italy. They speak about the lack of recognition of the education they received in their countries of origin, and the unskilled and ethnically segregated jobs that they are able to get. The Nigerian women experience greater racism since they are identified as black. This is hardly surprising if we consider Italy's colonial history and its legacy in contemporary Italy (Siebert, 2014; Giuliani, 2015). Such racist discrimination may lead to demonising 'the white man's welfare system' and may generate tensions between migrants.

> 'White migrants are always preferred ... people look at the colour of your skin.... And then prostitutes get everything, they are given houses and job opportunities.... What is this all about? They seem to support prostitution rather than families with children.' (Nigerian woman, 30 years old)

The video also tells stories of multiple discrimination, as in the case of Romanian women who had 'bad welfare experiences' and felt stigmatised on several levels: as women, migrants and caregivers. At the same time, it gives a voice to welfare workers who feel 'overwhelmed by having to work on too many different things at once', proving that the 'welfare is in crisis for Italians too' because of the lack of material and human resources.

The video underlines that health is not the primary problem faced by many migrants since the issues are not only physical and/or psychological. As Lombardi (2016b) clearly shows, health is closely linked to social conditions. For instance, concerning the higher abortion rate among migrant women, Lombardi (2016a, p 9) states that we can understand these phenomena only if we consider:

> ... migration factors (economic and social hardship, communication difficulties, irregularity, etc.); communication problems with health care providers; and the type of migratory project.... They are women with single, relatively recent and still unstable migratory projects, with no family in the country of arrival, who are employed in the domestic and the care sector and often with an irregular status.

The migrant women in the video endorse these connections very clearly, specifically:

- the fear of having the status of irregular immigrant, a condition that is difficult to overcome and easy to fall back into (for example, becoming irregular again, following the application of the Bossi–Fini law,[23] or because of the inefficiencies of the bureaucratic system in the renewal of residence permits);
- the extreme difficulty in finding decent housing (absence of social housing, significant housing price increases in recent decades, and severe discrimination faced by immigrants looking for accommodation);
- last, but not least, the difficulty in finding a regular job that can adequately cover housing and food expenses.

Reflecting on our experience, we see the research video as a first step in the direction of Janet Fink and Helen Lomax (2012). Drawing on a growing interest in the use of visual methods in the health and social sciences, these authors introduce a number of approaches, arguing that visuals contribute to, and extend our understanding of, social inequalities.[24] Among different visual methods, I will stress in particular the importance of 'photo-elicitation interviews' and focus groups, 'photovoice' and 'participatory videos' (Mitchell, 2011; Frisina, 2013) to unpack what health and wellbeing mean for migrants and to challenge 'othering' processes in welfare discourse and practice (Ortega–Alcazar and Dyck, 2012, pp 106, 120).

Speaking more generally, in what ways can we use our research video to stimulate wider public conversations? Following the suggestions of the migrant women and welfare workers who participated in the video and in the dissemination of our research, the video can be used both as a policy and as an advocacy tool. First, it can be shown to policymakers and welfare workers to stimulate discussion on how to incorporate the views and needs of marginalised groups (that is, irregular migrant women) in the formulation and implementation of health and social policies.[25] With regard to welfare workers in particular, I used our video during several training courses with intercultural mediators to generate insights on inefficient communication and misunderstandings, with the overall aim of improving welfare services. The video is a helpful tool in recognising both the importance and the necessity of dealing with the (sometimes latent) conflictual dimensions of intercultural mediation, as part of an anti-racist framework that aims to 'de-naturalise' or 'de-essentialise' differences and to fight structural inequalities.

Second, the video can be shown to migrants and native citizens as an advocacy tool for promoting civic participation. Limited access to welfare services is partly due to a lack of information, but also to the mistrust and fear experienced by many migrants, who feel excluded and disenfranchised as citizens. As suggested by the last part of the video (entitled Empowerment), it is important to adopt an active perspective with regard to citizenship: that is, to feel a citizen, to act as one, and to be recognised as such. Reaffirming a citizenship-based framework is ever more important in order to resist the disempowering and victimising features of a charity framework, which, in times of crisis, can contribute to reproducing representations of migrant women as victims of their race (as blacks), their religion (Muslim, for example) or ethnic background (eastern European) (Frisina, 2010; see also Chapter Ten of this volume).

An example of this approach is the video Prevenzione Amica Delle donne Migranti a Milano (Prevention, A Friend for Immigrant Women in Milan) (2015),[26] produced by the Municipality of Milan, Bracco Foundation and Opera San Francesco per i Poveri, a Catholic non-profit organisation. In this video about the issue of reproductive health, we hear the testimony of migrant women, but only through the voice of an Italian woman. The video shows photos of the faces and pregnant bodies of different migrant women, and the voice-over says that they are from eastern Europe and from South America. The women themselves cannot be seen or heard speaking. Through a series of photos, the video shows these women as victims and the recipients of the charitable assistance offered by the staff of the charitable Catholic organisation Opera San Francesco. In the video, we see a smiling monk with a voice-over saying 'Thanks to God, Opera San Francesco exists.... Here you can feel the presence of God.... Here there are good people who help poor people', thus possibly perpetuating the disempowering features of a charitable approach used when offering faith-inspired welfare services to migrant women. The video title (Prevention) refers to abortion, but it is never made explicit, particularly since it promotes the health centre of a Catholic organisation.

The gendered and moral crisis of the Italian welfare system

> Nobody can do an ultrasound scan [for free], not even Jesus! Nobody, not even Italians! You can have it only if you pay for it.... Nowadays ultrasound scans are a big problem for everybody. There are not enough doctors who can perform this examination in public hospitals.... It does not matter if you are white, black or green.... The real discrimination is based on money. (A gynaecologist in discussion with migrant women, WaVE research video)

According to Laura Pennacchi (2008), welfare systems have historically embodied an 'alternative morality' to the logic of market exploitation, but capitalist neoliberalism (Harvey, 2007) has recommodified many spaces of social life and has laid siege to the 'European social model'.[27] In his latest report on Italian welfare, Felice Roberto Pizzuti (2015) states that the structural roots of the 'great recession' (2008) resulted in growing inequalities (first of all by widening the gap between North and South). Neoliberal 'austerity politics' (so-called *politiche di consolidamento dei bilanci pubblici* [the consolidation policies of public budgets]) weakened the welfare system when it was most needed. Focusing on substantive, rather than formal, equality, we may argue that the current exclusion of many immigrants from the Italian welfare system continues to take place, despite their theoretical entitlement to the social services that are on offer.[28] Health inequalities concern all women who are irregular immigrants (Sardadvar, 2015), and the field of reproductive health is very revealing of this situation, not to mention the gendered and moral crisis of the Italian welfare system as a whole.

An article by Alessandra Sciurba on the issue of migrant women and abortion (2014) is a useful contribution in helping to recognise the structural inequalities that migrant women have to face. In the Italian case, the link between the feminisation of migration and the feminisation of the labour market was clearly revealed after the arrival of specific categories of migrant women – especially women from eastern

Europe, above all Romanian – who have found jobs as caregivers. It is no coincidence that abortions among these groups of women, who have no access to family planning or contraception, are among the highest according to statistics. Sciurba underlines how these women are subject to multiple discriminations related to gender, migrant status and type of employment.

According to Lia Lombardi (2016a, pp 9-10) and to a Ministry of Health report (Ministero della Salute, 2015), the current areas of concern relating to abortions among migrant women include:

- repeat abortions (very common among Romanian women);
- illegal abortions (estimated between 3,000 and 5,000 every year in Italy, and often unsafe because of the misuse of a drug for the treatment of ulcers);
- a steady increase in the exercise of conscientious objection by doctors, which hinders the ability to terminate a pregnancy and have an abortion within the timescales prescribed by law. This situation has prompted the European Committee of Social Rights of the Council of Europe to reproach Italy, stating that conscientious objection violates the right to health for women (see Article 11 of the European Social Charter).[29]

It is important to underline the increase in the exercise of conscientious objection with regard to abortions in Italy, since it reveals the tensions between religious and secular values as part of the gendered and moral crisis of the Italian welfare system. This shift is clearly linked to the hegemonic role of institutional Catholicism in the welfare area in Italy.

More generally – and although Catholic organisations are very important in the Italian welfare mix (a blend of state, market and third sector providers) – their role is controversial (Frisina, 2010). They seem mostly to adopt a conservative and primarily reactive approach with strong paternalistic characteristics. Catholic organisations 'fill in the gaps' and provide welfare for the 'needy', thus caring for segments of society that politicians ignore in their policy agendas, such as migrants. However, only a few Catholic organisations contribute to projects that aim either to transform society or achieve equality. If the aim of the welfare system is to redistribute not only goods but also power (De Leonardis, 2002), welfare workers should not only respond to needs, deficiencies or inadequacies, but should also make use of individuals' capabilities (Nussbaum, 2011) to promote the empowerment of all citizens. How does the social work of the Italian Catholic Church measure up to this?

Based on my research, I would argue that since the material and the symbolic are intertwined, especially in the area of welfare, cuts in social spending reinforce conservative values and generate new tensions and divisions in Italian society. In this context, Catholic hierarchies (Frisina, 2010) have become more active in the Italian public sphere, trying to regain the ground they lost in the 1970s, as illustrated by the case of the referendum on medically assisted procreation (Frisina et al, 2015), or in the debate on lesbian, gay, bisexual, transgender and intersex (LGBTI) rights and the recognition of same-sex unions (Ozzano and Giorgi, 2016). Moreover, conservative Catholics have publicly criticised 'the imposition of gender ideology in Italian schools'.[30] As a result, a cultural initiative against homophobia (Educating for Diversity at School, drawn up by the National Office against Racial Discrimination in response to European Union recommendations) was censored by the Italian Ministry of Education, University and Research after it was criticised at the Italian Episcopal Conference. With regard to this, the Italian sociologist Chiara Saraceno noted:

> Once again, through the voice of the head of the episcopate, Cardinal Bagnasco, the Catholic Church launched its denunciation against the 'gender theory', based on the assumption that it would promote confusion between male and female, generating a sort of 'trans-human'.... The words of Bagnasco reveal the persistence of theories and practices that, in the name of nature, tend to force men and women into a range of roles and rigid asymmetric destinies, which are likely to reduce the richness, variety and potentiality of human beings.[31]

During the WaVE fieldwork, these conflicting values may lead at times to new gender alliances – that is, across boundaries between women from different ethnic and religious backgrounds, as was the case with the demonstrations that took place in defence of Law 194 and family advice bureaux (Venice, 7 October 2006).[32] The most acclaimed speech during the demonstration was made by a social worker of Nigerian origin. She said:

> We don't want the help of self-righteous and moralist people who will attack the weakest and most defenceless women, such as immigrants, but we want more professional social workers, more psychologists, more gynaecologists, secular and free! Let's help immigrant women with prevention, do

> not threaten them when they have to make tragic decisions
> by themselves and they have no alternative other than the
> voluntary interruption of pregnancy: this means fighting for
> civil rights and for freedom. This is the fight of all women,
> Italian and immigrant!

However, forging transversal alliances across racial, ethnic, cultural and religious boundaries to fight against gendered discrimination with the aim of improving the social welfare of everyone, becomes harder (much harder) with the rise of populist and right-wing movements. Movements such as Lega Nord in Italy, which use discourses of 'us' (national and legitimate citizens) versus 'them' (foreigners and irregular migrants) in order to create scapegoats and to justify or explain the shortcomings of the Italian welfare system.

Eleonore Kofman and colleagues (2015) show how, in current European debates about the integration of migrants, the construction of 'us' and 'them' is always gender-oriented. Migrant women, previously invisible or seen as mere appendages of men, have become more visible, but they are often represented as a homogenised mass of uneducated and backward migrants and as victims of patriarchal cultures, as part of a trend of minoritisation (Nyhagen et al, 2012, p 106) and victimisation (see Chapter Ten). The more that discourses focus on Muslim women, the more the debate becomes 'culturalised', thus setting aside the socioeconomic dimensions with regard to the integration of migrants, including migrant women.

Feminist scholars are working hard to 'reshape post-patriarchal discourse on gender' and 'overcome [the] interpretative dualism on migrant and native women's victimization' (Bimbi, 2014, p 1). Neo-colonial discourses on migrant women create an illusion of living the gender equality of native European women, where women's self-determination is the undisputed norm regardless of whether violence against women persists, even in the most egalitarian European countries. To resist hegemonic representations of 'us' and 'them' (and not to reproduce the inferiorisation of migrants), welfare workers have started to recognise the experiences of post-colonial feminism (Romeo, 2012), Islamic feminism (Pepicelli, 2012) and transnational feminism (Pesole, 2012). The experiences (with all their nuances) of female intercultural associations, which have tried to revise their practices to include migrant women, are particularly instructive (Merrill, 2006; Bernacchi, 2015). There are promising signs attesting to the emergence of new intersectional gender alliances (across the boundaries of race, ethnicity, religion, age and class) in the fight against gendered discrimination and violence.

The case of Sumaya Abdel Qader is particularly interesting: she is an Italian woman of Palestinian origin, who founded the first organisation for young Muslims in Italy in 2001 (Frisina, 2007), and became popular thanks to her book *Porto il velo, adoro i Queen* (*I Wear the Veil, I Adore Queen*) (2008). A sociologist by training, she works as a social activist and is involved in the fight against gender-based violence.[33] She is on the frontline working with Aisha, a project that denounces violence and discrimination against women,[34] promoted by the Coordination of Islamic Associations in the area of Milan (CAIM),[35] which has promoted a leadership role for a new generation of Muslim Italians.[36] The project includes a social communication campaign against gender-based discrimination, with videos[37] and comic strips[38] (arguing that there is no religious justification for any violence against women, and calling for the development of new masculinities); sexual and affective education courses for young Muslims; and a course to train religious leaders (*imams*) in how to recognise gender-based violence and how to support women (that is, reporting violence, contacting anti-violence centres and supporting a woman's choice to separate, or obtain a divorce, from a violent husband).

Two important points emerged from a recent interview with Sumaya Abdel Qader:[39] the voicing of internal criticism about the complicity of Muslim communities in violence against women and more generally in everyday sexism, and the call for solidarity between women across boundaries. The latter point is illustrated in Takoua Ben Mohamed's comic strip showing a black-veiled woman holding the hand of an unveiled white woman's,[40] thus attesting to the emergence of an awareness that gender-based violence in Muslim communities is not an exceptional and isolated case.

The search for solidarities without borders and thus across ethnic, cultural, religious, political or economic boundaries will continue to be a challenging task for feminist activists and scholars. As these early developments have shown, studying the changing values of European welfare entails the study of new fields, such as the emergence of 'transnational forms of social protection' (Faist, 2013; Kofman and Raghuram, 2015). The moral crisis of welfare is not restricted to national boundaries. We will need to explore alternative moral codes based on practices of cooperation and solidarity among public and private welfare actors in countries that are both destination and arrival points for migrants.[41]

Notes

1. I am indebted to Lina Molokotos-Liederman, Lia Lombardi (University of Milan-ISMU Foundation), Chantal Saint-Blancat (University of Padua), Alberta Giorgi (CES, University of Coimbra) and Pia Karlsson Minganti (University of Stockholm) for their comments on this chapter. The Padua team was coordinated by Professor C. Saint-Blancat and included three researchers: Valentina Longo, Adriano Cancellieri and Annalisa Frisina. All translations from Italian into English in this chapter have been made by the author.

2. www.padovanet.it

3. The economic crisis of 2008 had a severe impact on the region; many migrant workers lost their jobs and experienced downward mobility (Sacchetto and Vianello, 2013).

4. www.padovanet.it/sites/default/files/attachment/C_1_Allegati_20021_Allegato.pdf

5. For more information on how Protestantism and Catholicism interacted with politics and class in the evolution of social policies in Europe and America, see van Kersbergen and Manow (2009).

6. Access to reproductive health services is not always available to the 17 million migrant women in EU countries, who have significantly higher fertility and abortion rates compared with their native counterparts (Lombardi, 2016a). There are about five million migrants in Italy (7% of the Italian population), among whom 52.7% are migrant women (Lombardi, 2016b, p 9).

7. In several European countries voluntary abortions among migrant women have fuelled heated debates. There have been controversies on high abortion rates in Italy, Spain and Norway, on the ability of undocumented women in France and the Czech Republic to have an abortion, and on voluntary abortion based on the gender of the foetus in Sweden and in the Netherlands (Lombardi, 2016a).

8. This issue is currently hotly debated both at national and at local level. See 'Padova, il 95% dei medici dice no all'intervento' (Padua, 95% of doctors say no to the intervention) (*Il Mattino*, 12 April 2016, p 9); 'Abortire in Italia è troppo difficile', (Aborting in Italy is too difficult) (*Corriere della Sera*, 12 April 2016, p 20); 'In Italia troppo difficile abortire' (In Italy too difficult to abort) (*La Repubblica*, 12 April 2016, p 21).

9. Racialisation is the process whereby dominant groups utilise cultural and biological features to construct levels of superiority and inferiority (Grosfoguel, 2004). On the cultural construction of migrant women in the Italian press and the importance of maternity and abortion, see Giorgi (2012).

10. www.who.int/reproductive_health/en/index.html

11. *Badante* literally means the one who provides care to someone, but has a derogatory connotation both towards the caregivers (migrants) and care receivers (elderly people).

12. In the 'global care chains', Italy is characterised both by the quantity, and by the specific employment, of immigrant women as caregivers, not only for the upper classes but also for those on middle and lower incomes, because of the absence of sufficient welfare measures. On how being a *badante* damages the health of working women, see Chiaretti (2005).

13. In the Padua case study, they were known as *Spazio Ascolto* (Listening Window) and *Ambulatorio Multietnico* (Multi-Ethnic Health Centre).

[14] Family advice bureaux (*Consultori Familiari*) were crucial in our research. They were founded as a result of the feminist political struggles in the 1970s and were planned primarily for women. They are regionally managed health facilities that were established by law in 1975, aimed at supporting individuals and families in matters relating to reproductive health and maternity (offering services ranging from psychological and social assistance to medical services). In practice, the number of advice bureaux and the quality of the work they carry out is insufficient because of lack of funding (Frisina and Cancellieri, 2012).

[15] On the characteristics of the 'social-capitalist' (or 'conservative/corporatist' or 'Mediterranean') Italian welfare regime and its commitment to the defence of the traditional family, see Frisina (2004).

[16] Childcare services do not cover the needs of Italian families (www.cittadinanzattiva.it/comunicati/consumatori/7983-c-e-un-nido-i-*nuovi-dati-sugli-asili-di-cittadinanzattiva.html*).

[17] As shown in the final part of this chapter, such fears are more common in Italian society today, thanks to Catholic 'attacks' on the so-called 'ideology of gender'.

[18] On how ethnicisation works in the same way as racialisation, see Gallissot et al (2001). On the ethnicisation of 'diseases of migrants' in the Italian welfare system, see Caputo (2005).

[19] 'Welfare e valori. Migrazioni, genere e religioni' (Welfare and Values. Migration, Gender and Religions), University of Padua, Department of Sociology, 7 June 2008. The goal of this 2008 conference was to encourage an exchange of 'good practices in the field of promoting health for migrant women'. The WaVE research team showed three videos: Getting Better (Ideadonna Onlus, ASL 3 e 4 Torino); 'Per la vostra salute, donne del mondo' (For Your Health, Women of the World) (Osservatorio sulle Diseguaglianze, ARS Marche, Associazione Senza Confini); 'Parole di donne, parole di salute' (Words of Women, Words of Health) (Albero della Salute, Regione Toscana).

[20] The video is available online at https://vimeo.com/153522148 (password: WAVE) and has four parts: 'Equal citizens? Welfare experiences' (5 minutes); 'Welfare in crisis for Italians too' (14 minutes); 'Our priorities' (10 minutes); and 'Empowerment: to feel like a citizen' (2 minutes 30 seconds).

[21] Thanks are due to Elena Radulescu of the association Columna and to Evelyn and Julius Emehelu of the Nollywood Beauty Shop.

[22] The original idea was to create groups of women of mixed origins. However, after the first meeting with Nigerian and Romanian intercultural workers, we realised the need to organise two separate discussions according to nationality (mainly because of linguistic reasons, since we wanted to include marginalised stakeholders who could not speak Italian). Thus we had two separate groups, one for Romanian and one for Nigerian women, and a third that included both Romanian and Nigerian women, as well as welfare workers.

[23] The Bossi-Fini law (189/2002) introduced the principle of 'contract to stay', an agreement between the migrant worker and the employer that is necessary to obtain, or renew, a residence permit. With this law the employer has the power to influence not only a migrant's working conditions but also conditions pertaining to residence. Moreover, the law lowered to six months the length of the residence permits in cases where the individual was unemployed.

[24] Fink and Lomax cooperated with Rose (2007) in the project Visual Dialogues, which aimed to generate 'an intellectually rigorous, policy-focused, visual research agenda while also stimulating wider public conversations about inequalities and the

role of the visual in sustaining and/or ameliorating these' (www.visualdialogues. co.uk).

[25] Migrant women who took part in the video imagined European policymakers to be an important audience because they thought that the problems they face should not be confined (and solved) at a national level only.

[26] www.youtube.com/watch?v=7pxjt6h_5r4. In addition to the video, a booklet in six languages was prepared and distributed through city clinics and information offices, and at the Opera San Francesco clinic, 'aimed at creating awareness among immigrant women of the importance of prevention and promoting pregnancy screening' (Fondazione Bracco, *A Short Past, a Long Future*: p 50), http://www. fondazionebracco.com/en/about-us/foundation

[27] Although there is no unified European welfare system, the European social model refers to 'the presence in the national member states of a system based on common values, such as the respect for fundamental rights, a shared solidarity, the provision of a safety net against some social risks, state intervention in social policies and the presence of social dialogue as a form of participation' (Colombo Svevo, 2005, p 96).

[28] Article 32 of the Italian Constitution states that 'the Republic safeguards health as a fundamental right of the individual and in the interests of the community; it grants free healthcare to the needy'. This article does not refer solely to (national) citizens, as other articles do, as it employs the term 'individual': social rights, as human rights, are to be granted to all, including irregular immigrants. This universal principle was explicitly acknowledged in 1998, when the provision of healthcare for irregular immigrants was introduced in the '*testo unico dell'immigrazione*' (single text on immigration) (see articles 34, 35, 36, 42, 43, 44).

[29] The Italian General Confederation of Labour, the largest labour union in Italy, filed a complaint two years ago stating that the few Italian doctors who perform abortions and respect Law 194/1978 are discriminated against and have 'various types of direct and indirect labour disadvantages'. The news that the European Council charged Italy with this offence was made public only after 11 April 2016, even though the government (which must now formally reply to the complaint) had been aware of this motion since 12 October 2015.

[30] www.catholicnewsagency.com/news/church-in-italy-fights-against-imposition-of-gender-ideology-in-schools-26494/. On the activism of Northern League in defence of the 'traditional family', see http://milano.repubblica.it/cronaca/2015/12/22/news/lombardia_la_lega_vuole_finanziare_un_numero_verde_contro_il_gender_nelle_scuole-129953680/#gallery-slider=125240744

[31] http://blog-micromega.blogautore.espresso.repubblica.it/2015/03/26/chiara-saraceno-l%E2%80%99anatema-contro-la-teoria-di-genere/*Repubblica*, 26 March 2015.

[32] The leaflet of the regional assembly of women in defence of Law 194/1978 condemned the proposal of a regional law as one that 'represents a violent attack against the self-determination of women and a heavy form of intimidation above all for young and immigrant women'.

[33] In other European countries, there are similar types of engagement. Muslim youth organisations with deeply involved and high-ranking female members fight against gendered-based violence and create transversal alliances; for the Swedish case, see Karlsson Minganti (2011, 2015) and Chapter Ten in this book).

[34] www.facebook.com/progettoAisha/info/?tab=page_info. For more information, see www.rai.tv/dl/RaiTV/programmi/media/ContentItem-d7f910b2-c0df-

47b7-9a1e-75f2e1f05ccc.html (00:19:50). The project was launched after a 7 km bike demonstration around Milan of veiled women protesting against the idea that Islam forbids women to ride bikes; http://video.repubblica.it/edizione/milano/milano-la-pedalata-delle-donne-musulmane-contro-discriminazioni-e-violenze/232080/231593

[35] www.facebook.com/pg/ilcaim/about/?ref=page_internal. See, for instance, the campaign for building a mosque in Milan (where young people are the main players): www.youtube.com/watch?v=eclrlIeTcAw&ebc=ANyPxKrQb44KLA2yIY0O S6Jfd2uS3mOkJeIhSp8HmbT6bzKmt7AT-8upjsAQJbBD99FmuKZYQZWe4_ NT5wDTC8d4SMOhB2mUeQ&nohtml5=False

[36] www.youtube.com/watch?time_continue=414&v=QvH4PQ-3_e4

[37] www.youtube.com/watch?v=BZP8lVRFpFA

[38] The comic strips are drawn by Takoua Ben Mohamed, a young Italian-Tunisian woman who created Fumetto Intercultura (Intercultural Comics), a website (https://ilfumettointercultura.wordpress.com) and a Facebook page (www.facebook.com/IlFumettoInterculturaTakouaBenMohamed) of comics against Islamophobia.

[39] www.huffingtonpost.it/2016/02/16/sumaya-abdel-qader_n_9242274.html

[40] 'You are free, you are not alone': www.facebook.com/progettoAisha/photos/a.9 19152111513853.1073741828.918914681537596/935027559926308/?type=3& theater

[41] On how policies can be changed to improve opportunities and outcomes for female migrants in Europe, see Anthias et al (2013).

References

Abdel Qader, S. (2008) *Porto il velo, adoro i Queen (I Wear the Veil, I Adore Queen)*, Milan: Sonzogno.

Anthias, F., Cederberg, M., Barber, T., Ayres, R. (2013) 'Welfare regimes, markets and policies: the experiences of migrant women', in F. Anthias, M. Kontos and M. Morokvasic-Müller (eds) *Paradoxes of Integration: Female Migrants in Europe, Volume 4*, New York, NY and London: Springer, pp 37-8.

Bernacchi, E. (2015) 'Intercultural feminist practices in Italy: challenging stereotyped and othering images of migrant women', *Periódico do Núcleo de Estudos e Pesquisas sobre Gênero e Direito*, Centro de Ciências Jurídicas – Universidade Federal da Paraíba, 2: 165-82, available at http://periodicos.ufpb.br/ojs2/index.php/ged/index.

Bimbi, F. (2014) *Symbolic Violence: Reshaping Post-Patriarcal Discourses on Gender*, Emerald Group Publishing, available at: www.emeraldinsight.com/doi/abs/10.1108/S1529-21262014000018B015.

Burawoy, M. (2005) 'For public sociology', *American Sociological Review*, 70(1): 4-28, available at http://burawoy.berkeley.edu/Public%20 Sociology,%20Live/Burawoy.pdf.

Caputo, B. (2005) 'L'etnicizzazione della malattia in contesto migratorio. Una prospettiva antropologica' ('The ethnicisation of disease in the context of migration. An anthropological perspective'), in N. Pasini and M. Picozzi (eds) *Salute e immigrazione. Un modello teorico-pratico per le aziende sanitarie* (*Health and Immigration. A Theoretical and Practical Model for Healthcare Agencies*), Milan: Franco Angeli.

Chiaretti, G. (2005) 'Badanti: Mal da lavoro mal da rapporti sociali' ('Badanti: sick of work or sick of social relations?') in G. Chiaretti (ed) *C'è posto per la salute nel nuovo mercato del lavoro? Medici e sociologi a confronto* (*Is There a Place for Health in the New Labour Market? Comparing Doctors and Sociologists*), Milan: Franco Angeli.

Colombo Svevo, M. (2005) *Le politiche sociali nell'Unione Europea* (*Social Policies in the European Union*), Milan: Franco Angeli.

De Leonardis, O. (2002) *In un diverso welfare: Sogni e incubi* (*In a Different Welfare: Dreams and Nightmares*), Milan: Feltrinelli.

Di Giulio, P. and Carrozza, S. (2003) 'Il nuovo ruolo del padre' ('The new role of fathers'), in A. Pinnelli, F. Racioppi and R. Rettaroli (eds) *Genere e demografi* (*Gender and Demography*), Bologna: Il Mulino.

Faist, T. (2013) *Transnational Social Protection: An Emerging Field of Study*, COMCAD Arbeitspapiere Working Paper 113, available at www.uni-bielefeld.de/tdrc/ag_comcad/downloads/WP_113.pdf.

Fink, J. and Lomax, H. (2012) 'Inequalities, images and insights for policy and research', *Critical Social Policy*, 32(1): 3–10.

Frisina, A. (2004) 'Welfare, church and gender in Italy', in N. Edgardh Beckman (ed) *Welfare, Church and Gender in Eight European Countries*, Uppsala: Uppsala University, pp 269–87, available at https://uu.diva-portal.org/smash/get/diva2:46831/FULLTEXT01.pdf.

Frisina, A. (2007) *Giovani Musulmani d'Italia* (*Young Muslims of Italy*), Rome: Carocci.

Frisina, A. (2010) 'What church for what welfare? Conflicting points of view within the Italian case-study', in A. Bäckström and G. Davie (eds) *Welfare and Religion in 21st Century Europe: Volume 1. Configuring the Connections*, Farnham: Ashgate, pp 147–66.

Frisina, A. (2013) *Ricerca visuale e trasformazioni socio-culturali* (*Visual Research and Socio-Cultural Transformations*), Torino: UTET Università.

Frisina, A. and Cancellieri, A. (2012) 'Padua case study report', in A. Bäckström (ed) *Welfare and Values in Europe: Transitions Related to Religion, Minorities and Gender, Volume 2. Continental Europe: Germany, France, Italy, Greece*, Uppsala: Acta Universitatis Upsaliensis, pp 205–36.

Frisina A., Garelli, G., Pace, E. and Scalon, R. (2015) 'The Italian Catholic church and the artificial-insemination referendum', in K. Dobbelaere and A. Pérez-Agote (eds) *The Intimate. Polity and the Catholic Church. Laws about Life, Death and the Family in So-called Catholic Countries*, Leuven: Leuven University Press, pp 93-124.

Gallissot R., Kilani M. and Rivera A. (2001) *L'imbroglio etnico in quattordici parole chiave (The Ethnic Imbroglio in Fourteen Keywords)*, Bari: Dedalo.

Giorgi, A. (2012) 'The cultural construction of migrant women in the Italian press', *E-Cadernos, CES*: 16: 66-91, available at https://eces.revues.org/1026.

Giuliani, G. (2015) *Il colore della nazione (The Nation's Colour)*, Milan: LeMonnier-Mondadori.

Grosfoguel, R. (2004) 'Race and ethnicity or racialized ethnicities?', *Ethnicities* 4(3): 315-36.

Harvey, D. (2007) *Breve storia del neoliberismo (A Brief History of Neoliberalism)*, Milan: Il Saggiatore.

Karlsson Minganti, P. (2011) 'Challenging from within: youth associations and female leadership in Swedish mosques', in M. Bano, and H. Kalmbach (eds) *Women, Leadership and Mosques: Changes in Contemporary Islamic Authority*, Leiden: Brill.

Karlsson Minganti, P. (2015) 'Muslim women managing women's shelters: Somaya, the Muslimwoman and religion as a resource', *Nordic Journal of Feminist and Gender Research (NORA)*, 23(2): 93-108.

Kofman, E. and Raghuram, P. (2015) *Gendered Migrations and Global Social Reproduction*, London: Palgrave Macmillan.

Kofman, E., Saharso, S. and Vacchelli, E. (2015) 'Gendered perspectives on integration discourses and measures', *International Migration*, 53(4): 77-89.

Lombardi, L. (2005) *Società, culture e differenze di genere. Percorsi migratori e stati di salute (Societies, Cultures and Gender Differences. Migration Patterns and the State of Health)*, Milan: Franco Angeli.

Lombardi, L. (2016a) *Reproductive Health of Migrant Women in Italy and Europe. Abortion, Social Conditions and Policy*, Milan: Fondazione I.S.MU.

Lombardi, L. (2016b) *Genere, salute e politiche sociali in Europa. La salute delle donne migranti tra diritti, accesso ai servizi e diseguaglianze (Gender, Health and Social Policies in Europe. The Health of Migrant Women, Between Rights, Access to Services and Inequality)*, Milan: Fondazione I.S.MU.

Magaraggia, S. (2013) "'Mio figlio di certo non lo educo allo stesso modo dei miei". Relazioni intergenerazionali e trasformazioni dei desideri paterni' ('"I don't raise my children as my parents did". Intergenerational relations and transformations of paternal desires'), *Studi Culturali (Cultural Studies)*, 10(2): 189-209.

Maneri, M. (2009) 'I media e la guerra alle migrazioni' ('The media and the war migration'), in S. Palidda (ed) *Razzismo democratico. La persecuzione degli stranieri in Europa (Democratic Racism. The Persecution of Foreigners in Europe)*, Milan: Agenzia X, pp 66-85.

Merrill, H. (2006) *An Alliance of Women. Immigration and the Politics of Race*, Minneapolis, MN: University of Minnesota Press.

Mezzadra, S. (2010) 'The gaze of autonomy. Capitalism, migration and social struggle', available at www.uninomade.org/the-gaze-of-autonomy-capitalism-migration-and-social-struggles.

Milne, E.-J., Mitchell, C. and De Lange, N. (eds) (2012) *Handbook of Participatory Video*, New York, NY: Altamira Press.

Ministero della Salute (2015) *Relazione sulla attuazione della legge contenete norme per la tutela della maternità e per l'interruzione volontaria di gravidanza, Legge 194/1978 (Report on the Implementation of the Law for the Protection of Motherhood and Voluntary Interruption of Pregnancy, Law 194/1978)*, Rome: Ministero della Salute, available at www.salute.gov.it/imgs/C_17_pubblicazioni_2428_allegato.pdf.

Mitchell, C. (2011) *Doing Visual Research*, London: Sage.

Nussbaum, M. (2011) *Diventare persone (Becoming a People)*, Bologna: Mulino.

Nyhagen, L. Predelli, L., Halsaa, B., Sandu, A. and Thun, C. (2012) *Majority–Minority Relations in Contemporary Women's Movements. Strategic Sisterhood*, London: Palgrave Macmillan.

Ortega-Alcazar, I. and Dyck, I. (2012) 'Migrant narratives of health and well being: challenging 'othering' processes through photo-elicitation interviews', *Critical Social Policy*, 32(1): 106-25.

Ozzano, L. and Giorgi, A. (2016) *European Culture Wars and the Italian Case: Which Side Are You On?*, London: Routledge.

Pennacchi, L. (2008) *La moralità del welfare. Contro il neoliberismo populista (The Morality of Welfare. Against a Populist Neoliberalism)*, Rome: Donzelli.

Pepicelli, R. (2012) 'Femminismo islamico' ('Islamic feminism'), in S. Marchetti, J. Mascat, and V. Perilli (eds) *Femministe a parole. Grovigli da districare (The Words of Feminists. Unravelling the Entanglements)*, Rome: Ediesse, pp 97-100.

Pesole, E. (2012) 'Femminismo transnazionale' ('Transnational feminism'), in S. Marchetti, J. Mascat and V. Perilli (eds) *Femministe a parole. Grovigli da districare* (*The Words of Feminists. Unravelling the Entanglements*), Rome: Ediesse, pp 106-10.

Pizzuti, F.R. (2015) *Rapporto sullo Stato Sociale 2015. La grande recessione e il welfare state* (*Report on the Social State 2015. The Great Recession and the Welfare State*), Naples: Simone Editore.

Romeo, C. (2012) 'Femminismo postcoloniale' ('Post-colonial feminism'), in S. Marchetti, J. Mascat and V. Perilli (eds) *Femministe a parole. Grovigli da districare* (*The Words of Feminists. Unravelling the Entanglements*), Rome: Ediesse, pp 101-5.

Rose, G. (2007) *Visual Methodologies*, London: Sage.

Sacchetto, D. and Vianello, F.A. (eds) (2013) *Navigando a vista. Migranti nella crisi economica tra lavoro e disoccupazione* (*Migrants in the Economic Crisis. Between Work and Unemployment*), Milan: Franco Angeli.

Sardadvar, S. (2015) 'How migrant status affects health beyond socioeconomic status: evidence from Austria', *International Migration Review*, 49(4): 843-77.

Sciurba, A. (2014) 'Libere di scegliere? L'aborto delle donne migranti in Italia tra politiche migratorie, sfruttamento lavorativo e casi estremi di abusi e violenza' ('Free to choose? Abortion among migrant women in Italy. Between migration policies, labour exploitation and extreme cases of abuse and violence'), *About Gender*, Special Issue: Il corpo delle donne, l'aborto, i diritti riproduttivi. Bilanci e prospettive (Women's bodies, abortion and reproductive rights), 3(5): 245-74.

Siebert, R. (2014) 'Il lascito del colonialismo e la relazione con l'altro' ('The legacy of colonialism and the relationship with the other'), in T. Grande and E. Parini Giap (eds), *Sociologia* (*Sociology*), Rome: Carocci.

Tognetti Bordogna, M. (2004) *I colori del welfare. Servizi alla persona di fronte all'utenza che cambia* (*The Colours of the Welfare State. Personal Services in the Face Change*), Milan: Franco Angeli.

van Kersbergen, K. and Manow, P. (2009) *Religion, Class Coalitions, and Welfare States*, Cambridge: Cambridge University Press.

Zajczyk, F., Ruspini, E., Crosta, F. and Fiore, B. (2007) 'Fathers in Italy', in *Pariteia. Promoting Gender Equality in Active European Citizenship. Final Report of Action 1 – A Survey*, Amsterdam School for Social science Research and University of Milano–Bicocca, available at www.verwey-jonker.nl/doc/participatie/finalreport.pdf.

Part Four:
Drawing the threads together

Welfare and values in Europe: insights drawn from a comparative cross-country analysis

Effie Fokas

Introduction

This chapter works on two levels. On one level, it is a summation of the comparative dimensions of the Welfare and Values in Europe: Transitions Related to Religion, Minorities and Gender (WaVE) project, and applies a comparative lens to the material emanating from the 13 case studies that formed its core.[1] On the second level, the chapter provides a framework though which the threads in the preceding chapters can be brought together. Clearly, the two overlap in so far as the chapters gathered here build on the original project very directly, developing its themes in light of the social changes that have taken place since 2009 and of the growing literature in the field. The exemplification, however, will be wide-ranging in order to display the impressive scope of WaVE and the questions provoked by its findings.

As suggested by the project's subtitle, three major and *interconnected* dimensions of social change in Europe are identified and examined through the prism of welfare – that is, changes related to religion, minorities and gender. It is no exaggeration to say that these dimensions of social change have seen *rapid* transformation in the past few years and months, transformations so momentous as to threaten core conceptions of social solidarity in Europe. As one might expect, this questioning of the theory of a 'social Europe' has been accompanied by an even more alarming unravelling of a 'social Europe' in *practice*, particularly as the severe financial crisis that has affected Europe for the past decade or so has been exacerbated by the added layer of the refugee crisis of recent years (sparked especially by the war in Syria but not limited to it). Across Europe we have seen welfare systems build thick and exclusionary walls and value systems implode. With regard to the latter, for example, Danish, Swiss and Swedish conceptions of national identity linked to the values of tolerance, opportunity, and welcome, respectively, have been severely challenged by the refugee crisis.[2]

There is a special need for comparative study of these developments, particularly as they comprise a religious dimension. As noted elsewhere in this volume (see especially Chapters Two and Five), religion is undergoing a process of globalisation, provoking, simultaneously, a series of reactions or counter-movements: both tendencies increase the need for comparative and transnational studies. Today, as at the start of the WaVE project, a snapshot of European society reveals a number of controversies pivoting on conflicts – perceived or real – between religious minorities and majorities in Europe. And welfare provision (that is, the question of who should provide what, to whom, and for what reasons) has migrated to the heart of these issues. Negative attention directed at the Muslim presence in Europe continues to permeate many of the debates in this area, most conspicuously through issues such as the wearing of headscarves in public schools and places of employment (seen to threaten both secular and gender-equality values),[3] and tensions concerning the building of mosques. The Muslim presence in Europe is indeed a catalyst for debates on conflicts over values, and an especially interesting (and profitable) focal point for the mass media, which tend to overemphasise the 'Muslim factor'.

This generalised image is, however, highly inadequate. First, conflicts over religion and values are not limited to minority–majority relations, nor to Islam in Europe. In Europe at least, we are also witnessing – parallel to, or as undercurrents of, these developments – major tensions between religious and secular worldviews. Debates between secularists and religionists, or *post*-secularists, continue to proliferate. Meanwhile, there is significant tension *within* religious and secular worldviews so that neither can be viewed as a monolith. Further, the generalised image of a values conflict centred on Islam lacks critical nuance – for example, the extent to which conflicts of *interests*, rather than conflicts of values, are at play in different circumstances. Attention to such nuance in the WaVE case studies, nuance best achieved through empirical, bottom-up research, has challenged the generalised image of an Islam-based values conflict. In fact, as will become clear in the following pages, the WaVE research indicates that most majority–minority interactions in the domain of welfare lie somewhere between the categories of 'conflict' and 'cohesion', in a large grey area that requires very careful navigation.

The twin aims of this chapter are to highlight certain patterns found in the case study data collected both during and after the WaVE project, and, on this basis, to offer insights gathered regarding practices, tendencies, mechanisms and so on leading to conflict or cohesion in, or influencing the large grey area in between, minority–majority relations. The chapter is structured as follows. First, it sets out the WaVE project research design and explains certain implications of the project's methodology choices. Second, it outlines briefly the concepts of welfare and values as motivators for the WaVE research. Third, in a section entitled 'findings', it presents (necessarily selective) results from the research conducted in first three parts of the book, roughly divided in accordance with the project's general themes (although the themes overlap in many cases):

- Religion – what is the role of religion in the context of welfare and values, in terms of religiously provided majority welfare[4] and/or religiously defined minority welfare needs?
- Minorities – what is the experience of minorities within this framework, in terms of problems in access to welfare provided, differing welfare needs, and/or establishment of their own welfare networks?
- Gender – are there specific minority and/or majority gender values influencing the provision and/or use of welfare? Are there gendered welfare needs and if so, how do these influence minority–majority relations?

This brief presentation of the three main thrusts of the research is followed by reflections on social cohesion in relation to welfare. Here the focus is on two themes that call for careful analysis and around which many of the cross-relevant sub-themes cluster: majority policy (and practices) in relation to minorities; and minority social networks and integration. Finally, the chapter closes with an exploration of factors arising from the data that influence minority–majority relations in both positive and negative ways.

Opportunities and challenges of the research design

The study was carried out in 12 European countries, as set out in the introduction to this volume: Sweden, Norway, Finland, Latvia, England, Germany, France, Poland, Croatia, Italy, Romania and Greece. A mere glance at the list of countries is suggestive of the great diversity of experience in the domains of welfare, religion, minorities and gender in these various parts of Europe (see Part Two). In particular, the inclusion of four post-communist contexts entails a profound diversification of the material examined. As Siniša Zrinscak argues in Chapter Seven, these cases allow an examination of special features related to majority contexts formed by collectivistic religions (Jakelic, 2010) – features, however, that are different from the Greek case of collectivistic religion because of the communist experience. The transition from the communist welfare state to the current welfare systems has in each case been a momentous one. The experience of these countries is fundamentally different from that of our other case study countries. This is so with respect to minority presence (centuries old, and which by and large also means a lack of state welfare measures designed specifically for minority needs) and to the prevalence of emigration, rather than immigration, which is most relevant in the other cases in the WaVE project. Further, accession, or potential for accession, to the European Union (EU) is a conspicuous factor of change in the post-communist countries.

In order to facilitate our aim of grasping welfare and values 'on the ground' and as reflected in practice, we chose to conduct qualitative empirical research in the form of in-depth fieldwork carried out in one medium-sized town in each country case (see Chapter One of this volume). From quantitative studies and values surveys we have information about the values claimed by different groups of people. But these are often abstract notions and they tell us little about whether, in practice, differing values are, or are not, leading to conflict and thus damaging social cohesion. Values do not exist 'in the air', as it were, but are grounded in everyday life and interactions, and they need to be examined as such – that is, on the ground and through qualitative research – if they are to shed light on actual, lived social cohesion and/ or conflict. As van Deth and Scarbrough argue:

> Values are embedded in other things – in ways of thinking, talking and acting, in judgements, decisions, attitudes, behaviour, and the like. We can conceptualise values as separate from these other things, but we cannot 'get to them' separately from their place in other things. Values cannot be researched on their own because they do not stand on their own. (1998, p 31)

Thus the study was inductive in its approach. Specifically, researchers were set the task of *observing* majority–minority interactions in the domain of welfare and, based on the patterns observed, to offer analyses on the causes of conflict and/or cohesion between majorities and minorities (focusing on mechanisms in each case). As discussed in Chapter Two, contextuality was a guiding principle, so that in each case researchers focused on particular groups and themes bearing special relevance to the town in question. Accordingly, the diversity of the case study towns and countries is reflected in the diversity of the research areas covered. The different minority groups studied form a complex grid of religiously, ethnically and/or linguistically, gendered, or otherwise defined groups. The 13 cases include Muslims (both 'old' and 'new', native and immigrant, first generation to fourth generation), Roman Catholics, Greek Catholics, Protestant groups (mainly Evangelical and Pentecostal), and Russian Orthodox and Greek Orthodox groups; Roma and travelling communities; Finnish and German repatriates (recent returnees from the former Soviet Union and former eastern bloc countries); Russian-speaking communities; Russian, Ukrainian, Polish, Albanian, Bosnian, Romanian, Greek, Turkish, Algerian, Moroccan, Nigerian, Pakistani and Indian immigrants; female labour migrants; and male labour migrants. The list of themes explored in the various cases is also diverse, including immigration policy, reproductive health policy, care for elderly people, educational programmes, employment policy, the administration of benefits and the administration of reproductive health.

As already argued, the advantages of our particular research design are many. First, qualitative studies offer the opportunity for gathering large amounts of varied, in-depth information. By conducting qualitative studies in particular towns, we have been able to glean nuanced information about our cases, and to find that information embedded in its natural context.[5] The material gathered reflects more closely the local realities on the ground in each case. Further, as a result of having contextuality as our guide, the research offers a more complete and realistic perspective of the range of arenas of minority–majority interactions and thus a better grasp of the types of problem that might be encountered, and the types of solution found, in efforts aimed at achieving social cohesion in diverse societies across Europe. A strict standardisation of research topics across all cases would have resulted in a far less nuanced perspective for the researchers.

However, the significant opportunities offered by WaVE's research design also entail particular challenges and limitations, such as those raised by Pål Repstad in Chapter Two. In short, as Repstad explains, there is an inherent tension in comparative studies between rigid standardisation and isolated case studies: while a minimum level of standardisation is necessary in order to glean insight into patterns and mechanisms, exaggerated standardisation may miss the real situation on the ground in terms of important local or national contextual factors. In the WaVE project we made a conscious decision to favour flexibility, but within certain broadly defined constraints that would permit inferences to be drawn regarding patterns and mechanisms observable across all or most of the case studies. These inferences are presented in the following sections.

Still, it is worth noting at least some of the practical challenges faced in the WaVE approach to research methodology. First, defining certain terms in a universally applicable manner across these diverse cases was exceedingly difficult – for example, 'majority' and 'minority', 'welfare', and 'values'. These, together with other concepts critical to the WaVE research, such as 'social cohesion' and 'religion', were managed with an open approach: we did not choose one definition to follow for all case studies, but allowed for a rich variety of definitions to arise from the various contexts, national as well as local. This open approach was certainly more challenging for the researchers and rendered comparison more difficult, but it formed an important part of the contextuality underpinning our research.

A second challenge follows from this: comparison across the cases was necessarily more abstract than would have been the case if we were comparing the same groups and the same issues across all cases studies. The level of abstraction in our comparison, however, yielded valuable insights – as we shall see later in this chapter – in terms of the role of religion, minorities and gender in conflict and/or cohesion in the welfare domain. Thus while a certain degree of specificity, neatness and systematisation in the comparison may have been sacrificed with the selected research methodology, it may be argued that the opportunities offered by our approach outweighed the limitations because of the enhanced need, in our field of study, to understand in a true-to-life way what was happening on the ground on a daily basis. Identifying patterns and mechanisms may be a modest aim, but such identification, when grounded in quality research, is an invaluable resource to social scientific understandings of the realities around us. And enhanced insight into these realities, I would argue, is especially pertinent in our quest to attain a deeper understanding of how greater social cohesion can be achieved between (and within) majorities and minorities in diverse societies.

Juxtaposing welfare and values in WaVE

Welfare, it may be argued, is a quintessential European value, bearing in mind that each European nation has its own characteristics in this regard, with different hierarchies of welfare values in each case. Gender equality, for example, stands out as a core value in Swedish welfare, while people take to the streets in Greece and France over proposed changes to free universal tertiary education as a basic right.[6] Meanwhile, European state welfare provision is, at root, aimed at social cohesion, in as much as welfare systems are based on structures of interdependence between the members of a community, as embedded in citizenship laws and expressed through a sense of belonging. Increasingly, however, in the context of growing diversity and, particularly, in the context of the current financial and refugee crises, debates arise over whether diversity in itself *inhibits* the ability of welfare systems to foster the overall goal of social cohesion.

Once again, a second question follows from this: is it the mere presence of difference that is the key factor in the challenge to social cohesion, or is it the presence of different, perhaps competing, *values*?

As can be seen in the previous chapters, the WaVE project develops a bridge between welfare and values through the questions it poses: which values are embedded in majority and minority welfare provision and welfare needs? And what are the results in terms of 'conflict' or 'cohesion' between majorities and minorities (or, indeed, within society at large)? And, finally, what role – if any – is played by religion in this context? I turn now to the findings related to these questions under the topics of religion, minorities and gender. Given the range of examples in our material, the following sections are most easily read with Map 1.1 to hand.

Religion

Majority religion welfare actions and attitudes towards minorities

The considerable role played by majority churches in welfare provision across Europe has been established in other research (and by several members of the WaVE research team though the Welfare and Religion in a European Perspective: A Comparative Study of the Role of the Churches as Agents of Welfare within the Social Economy [WREP] project). In fact, in some cases the majority church provides 'gap-filling' welfare services that even the state does not provide – for example, in Thiva, the only homes for elderly people are run by the church, and the same applies to children's afterschool clubs in Lahti (Finland) and facilities for homeless people in Przemyśl (Poland). In the latter two cases, the strong role of the church is likely to stem from the position of these churches in relation to national identity and to the state; indeed, to a large extent these churches are seen as part of the state, hence – for better or for worse – their welfare services are seen as part of the state welfare apparatus. According to one Greek Orthodox monk, this is certainly 'for the worse', as the church should not be viewed as 'an arm of the state'. A second reason for the strong role of the church in these examples, however, is the relative weakness of the state welfare system, leaving as many gaps as it does in both national cases. Interestingly, though, the Finnish case offers a noteworthy example of such gap filling even where the welfare state is comparatively very robust. In Lahti, for example, churches help to conceal state weaknesses by offering basic language courses to immigrants.

To what extent is it problematic that majority churches are the sole local providers of certain welfare activities? One potential problem is that in several cases (Przemyśl, Medgidia [Romania], Thiva [Greece] and Sisak [Croatia]) the majority faiths are involved in addressing the most basic of minority needs, such as offering food, clothing and blankets, but in each case, most such activity is very much ad hoc and driven by particular individuals rather than embedded in a systematic approach to welfare provision. Of course, ad hoc means *not* universal, thus receipt of such welfare assistance may depend on luck, who one knows, and so on. In the case of Thiva, for example, Pakistanis and Indians are not privy to some of the most generous of religiously provided welfare because of their limited Greek and lack of social interaction with the majority population, which means they are not informed by word of mouth, as are the other minority groups benefiting from such services. At the same time, the informality of such welfare services may also be seen as an advantage, in their relative flexibility and ability to 'work between the cracks' between unbending organisational, institutional and bureaucratic limitations.

A second potential problem in majority church-provided welfare services is the notion that the help comes with 'strings attached', and an expectation that the recipients – regardless of their faith orientation – will also participate in religious services and activities offered alongside welfare assistance. The welfare provision of the Catholic Church in Przemyśl was described as having 'some religious elements': in one home for single mothers and children, there is no official requirement that the boarders take part in the rosary prayer, but research participants expressed a sense of pressure to participate – if not external pressure, then internal, out of a sense of gratitude and indebtedness towards the nuns who run the home. In Schweinfurt (Germany), one representative of a church welfare service states: "It is understood that we talk about God here and when one goes along with that it is ok. Even if a man entertains Buddhist thoughts, that is his choice, but he has agreed to go along." Meanwhile in Gävle (Sweden), where one might assume a much more discrete majority church presence (see Chapter Five), the influence of a Christian ethos and culture on the education system is still considered so strong as to be problematic for some non–Christian minorities (though more so perhaps for vocal secularist groups). One symbolic example is the use of Lutheran churches for public education graduation ceremonies. Here we find resonance with the observation of Statham and colleagues (2005, p 429):

> Although European societies see themselves are broadly secular, Christian religions often play important institutional, social and political roles, regardless of how many or how few people actually believe or practise the religion. These institutional arrangements define pre–existing conditions and the political environment into which migrant religions have to find a space for their community.

Indeed, the welfare domain is highly revealing of a broad range of norms across Europe, seemingly banal until they encounter difference, such as may occur with mass immigration.

As is clear from Chapters Six and Eleven, the Italian case offers a much more blatant example of majority religions norms influencing minority welfare and, critically, also majority welfare, via Catholic Church attitudes to abortion. Here, tensions arise over immigrant women's high rates of, and demands for, voluntary termination of pregnancies, and the Church's influence over reproductive health in general. The fact that a large percentage of the demand for this service comes from immigrant women is a breeding ground for ill feeling, particularly on the part of the civil servants working with reproductive health issues, towards the minority population seeking abortions. Meanwhile, the fact that a large percentage of doctors (80% and seemingly growing year on year) refuses to perform abortions on the grounds that their (majority Catholic) faith condemns it, indicates the *publicness* of Italy's dominant religion. The issue thus permeates both the public and the private domain, reflecting the Catholic Church's influence even within welfare provision structures. At the same time, this case highlights the internal plurality of majority religion, as liberals and traditionalists struggle against one another over the issue of reproductive health. Indeed, the Italian case offers an example of how value conflicts may arise *within* a particular group (here, the majority) rather than between the majority and minorities.

According to Hunsberger and Jackson (2005), more religious people express prejudice (in terms of self-reported negative attitudes towards stereotypical perceptions of various categories of 'others') than non-religious individuals. Theoretically, this could have a negative influence on the openness of religious welfare provision to minorities, in so far as religious organisations reflect individual members' prejudices. Still, such a claim would have to be assessed against differences across national, religious and generational categories to avoid a monolithic perspective of 'religious people'. More interestingly for our purposes, Hunsberger and Jackson's study suggests that religion-based prejudice against minorities is likely to be intensified if and when members of the majority religion perceive themselves to be in conflict with other religious (or non-religious) groups for limited resources: for example, 'the (often erroneous) perception that immigrants create competition with members of host populations for jobs can create prejudice against these immigrants' religion in particular' (Hunsberger and Jackson, 2005, p 818). In other words, what could easily be interpreted as a conflict of religious values is, in fact, a conflict of *interests*, over limited resources. The case of Sisak offers an example of such prejudice, with certain respondents complaining that anyone who is not Catholic is not considered Croatian and, hence, is not offered equal rights, particularly in the area of employment competition. The case of Evreux (France) offers a counter-example, of cohesion and cooperation between Catholic, Protestant and Muslim representatives in a particular part of town, focused on helping to protect undocumented immigrants from being discovered and potentially deported.

Minority religious needs and practices

First, it is important to point out that in terms of minority religions, minority status in and of itself often leads to group identification on the basis of religion; this is all the more likely in so far as immigrant communities are detached from core public institutions promoting civic values and tend, instead, to rely on their religious institutions and family networks as a 'community support system' (Statham et al, 2005; see also Chapter Eight). That said, an important and recurrent observation in the WaVE study is that the (externally imposed) religious identification of groups is often stronger than the internal realities of the given group's merit. In other words, minority groups who may perceive of and identify themselves with reference to a broad range of categories are often perceived of and defined by others (for example, the majority population) in one dimension – that is, with reference to their religious identity. This tends to be a product of one of two things (or a combination of these): 'representatives' of these groups are often more religiously vocal and conservative than the average member, and the mass media often emphasise the religious definitions of these groupings over other definitions. In other words, what we as researchers may define as religious needs may, by the groups themselves, be expressed as ethnically or otherwise defined needs.

In terms of the examples we have identified as religiously defined minority needs, a main issue that arises is the need for cultural competence of welfare workers and authorities in the welfare arena (an issue to be addressed more thoroughly in the next section), which includes knowledge of religious traditions, needs and so on. The Gävle case offers an example of tackling this issue in the introduction of an inclusive calendar at a local school where the religious holidays of all faith groups represented in the school are observed. Culture is easily mixed with religion in this area of specific minority needs, and one example serves to prove the point: in Drammen (Norway), homework assistance programmes, originally introduced to provide after-school assistance to minority children in areas where their learning was weaker than that of majority students, evolved in one case (that of a separate 'boarding school' version of this programme) to include lessons in culture and tradition, *and* in religion. Provision of food in schools in accordance with religious traditions is, indeed, one type of a religiously defined welfare need. But it is notoriously difficult to distinguish, from an external perspective, between religious and cultural needs. And, perhaps arbitrarily, some of what we have labelled as the latter appears in the following section.

Minorities

Minority welfare needs, met and unmet

The range of minority welfare needs across the cases in this study is extremely broad. This to some extent reflects the breadth of development of national welfare systems (discussed previously), but it is also a factor of the status of the minority individual or group in question (financial, marital and educational status; age; immigrant status (documented or undocumented); employment status; level of skills, and so on). In Germany, individuals who arrived as guest workers now face difficulties in terms of extremely low levels of permissible pension. The Romanian case is perhaps the most acute, with extreme poverty (albeit among both majorities and minorities) and an especially weak welfare system (with only four social workers in the entire case study town which is of just under 44,000 individuals). The Greek and Italian cases reveal similar characteristics by virtue of their large contingents of undocumented immigrants, for whom 'illegal' status renders concepts such as health and general welfare benefits offered by the state as something of a luxury: their welfare priorities are acquiring residence and work permits, accommodation and employment – in short, the right and ability to remain, live and work in their respective immigration destinations. In most cases, undocumented immigrants are barred from access to much (if not all) state welfare provision. Medical emergency services are usually an exception, offered universally to all in need, but even here practice often differs from theory. Thus, depending on the status of the minority individual, and in conjunction with the welfare situation of the host county, there may be a whole range of systemic barriers to welfare access.

Such barriers, however, are as much practical as systemic. One poignant and repeated example noted in Chapter Four is the lack of information about available programmes reaching minority communities, usually because of their poor knowledge of the majority language but also because of limited communication with majority individuals and structures. This problem surfaces prominently in most of the WaVE case studies. One illustrative example comes from the case of Thiva, where one programme for Greek-language training was advertised through posters in store windows throughout the town, but only in Greek and therefore inaccessible to those in most need of the language courses. In Darlington (England) (see Chapter Nine), the provision of information and a recommendation by a midwife (a trusted individual with whom some degree of contact was inevitable) was needed for some minority women to seek out certain welfare provisions offered in the locality.

In yet other cases, minority communities are fully informed, but the provision offered is not quite what they need or want. As discussed in Chapter Eight, a strong focus on the family and religious or ethnic community provides an important clue as to why this is the case: hence the relatively few Greek and Turkish immigrants using state services of care for the elderly in Reutlingen (Germany). In both cases, 'sending' family members to a state institution is taboo and was often interpreted as a lack of love and respect for the elders in question (the latter being a very highly ranked value in these cultures, as noted also in the Darlington and Medgidia material). In Schweinfurt, a minority-run welfare organisation (Friendship) placed emphasis on the importance of German-language capability for returnees from the former Soviet Union but faced the problem of a lack of motivation on the part of recipients, who complained about their limited chance of finding work in Germany in any case (so why learn German?), and explained that they had a sufficiently large circle of family and friends who spoke Russian, so there was no immediate need to learn German.

Overall, a frequently expressed minority welfare need is to have access to culturally aware and linguistically capable (in the minority language[s]) professional helpers. In the Drammen case study, a need for psychologists in these categories is identified. In Darlington, minorities' requests along these lines have clearly been 'heard' by officials, who nevertheless find it difficult to recruit welfare professionals from minority cultural, ethnic or religious backgrounds (indicating a potential vicious cycle: the family- and community-oriented approach of minority groups means that all needs should be cared for within the family, but when needs arise that *cannot* be cared for in the family, it is difficult to find competent same-culture help, because the culture does not encourage welfare activity beyond the immediate family). In Reutlingen, there was a broad discussion about 'intercultural care' for elderly people, but a real solution to managing this has not yet emerged. Because minority groups by and large avoid making use of homes for the elderly, if at all possible, these institutions are ill equipped, in terms of intercultural knowledge, to handle the relative few cases of minority users that do arise. Once again, a vicious cycle ensues. The Schweinfurt case, however, offers a successful example of a Turkish member of the town's Advisory Council on Foreigners acting as a 'cultural broker' for Turkish and Muslim users of welfare services, and resolving a seemingly constant flow of misunderstandings that arise between workers in the welfare services on the one hand, and the minority users on the other.

In Evreux, the lack of cultural competence of welfare structures – and of the broader society – stand outs as especially problematic, in particular, the indication of minorities by their ethnic, rather than religious, identities by welfare structures and the public at large. In Gävle, the Family Centre established by the local authority fails to attract the desired participation of the targeted groups of immigrants in the activities established for them (courses in cooking, meetings places for immigrant women, and so on). According to the Swedish research team, this could be the result of these programmes being a clear reflection of dominant Swedish values: as one researcher put it, "they are directed more towards giving than towards listening for the voices of the newly arrived persons as citizens with both resources and needs". (As seen in Chapter Nine, a similar plan in Darlington for cooking classes for Traveller women was abandoned for fear of offending the women concerned.)

One possible factor in the lack of communication between majority welfare institutions and minorities, and limited knowledge of the latter's needs, is spatial segregation, which occurs in many cases. In Evreux, Medgidia, Thiva and Gävle in particular, there are strong tendencies towards the ghettoisation of particular groups. The trajectory of the development of each of these ghettos is different, but the results are similar in terms of symbolic distance from the majority population (even where ghettos are in the centre of town). Such symbolic, and very often real, distance is especially conspicuous in the case of the Roma, and particularly so in the Polish case. Here the relationship between the local majority and the Roma is described as 'lack of mutual adaptation and understanding' – a description that could apply to the Roma in other case studies as well. Lack of education is pinpointed as the root of the problem, but the majority and the Roma explain this differently: the 'stricter' majority perspective is that the Roma are uninterested in education and lazy; the 'softer' majority perspective is that the Roma lack mobilisation and lack sufficient appreciation for education. The Roma themselves cite a lack of understanding of Roma children's needs, alongside the verbal abuse of the children, poor health and an unwillingness to attend school because of the poor treatment received there, and the lack of necessary clothing or equipment. Thus the impasse resulting from lack of mutual adaptation and understanding remains in place. This evidence is corroborated by the results of other research on the Roma, which reveals the *circularity* of the relationship between stereotypes, labelling and politics (Sigona, 2005), a cycle that is difficult to break.

Finally, certain majority welfare–providing efforts can lead to yet more problems rather than solutions. The Darlington case offers an interesting example of how good intentions can go astray: local authorities, forced to meet national integration targets, may be required to take decisions against their better judgement (the latter being contrary to national integration policies and based on their close contacts with, and understanding of, the local community). As a result, minorities are placed in an uncomfortable position, which, in turn, may lead to tensions and conflicts between groups. To give but one example, local authorities were obliged to act against their better judgement in order to implement a national-level policy calling for a meeting between diverse minority groups that were unlikely to see eye to eye. The plan backfired by producing more discord than anything else. A recurrent theme, then, is the need for greater understanding and awareness of the characteristics and needs of minorities on the ground and the development of policies accordingly. The insider knowledge and first-hand insights of local-level representatives of welfare agencies should not be underestimated, still less ignored.

Minority networks: tending to own needs

Most minority communities have their own welfare networks, although these vary significantly in levels of formality and structure. To a large extent, these networks develop in response to the particular needs of minority communities as they arise. For example, the aforementioned homework assistance programmes in Drammen (see also Chapter Three) were established by the local Turkish minority in order to offer extra assistance as the need arose for Norwegian language learning. Minority parents have praised the programmes for their additional role in keeping their children safe, protected and off the streets, where drug use is a problem in the locality. One of the homework assistance programmes was in fact extended to act as type of boarding school, but only for boys. The latter provoked an intense media reaction, criticising the separatist tendencies perceived in this development, and in some cases feeding fears of possible extremist tendencies. Possibly as a direct reaction to the debates provoked by the establishment of the boarding school, the Drammen local authorities decided to establish after-school homework assistance programmes in all its schools.

In general, minorities' desire for their own welfare institutions is perhaps most acute in the realm of education. For example, separate Saturday schools have been established in Reutlingen for the children of USSR repatriates, seeking to provide more creative, art-focused courses as well as to teach children Russian, adopting across the board a more rigorous and robust teaching style than that – according to this group – offered by the German education system. Similarly the Russian-language high school in Ogre serves the purpose of uniting the Russian-speaking population and preserving Russian cultural values (the schools are not new, but the Russian-speaking population actively seek their continued operation). A counter-example in the Roma case study in Przemyśl concerns a separate school being established by the local authorities against the will of the Roma themselves, who prefer that their children not be segregated; the school eventually closed because of lack of attendance.

Whether separate minority welfare institutions (including educational services) lead to greater integration into, or segregation from, the majority society is a matter of debate. In Gävle, immigrants are encouraged by majority institutions to form their own organisations in democratic forms so as to better integrate into Swedish welfare society and its structures and procedures. Trends in the formation of social networks around a culture of origin reflect what Castles and Miller (2003, p 39) describe as helping people to 'maintain self-esteem in a situation where their capabilities and experience are undermined' (see also Schrover and Vermeulen, 2005). One minority representative in Schweinfurt describes minority initiatives, particularly in the realm of education, in just these terms: maintenance of minority culture in conjunction with enhanced education is required for minority self-esteem, which, in turn, leads to increased participation of minorities in the public sphere.

In the case of Reutlingen (see Chapter Eight), in the realms of education and social work, minority communities express their eagerness to organise their own welfare networks rather than simply receive help from others, and they rally for more public funding for their own programmes. For instance, youth crime is one particularly challenging problem in the locality; certain minority groups feel they could be used effectively as a resource, establishing their own initiatives against youth crime that would be more successful in addressing the causes of such crime within their communities. This is one of many examples in which minority communities seek recognition as a resource for what they have to offer to the broader community; this links well to the Gävle illustration above, regarding the need to listen carefully to minorities' expressed needs and to recognise the resources that they can offer in addressing social problems.

In fact, in Przemyśl and in Lahti, there seems to be well-developed activity along these lines. In the former, participation in welfare provision is presented as an important part of social integration. Minority organisations (particularly Protestant groups) wish to be recognised not only as a useful resource, but as a *partner* – that is, as an equal contributor to the resolution of local welfare issues, in partnership with the local state structures. Symbolic of their exclusion in this domain is their difficulty in securing public spaces for their welfare activities. Indeed, *space* – access to public spaces by minority organisations – is another significant factor in minority integration and goes hand in hand with the need for recognition and for the operation of their own welfare networks (this issue arises in several case studies). Space in this sense has both physical and metaphorical significance.

The situation in Lahti regarding Protestant groups' welfare activities is similar to that in the Polish case study, in terms of how minority activity in the welfare domain is seen as a way to integrate minorities into local society. In this case, however, some minority faith groups (such as Pentecostals) have their own venues and sometimes offer these for use by immigrant groups, thus encouraging their volunteering and citizen participation.

Gender

Gender and majority values

Some of the most mediatised and socially *divisive* welfare challenges in Europe are emerging around the gendered needs and values of religious minorities (and, especially, of Muslim women): these range from the debate about whether it is appropriate to wear a headscarf (in the sense of this being a barrier to education and employment for Muslim women) to more controversial issues, such as polygamy, female circumcision and divorce under Sharia (Islamic) law, which 'contradict most liberal states' legal and moral understandings of equality, between individuals, and men and women' (Statham et al, 2005, p 431). In fact, much of what is often (however inappropriately) described as a 'return' of religion has been channelled through issues surrounding the body and rights of minority women (headscarves, forced marriages, honour killings and so on) – issues that have provoked broader debates about sexuality and women's bodies in the public sphere.

These particular issues do not appear in the WaVE research as such, although they likely exist in the background through their influence on respondents' perspectives (a 'spill-over' effect of European and global-scale issues that may not even be present at the national, much less local level). In this volume, however, we have included the fascinating study of Somaya, a refuge for women established by and for Muslims – an identity that has gradually been modified as a result of subtle and persistent pressures, leading the researcher to a series of further reflections on the relationship between welfare, religious diversity and feminism (see Chapter Ten). This example provides much food for thought as the unintended consequences are worked out to the disadvantage of Muslim women.

This apart, a number of more practical issues arose in WaVE, among them the wish of Muslim women in Reutlingen to be able to use a public swimming hall for girls and women only at certain times, as they do not allow their daughters to participate in mixed groups, yet want them to be able to swim. Calls for separate-sex swimming lessons also factor into the Gävle case. In fact, the Swedish case is perhaps the most conspicuous in terms of welfare values related to gender, given that the promotion of gender equality and individual autonomy is intrinsic to the welfare system as a whole. Here majority–minority 'tensions' arose in relation to education, specifically the Swedish value of same and equal rules for men and women, boys and girls. For example, in addition to the issue of swimming lessons, the Swedish openness to sexuality was met with resistance from Muslim parents in Gävle who did not want their children to shower and change in front of others (to avoid nudity), and had a negative reaction to the use of drawings and models of naked bodies in biology classes. Also in the domain of family care, notably at the Family Centre established in Gävle, contrasting gender values were evident in the relative inactivity of fathers (not only Muslim men but those from immigrant groups in general) in contributing to the care of young children (for example, in taking care of small children so as to free the mother to attend support group meetings; instead, the mothers tended to bring their small children with them to such meetings).

It is tempting to interpret all of the above through the lens of a gendered value conflict related to Islam. However, such developments are by no means restricted to Islam and to Muslim communities; in other case studies, conservatism and gendered values are introduced by different minority groups, and indeed by majority individuals in more patriarchal societies. Stereotypes and culturalist interpretations abound. For example, Nigerian men are described by one welfare worker in Padua as uninvolved in the care of children. Such stereotypes are often produced and reproduced by welfare agents, and in some cases are promoted by the minorities themselves, as some migrants tend to present their own cultures in a somewhat static way.

Such stereotypes can, however, go both ways, as minority groups issue their own judgements of majority society in the realms of gender and family values, or of younger generations within their own minority group. For example, certain Polish and Romanian women in Thiva judged their own value in relation to Greek women on the basis of who cooks and cleans more for their men. Greek and Turkish women in Reutlingen noted that women from younger generations did not play a sufficiently strong role in the home caring for the family. In Sisak, older Muslim women emphasised the need to preserve their cultural values and criticised younger women in this respect, noting in particular younger men who marry Croat women and adopt Croat values and traditions. Meanwhile, in Lahti, Lutherans praised immigrant communities for their strong family values as compared with the majority Finnish tendencies, which are considered less family-oriented.

This brings us to the question of generational tensions as regards the roles of both men and women. Beyond the examples explored in Chapters Eight and Nine, conflicts or potential conflicts were frequently identified by respondents over different gendered values between one generation and another. Clearly these developments resonate with debates within western European societies over what has been controversially labelled as the 'selfish [female] sex', which is considered to be responsible for gaps in care for children and elderly relatives. The accusation in the representative literature is that 'the elderly and vulnerable are paying the price for a generation of professional working women' (Wolf, 2006). In this sense, many minority women consulted in the WaVE study found themselves exposed to two opposed accusations: internally, among their communities, they were criticised for not providing continuity in their cultural values and traditions (including gendered values), and externally they were often criticised as the bearers of those aspects of culture considered most foreign and antithetical to 'western European values'. More broadly, this corroborates with the observation by Yuval-Davis and colleagues (2005, p 519), that it is immigrant women who are most often implicated in the maintenance of (or, at least, in the failure to 'overcome') traditional practices such as arranged marriages, authoritarian gender and generational relations, and religious practices.

Gender between religious and secular values

The aforementioned are mainly examples of gendered values concerning culture and tradition. There are also cases of explicit gendered values linked to religion, as we have seen in the case of Padua (Chapter Eleven), where tensions develop between majority and minorities over reproductive health issues strongly influenced by the Catholic Church. However, the issue unfolds to reveal fault lines other than that between majority and minority: secular versus religious values; progressive versus conservative religious values; and women of all religious and ethnic backgrounds uniting behind women's right to choose abortion, aligned against those who advance conservative religious values in so far as the voluntary termination of pregnancy is concerned. Here the high percentage of immigrant demand for abortions is used to question the rights of *all* women. In this particular 'grey area', women of various religious and ethnic backgrounds (including Catholic) are united in opposition to a particular conservative Catholicism.

Gendered differences in access to and provision of welfare services

In several cases, it is clear that within minority communities, women often have their first and perhaps only contact with the local welfare system through needs arising in relation to pregnancy, childbirth and childrearing. As such, the importance of welfare services aimed at women, in terms of potentially influencing minority welfare as a whole, is considerable. In Darlington, for example, we saw that minority women's first contact with welfare services is often through pregnancy or childbirth, from which point they are introduced, through referrals, to a world of options such as language learning and other courses. Trust factors are highly important here, established only through initial positive experiences in their contact with the system, which could eventually lead them to allow 'foreigners' to care for their children while they worked. In Padua also, women's reproductive health needs exposed them to other areas of help and influence, for them and for their families in general. And in the Polish case, women were sometimes the only family members to have contact with the welfare services, as they were more likely to seek help for their own needs and would struggle on behalf of the entire family for their needs as well. All of these are good examples of interconnections (here, between gender and minority status) fostering positive interactions between various groups rather than problematic outcomes (Staunæs, 2003).

The Padua case described here is an example of 'women's solidarity'. A similar such positive example concerns the Association of Ukrainian Women in Przemyśl, where minority women come together to address minority women's needs – here, once again, women are the main providers and recipients of welfare aid. In the Finnish case, Ingrian women too are active and well connected in social networks and are recipients of local welfare aid, whereas Ingrain men are described as passive. In Thiva, the Pakistani and Indian populations are almost exclusively men; they have formed their own associations and do not seek welfare support from local authorities and local voluntary institutions, although this is mainly because they lack information about such services (again, because of communication and language barriers).

Reflections on welfare and social cohesion

All this material, when considered comparatively, yields important insights into the relationship between welfare and social cohesion. There are insights to be drawn, first, regarding policies and practices – specifically, majority policy (and practice) towards minorities – and second, regarding the role of minority social networks in integration. This section as a whole should be read in the context of the limitations set out in Chapter Four.

Majority policy (and practice) towards minorities

Two conspicuous problems traced across our case studies in terms of majority policy and practice towards minorities concern language and media. Majority policy in most cases, albeit to different degrees, has largely failed to overcome limitations in potential cohesion between majorities and minorities in terms of language. Communication and language problems present difficulties with regard to frequency and type of contact with local welfare services; difficulties with accessing majority language-learning classes; and, more generally, a lack of understanding, on the part of the majority, of minority culture and minority needs.

The problem is compounded by the fact that in this environment, stereotypical and culturalist perspectives thrive, often with the support of the local and/or national media. Indeed the role of the media appears frequently, particularly linked to the dissemination of stereotypes but also to the inflammation of tensions. Most interesting, however, is what we *do not* see in the findings, which makes us more aware of the particular role played by the media in majority–minority relations, because the picture gleaned from our case studies is quite different from that described in the introduction to this chapter, and that seen in national and global media. In general, our research data offer a much more nuanced picture of the everyday significance of religious values in majority–minority relations. Certainly, we were not overwhelmed with an image of Islam as causing barriers to cohesion between Muslims and majorities in our individual case studies. By and large, other minority groups proved equally if not more challenging to local majorities than Muslim groups.

A further domain of policy and practice playing an important role in social cohesion, or lack thereof, *especially* in the Italian and Greek cases, is immigration policy. The situation of undocumented immigrants was precarious at the time of the WaVE research (and is infinitely more so today), and immigration policies have proven incapable of providing documentation of (and eventual access to welfare for) migrants and refugees. Here a lack of state resources is conspicuous, notably, but not exclusively, in the Greek and Italian cases. Illegal immigration is widespread. And just as many local economies have tended to adapt to the presence of undocumented immigrants, so also have local populations recognised the need for migrant labour. Within this situation, which is particularly difficult for many immigrants, interesting examples of majority–minority cohesion arise in our research and corroborate the 'contact hypothesis' – that is, that increased contact with people of other ethnic and racial backgrounds leads to increased tolerance and social solidarity. The WaVE research has offered examples of increased and closer contact leading to fondness of one's neighbour, even if prejudices remain about the 'other' members of the particular ethnic or religious group; of majority individuals helping minority individuals through the difficulties related to immigration policy (often in the context of employer–employee and landlord–tenant relations, or among neighbours); and of a sense of solidarity between minority and majority individuals united in opposition to the problems of 'the system'. In all of these instances, we should recognise the important role of the individual and interpersonal contact (*particularism*). In this and in several other domains of welfare provision, our research has shown the critical function of particular individuals in majority–minority interactions.

Finally, and intimately connected to policy on immigration and minorities as well as to the role of the individual, is the role of 'professional helpers' or, as Michael Lipsky (1980) calls them, 'street-level bureaucrats'.[7] According to a classic study by Lipsky, welfare policies (including immigration policies) are *not* best understood as made in legislatures. Rather, much more relevant to minorities' realities are their daily encounters, in crowded offices, with street-level bureaucrats: Lipsky argues that 'the decisions of street-level bureaucrats, the routines they establish, and the devices they invent to cope with uncertainties and work pressures, effectively *become* the public policies they carry out' (1980, p xii). These civil servants are, characteristically, limited in their ability to meet minority needs, especially because of the ratio of workers to clients or cases, and indeed because of time constraints. In cases where illegal immigration is prevalent, encounters with professional welfare workers may have a negative effect on many aspects of minorities' experiences, delaying their legal entry into the labour market and, therefore, extending their precarious positions in their host societies. Here too, then, the underlying theme is particularism.

Further, it is important acknowledge 'the other side of the coin' – namely, the dissatisfaction such situations entail for the welfare workers themselves, who are inevitably overworked, underpaid and frustrated over their inability to come anywhere near to doing their jobs properly. Moreover, dissatisfaction and frustration on their part often translates into less-than-friendly attitudes towards the minorities whose needs they are there to serve, and may also translate into frustration with the minorities themselves and to development of (or submission to latent) stereotypes. Frustration may also arise among welfare workers in situations where they feel that the recipients of their efforts are not worthy of their help. And in all such cases, an added problem is that these welfare workers, who could play such a useful role in helping to improve policies towards minorities by informing institutions and political leaders of major pitfalls, are often too frustrated and overburdened to do this.

Minority social networks and integration

In terms of the social networks of minority groups and the role of these networks in the integration of minorities into majority society, the significance of the family forms a 'red thread', linking almost every one of our case studies. In the vast majority of the cases, minority groups reveal a focus on caring for their own, starting with the unit of the immediate family, and spreading out to extended family and friends and thus to the local ethnic, religious or linguistic community to which they belong. In other words, they practice the principle of subsidiarity. In many cases, minority groups attach to this caring function the act of passing on language, culture and traditions. At times, these tendencies become the centre of debate, bringing together two clashing perspectives. On the one hand, these social networks are seen as supporting minority integration into majority society by increasing minority self-esteem, recognising and encouraging the use of minorities' own resources, and symbolically at least setting minority welfare services in the same domain as other majority-provided welfare services (in other words, treating minorities as equal partners in the welfare domain). On the other hand, such minority social networks are perceived as structures that further segregate and isolate minorities from majority society. The discussion in Chapter Eight on the Turkish association in Reutlingen makes precisely this point, which is echoed in rather different way by the dilemma faced by the women's shelter discussed in Chapter Ten. The need to downplay the religious specificity of this organisation and to render it more 'mainstream' was clearly a response to the perceived risk of segregation and isolation.

A principal reason for minorities' preference for their own welfare networks may be the symbolic meaning attached to their establishment and the sense of belonging that comes with the gaining of a community's own *space* for its welfare activities. This is also an issue of dignity, and conforms to the norms of majority society, which organises itself into its schools, programmes, facilities and so on. A further reason may be the simple fact that having specific welfare networks allows minorities to 'to do things their way', family- and tradition-focused. It is this latter reason that gives rise to the debate and controversy around the question of differing, and possibly conflicting, majority and minority values. But the question also arises: who is to say that minorities' ways are 'wrong'? Here the multiple modernities approach to diversity instructs us to broaden our perspectives in order to include alternative forms of modernity arising in other cultures. At the same time though, in seeking to analyse 'minorities' ways' as right or wrong, which voices will be listened to? Minority groups are certainly not monolithic and internal divisions abound. The risk is that, from an external perspective, it is easy to hear the most vocal of representatives who are often also the most (religiously and otherwise) conservative, and who tend (for the same reasons) to receive more media attention.

Further, these debates raise the broader question of who is best placed to determine what is 'good' or 'bad' segregation. Is emphasis on caring for one's own an endorsement of segregation, or an admirable value? Is it ideological, or practical (noting that these epithets may mean different things for different people)? And how critique-worthy is, for example, the desire to protect children from the social ills present in majority society? The other side of the coin is the difficulty in determining where to draw the line between a 'healthy' preservation of traditions that leads to increased minority group confidence and the continuation of 'unhealthy' (according to the majority) practices such as arranged marriages or those between close relatives. A cross-country comparative approach to the WaVE research has brought all these questions to the fore.

It has also raised a further question: how tolerant are majority societies to difference? Are majority societies working towards integration, or assimilation, or in fact towards segregation? Our research results point to an ambiguity on this point. Programmes labelled as aiming towards integration often mask deeper value orientations – those that create ambitions for assimilation instead. This does not necessarily (nor often, in our cases) result in substantive *conflict* between majorities and minorities. Nor, however, does it help to diminish misunderstandings between the two, or to address, as fruitfully as possible, the welfare needs of minorities. Further, it fails to take sufficient account of the positive resources that minority groups represent, one of which could in fact be a focus on the family.

Conclusion: patterns and trends

I now draw together those patterns and tendencies that are discernible when applying a comparative lens to the case study material –

specifically, patterns in welfare provision that lead to greater cohesion or conflict. A second point follows – that is, the tendencies towards conflict or cohesion caused by *values* in welfare provision and needs.

The factors that can be identified as having more or less *positive* results in the direction of increased social cohesion are, by and large, ambiguous. For example, the fact that majority religion welfare provisions often fill major gaps left by the state is positive in the sense that at least these important services are made available to minorities. However, the services sometimes come with 'strings attached', for example, in terms of expectations that recipients will partake in 'religious goods' offered alongside welfare aid (church services, prayer meetings and so on). Moreover, majority religion welfare services often operate in an informal, ad hoc way, so that there is still no universal coverage of the particular welfare needs they address. Second, the role of the individual and interpersonal contact is critical in meeting the welfare needs of many minorities: relationships developed with neighbours, employers, civil servants and so on are often extremely effective in getting around bureaucratic or other barriers to access to welfare, and are also important in fostering a sense of cohesion with the majority individuals in question. However, here again we find particularism (rather than universal coverage) and luck (who you happen to know) playing a large role in whether minority needs are met or not. Third, and most ambiguous, is the role of independent minority welfare networks. Whether or not such networks lead to greater social cohesion or, rather, to the segregation of minority groups is debatable and depends on one's vantage point. Minority groups, however, tend to perceive of such networks as effective in terms of dealing with their primary needs (for example, maintaining their culture and religion and (sometimes as a result) family cohesion; allowing them to be used as resources and thus ideally to be treated as equal partners in the welfare domain; and, related to the latter, strengthening their self-esteem. The chapters in Part Three of this book furnish multiple examples of all three.

In terms of factors that lead to more or less *negative* results in terms of social cohesion between majorities and minorities, we have seen that these are in many cases interrelated. A lack of cultural competence among majority individuals and institutions providing welfare to minorities often leads to inappropriate, or ineffective, welfare provision. We find many cases of external labelling, so that the labels applied to minorities by the majority welfare services are often different from minorities' self-definitions. Related to this are tendencies towards stereotyping and culturalism, whereby in the absence of cultural competence as regards minority identities and needs, culturalist reductionism and stereotypes abound, leading again to inappropriate and ineffective welfare provision, and having a negative effect on the potential for healthy majority–minority interactions and relations. One factor that frequently exacerbates this problem is the media, which often create or promote stereotypes, essentialise minority identities, and overemphasise conflict and tensions. Another factor influencing lack of cultural competence and stereotyping is the spatial segregation of many minority groups – here both physical and metaphorical distance between minorities and majorities significantly limits substantial interaction and thus understanding between majorities and minorities. And related to this are language and communication barriers, which have already been addressed at length but must be emphasised again here as crucial factors in majority–minority relations.

Meanwhile, across the case studies we also encounter failures to use insider knowledge, where available. For example, local welfare workers are often best placed to influence national welfare policy, which sometimes ignores the insights and expertise of those working at the local level. Another problem relates to the role of professional helpers, those civil servants administering public welfare to minorities who are often overburdened and ill prepared for the challenges of handling minority needs. The latter is intimately linked to immigration policy, which is often poorly formulated (particularly in its ability to handle undocumented immigrants in a constructive manner), thus exacerbating the problems of the professional helpers, and influencing in turn the experience of minorities and their access to public welfare services.

In terms of tendencies towards 'conflict' or 'cohesion' arising from *values*, the most conspicuous area of conflict in the domain of welfare relates to minority social networks. The values embedded in many such networks (tending to members' own needs; conservative cultural or religious values such as sexual modesty and segregation of activities for boys and girls; and so on) sometimes clash with majority values in particular settings (for example, liberal approaches to sex; autonomy for both women and men over their own bodies; and the integration of all social networks into a broader, shared national system). And as noted earlier, the mere existence of some such networks is, from certain (majority) perspectives, seen as a segregating factor. However, we have also seen examples of conflicts of this nature that are ultimately precursors to greater social cohesion, as they provide both the majorities and minorities in question with an opportunity to better understand and appreciate one another's perspectives. In these cases, contact (communication) – which may be tense to begin with – is necessary in order to achieve mutual understanding.

Certainly, women's bodies and rights are often the focal point for debates regarding conflicting majority and minority values, although by and large the content and intensity of the issues raised in our research are quite different – and a great deal more subtle – from those portrayed in the media. Conflicts over values also arise in the form of generational clashes *within* minority groups. As we have seen, these clashes often have a gender dimension, as differences arise over the role of younger women in the household and the extent to which they cook and clean and so on.

Finally, in terms of welfare values leading to cohesion, a crucial and very banal point is simply the extent to which majority welfare provision is aimed at social cohesion – in other words, welfare provision extended to minorities, offering rights and benefits in an effort to enable better integration into society, leads to an enhanced sense of belonging. In spite of all the flaws and weaknesses of such efforts (many of which are outlined here), they may still be detected as the driving force behind much majority welfare provision. The same can be said for minority welfare provision that is aimed at social cohesion, as in many cases minority (often, but not exclusively, religious) welfare services play a significant role in offering help to members of both majority and minority communities, for example, in the area of alcohol abuse. In such cases we see solidarity developing around a particular welfare need. Finally, our research found several positive examples of women's solidarity, in particular, developing around specific needs. Here the values expressed are women's rights and women's *ability* to help support one another's needs, and the alliances that develop often cross ethnic and religious boundaries and unite women of different backgrounds behind their shared concerns.

This reference to patterns emerging through the research and of insights gathered is not – and cannot be – exhaustive. Indeed, the information generated by the WaVE project is above all rich and complex, with one of the major lessons emerging being that the European situation in so far as welfare and values is concerned is, in fact, far more nuanced than is often portrayed, not only by the media but also by much academic literature. The WaVE project's reliance on street-level information, through the case study approach and intensive qualitative study, has proven critical to the ability to generate insights faithful to the situation on the ground in various national and local contexts.

As indicated in this chapter, the WaVE research has shown us that most majority–minority interactions in the domain of welfare lie somewhere between the categories of 'conflict' and 'cohesion', in the large grey area in between. Here we have found resource factors, such as time, space and money, key to the actual interactions between majorities and minorities alongside more everyday factors, such as the role of the media, communication (that is, language), immigration policy, employment policy and the efforts of 'professional helpers'. Furthermore, we have also seen different 'dimensions' of conflict or tension – for example, between different minority groups (rather than between majority and minority), or between different generations of the *same* groups. The same applies with dimensions of cohesion. Thus, as a whole, our research questions the very notions of conflict and cohesion and identifies complex (rather than dichotomous) relations between the two whereby, for example, conflict may be a necessary precursor to long-term cohesion. Critical to our work in the WaVE project has been careful attention to this large grey area, comprising active resource factors and pointing to different dimensions of conflict and cohesion beyond majority–minority relations and to different relationships between conflict and cohesion. These insights, gleaned from researchers committed to learning from the realities on the ground in 13 case studies, will, we hope, serve as a firm basis for future research at the intersection between welfare and values.

That said, an immediate question immediately presents itself. Can such (relative) optimism be sustained in the aftermath not only of the 2008 global financial crisis and the 2015-16 influx of migrants, but of Brexit,[8] which visibly calls into question many of the values presented here? Without doubt, new and very demanding challenges are emerging both for Europe as a whole and for its member states – a theme that is addressed in the final chapter of this volume.

Notes

[1] In this respect the text has benefited enormously from the comments made by WaVE project members on early drafts. Still, the chapter reflects the author's own interpretations of the material, and any resultant weaknesses in the text are her sole responsibility.

[2] The Swedish deputy prime minister Åsa Romson notably cried in a televised announcement of new measures to deter asylum seekers – measures reversing Sweden's open-door policy towards people fleeing war and persecution. See www.theguardian.com/world/video/2015/nov/24/asa-romson-sweden-deputy-prime-minister-cries-announcing-refugee-u-turn-video

[3] The most recent opinion issued by the Advocate General of the Court of Justice of the European Union (31 May 2016), approving of a company ban on its employees'

wearing of headscarves, has itself provoked a strong media reaction; see http://curia.europa.eu/jcms/upload/docs/application/pdf/2016-05/cp160054en.pdf; www.lawandreligionuk.com/2016/06/01/hijabs-in-the-workplace-a-g-kokotts-opinion-in-achbita; www.telegraph.co.uk/news/2016/05/31/bosses-can-ban-headscarves-and-crucifixes-eu-judge-says; www.theguardian.com/world/2016/may/31/senior-eu-lawyer-backs-workplace-ban-on-muslim-headscarves; www.independent.co.uk/news/world/europe/eus-top-judge-backs-workplace-ban-on-headscarves-a7058251.html; www.nytimes.com/2016/06/01/world/europe/eu-legal-opinion-upholds-employers-ban-on-head-scarves.html?_r=2; http://blogs.wsj.com/brussels/2016/05/31/eu-companies-can-ban-headscarves-as-part-of-broader-policy-court-adviser-says

4 Note, by 'religiously provided welfare' I mean welfare provided by religious institutions or groups, rather than welfare provided through religious means or with religious messages (the two do not necessarily overlap).

5 The WaVE researchers owe special thanks to Pål Repstad (2006) for these insights, shared in a paper presented at the WaVE junior researchers' meeting in Padua, 14–17 September 2006. As Repstad notes, 'natural' belongs in inverted commas because there is inevitably an element of the researcher's construction and interpretation of the information.

6 To be precise, in the Greek case the reactions largely reflect opposition to the way in which degrees from private universities receive equal accreditation to those from public universities.

7 These are civil servants working in schools, police forces, welfare departments and other agencies who are responsible for, and have wide discretion over, the allocation of benefits and public sanctions (Lipsky, 1980: p xi). I am grateful to Pål Repstad for bringing this text to our attention. See also Psimmenos and Kassimati (2003).

8 Shorthand for the process of the UK's withdrawal from the EU following a referendum in June 2016.

References

Castles, S. and M. Miller (2003) *The Age of Migration* (3rd ed), Basingstoke: Palgrave Macmillan.

van Deth, J.W. and Scarbrough, E. (eds) (1998) *The Impact of Values*, Oxford: Oxford University Press.

Hunsberger, B. and Jackson, L. (2005) 'Religion, meaning and prejudice', *Journal of Social Issues*, 61(4): 807–26.

Jakelic, S. (2010) *Collectivistic Religions: Religion, Choice, and Identity in Late Modernity*, Farnham: Ashgate.

Lipsky, M. (1980) *Street-Level Bureaucracy. Dilemmas of the Individual in Public Services*, New York, NY: Russell Sage Foundation.

Psimmenos, I. and Koula, K. (2003) 'Immigration control pathways: organisational culture and work values of Greek welfare officers', *Journal of Ethnic and Migration Studies*, 29(2): 337–71.

Repstad, P. (2006) 'Notes on the advantages and limitations of qualitative methods', Paper presented at the WaVE junior researchers' meeting in Padua, 14–17 September.

Schrover, M. and Vermeulen, F. (2005) 'Immigrant organisations', *Journal of Ethnic and Migration Studies*, 31(5), September: 823–32.

Sigona, N. (2005) 'Locating "The Gypsy problem". The Roma in Italy: stereotyping, labelling and "nomad camps"', *Journal of Ethnic and Migration Studies*, 31(4): 741–56.

Statham, P., Koopmans, R., Giugni, M. and Passy, F. (2005) 'Resilient or adaptable Islam? Multiculturalism, religion and migrants' claims-making for group demands in Britain, the Netherlands and France', *Ethnicities*, 5(4): 427–59.

Staunæs, D. (2003) 'Where have all the subjects gone? Bringing together the concepts of intersectionality and subjectification', *NORA Nordic Journal of Women's Studies*, 11: 101–110.

Wolf, A. (2006) 'The selfish sex', *The Times*, 29 March, p 4.

Yuval-Davis, N., Anthias, F. and Kofman, E. (2005) 'Secure borders and safe haven and the gendered politics of belonging: beyond social cohesion', *Ethnic and Racial Studies*, 28(3): 513–35.

THIRTEEN

Afterword

Grace Davie

Revisiting the material from the Welfare and Values in Europe: Transitions Related to Religion, Minorities and Gender (WaVE) project in the months following Brexit is a sobering experience.[1] WaVE 'took off' in 2006, two years after the most significant enlargement in the history of the EU, which was followed in 2007 by further expansion. These were days of optimism, confidence and growth both for the EU as a whole and for its constituent nations, sentiments expressed in economic, political and cultural life. A decade later, a very different picture is emerging in which the supposed dominance of Brussels is increasingly resented, where nationalist parties are becoming stronger almost by the day, and where migration is not only considered 'out of control', but also a security threat. As Effie Fokas has reminded us (p 261), right across Europe we have seen welfare systems build thick and exclusionary walls and value systems implode. The aspirations of WaVE – not to mention the values that it sought to unpack – are, it seems, in peril.[2]

The contrast appears sharp, but the cracks were showing well before the end of the research period (2006-09); they were epitomised in the global financial crisis of 2008 that eroded almost overnight the confidence of previous decades. Austerity followed, more so in some places than others, bringing with it not only economic recession but also sharp reductions in welfare measures just when they were needed most. The debates surrounding the Greek case were particularly intense, as Grexit (the withdrawal of Greece from the Eurozone) became a real possibility. The full story lies beyond the scope of this Afterword, but its essence can be captured as follows, noting that perceptions count for as much as facts in these vignettes. From the Greek point of view, an over-mighty 'Europe' imposed stringent conditions on Greece in return for loans, without which the Greek economy could no longer function. That said, it could barely function anyway as unemployment soared, especially among the young. The population turned back to the family for support, often beyond what was reasonable, as meagre pensions were stretched to support several generations. Suffering was widespread.[3] From the point of view of Brussels (and indeed much of northern Europe), Greece was paying the price of decades of political mismanagement – specifically a failure to live within its means, not least with respect to welfare (most notably pensions). Why should hardworking northerners pay for this excess? The question is a real one. Beneath both scenarios, moreover, lie the failures of the Eurozone: its inadequacies were laid bare as its tightly-connected but all too disparate economies were brutally exposed to the financial crisis.

In 2011, pro-democracy demonstrations erupted in Syria, as part of the movement known as the Arab Spring. Initial optimism was, however, short-lived. Government crackdowns turned peaceful protests into violent ones, justifying an escalation of force. As in the case of Grexit, the details far exceed this chapter. That said, the intensification of violence right across the Middle East accounts directly for the sharp increase, indeed exponential growth, in the numbers of migrants entering south and south-east Europe (the peak came in 2015). Already challenged, Greece – together with Italy – was once more caught at the sharp end, finding itself a principal player in a humanitarian crisis of major proportions, not this time of its own making (see Chapter Six). Further north – the hoped-for destination of many migrants – different European societies reacted variously, some resentful from the outset, others initially welcoming but then more resistant as the pressure increased, and all progressively anxious as the numbers spiralled and it became more and more difficult to distinguish 'genuine' asylums seekers from economic migrants – recognising that both groups of people were desperate for help. Growing tensions in Turkey simply made a difficult situation more complex.

Into this heady mix came the UK referendum on membership of the EU. At one level, this was an ill-conceived attempt to overcome differences in the British Conservative Party, honouring an ill-advised election pledge. At another, it became the vehicle through which the British population expressed a whole series of resentments – economic, political and cultural. By no means were all of these directed at the EU, but the latter became a target for their expression. In fact, the referendum uncovered fault lines in British society that ran right through the political parties as we know them, dividing one part of the UK from another and revealing a widening gap between metropolitan London and the rest of the country. More insidiously, it exposed resentments towards migration, magnified by a failure (at times wilful) to recognise the contributions that migrants make to the British economy. Rather migrants were seen as a drain on already scarce resources. Central to the whole debate has been the question of entitlement – to jobs, to housing, to education and to welfare – in other words a question critical to the aims and objectives of WaVE and the research associated with it.

At one level, therefore, the events of the past half-decade have undermined the relative optimism on which WaVE was based – that solutions could be found to the difficult questions facing an expanding Europe at the turn of the millennium. But at another, it has rendered the approach adopted by WaVE all the more relevant if we are to probe beneath the stereotypes presented by the media and to discover the all-too-human issues that lie beneath the headlines – issues that must be resolved at the level of everyday life in real communities the length and breadth of Europe. The emphasis on locality will be central to this work, as the recently arrived find their way – or, as is more likely, are directed – to particular places that are not always properly prepared to receive them. The intricate interconnections between religious and secular agencies will be at the forefront of efforts to make such people welcome and to find ways of accommodating their inevitably complex needs. With this in mind, re-reading the case studies brought together in this book (and the project on which it is based) is salutary.

There are two further reasons why the WaVE research constitutes an important landmark. The first recognises that the work that we have carried out is, in fact, a subset of a larger issue: that is, the profound ambiguities surrounding not only religion and welfare, but religion itself in 21st-century Europe. The second reason reflects the part played by WaVE in the establishment of a new academic discipline, as the links between religion and welfare become an increasingly important area of interest for a wide variety of scholars. Each of these questions are taken in turn.

It is clear that two rather different things are happening at once in the religious life of Europe, a situation described at length by Grace Davie (2006, 2015). On the one hand, there is a continuing process of secularisation – a trend that can be seen right across the continent, albeit differently in different places. It is, for example, noticeably more advanced in north and west Europe than it is in the south and east – a point already discussed in Part One of this book. Secularisation remains, however, a dominant trend. At the same time, the significance of religion in public debate is growing, both in Europe as a whole and in many of its constituent nations. An important driver in this respect is the growing diversity of Europe's religious life and the difficulties experienced in accommodating the needs of many different minorities. WaVE speaks directly to this agenda, once again undermining stereotypes and pointing to positive as well as negative outcomes in these protracted and difficult debates.

At a more general level, it is important to grasp the juxtaposition of these contradictory trends and the consequences that follow from this. Religion has indeed re-entered the public square and demands a response. But at the same time, an increasingly secular population (the consequence of the drift away from the churches) has difficulty in dealing with these issues, in the sense that most, if not all, Europeans are rapidly losing the concepts, knowledge and vocabulary that are necessary to address the difficult questions that arise in the management of difference. What follows is a public conversation about religion, which is of poor quality – at best ill-informed, frequently ill-mannered and at times dangerously provocative. It is this situation that must be addressed if we are to engage with clarity issues of extreme importance to the functioning of Europe's democracies.[4] These include the tensions between freedom of religion and freedom of speech; the limits of toleration; the relative merits of assimilation, integration and multicultural autonomy; and complex questions about security. To pretend that there are easy answers is naïve – the more so in a situation as tense as that in the months following Brexit, a period inflamed by a string of terrorist incidents in different parts of Europe.[5]

WaVE, and it predecessor – Welfare and Religion in a European Perspective: A Comparative Study of the Role of the Churches as Agents of Welfare within the Social Economy (WREP) – have made a real contribution in this respect. Indeed, they have gone further than many enquiries in this field in addressing very directly the religious dimensions of the welfare debate – specifically the theological assumptions that underpin both motivation and praxis in this field (see Chapter Five). In so doing, these projects situate themselves in a distinctively Weberian trajectory, recognising religion – and, more specifically, religious beliefs – as an independent variable in this particular field. The work of religious agencies should not be seen simply as reactive; it is rather an outworking of specific bodies of religious understanding, applied in rapidly changing circumstances. Up to now, however, the theological emphasis has largely focused on the majority churches under review (see Ekstrand, 2011). Rather more recently, we have been reminded that this aspect of our work needs to be extended further if we are to understand fully the contributions of religious minorities in this field – an element of our work as yet incomplete.[6]

Whatever the case, it is clear that academic interest in the field of religion and welfare is growing fast. This can be exemplified from the

British case. The following paragraphs list a wide range of contribution and a selection of themes that arise from them. Similar (and extensive) catalogues are found in many other European societies and are indicative of a widespread change of mood, as scholars from many disciplines come together to explore a field that was not anticipated in the expansion of social science (and its applications to social policy) that took place in the period following the Second World War. In parenthesis it is worth noting a similar trend in both religion and healthcare and religion and law, brought about for exactly the same reasons. Quite simply there is 'a need to know' about such matters in 21st-century Europe, a need that is accelerating as the decades pass.[7]

To substantiate this claim, we can cite the following contributions to the debate surrounding religion and welfare in Britain: Harris (1998), Prochaska (2006), Dinham (2009), Dinham et al (2009), Beaumont and Cloke (2012), Jawad (2012), Dinham and Francis (2015), a themed section in *Social Policy and Society* (2012),[8] a collection of opinion pieces brought together in Spencer (2014), a further discussion on Catholic social thought and Catholic charities (Ryan, 2016), and the continuing work of the William Temple Foundation.[9] Added to these are a string of government and voluntary sector reports, some national and some regional.[10] The formats of these contributions vary: some texts are single-authored and develop distinctive themes; others are compilations of case studies with reflective pieces fore and aft. Either way, the disciplinary range is wide. It includes different branches of theology and ethics, economic and social history, economics, studies of civil society, organisational dynamics, social policy, political and sociological analysis, and political and social theory. Equally varied are the viewpoints of the authors. Some come from inside the faith communities and care deeply about the future of such bodies; others have encountered the abundance of faith-based organisations in the course of their fieldwork and wondered how to incorporate such groups in their analyses. This, moreover, is a rapidly developing field in which new ideas are emerging all the time.

That said, a number of themes recur. On the first point everyone agrees: there is a huge amount of activity in this field for the reasons set out in Chapter One. A second set of issues concerns the appropriateness, or otherwise, of faith-based provision in welfare – a topic that provokes heated debate. As we have seen, societal responses range from warm approbation to serious critique. Searching questions arise in these discussions. These include sensitive issues surrounding inclusion, exclusion and conditionality, and issues relating to professional codes, training, evaluation and quality control – all of central concern to

WaVE. Dinham and Francis (2015) dig deeper still, raising questions that recall an underlying theme of this book. In Britain in the mid-20th century, the welfare state displaced religion and religious sensibility as the primary language of care. Some 60 years later, an increasingly mixed economy of welfare has readmitted religiously based actors, almost by accident. An entirely new situation has begun to emerge: much greater diversity than previously, alongside a diminishing capacity to address the implications that follow – hence the ill-informed and ill-mannered debate mentioned earlier. There is therefore an urgent need to re-skill both public professionals and ordinary citizens in order to deal with the issues as they present both in and beyond the world of welfare.

It is precisely this challenge that motivated the team(s) responsible for WREP and for WaVE and – subsequently – the editors of this volume. Such questions are more likely to proliferate than to diminish in the aftermath of Brexit, recognising that this is not simply a British question. The fissures exposed in the UK referendum are clearly evident in a range of European societies that – at one and the same time – will be exposed to increasing demands for welfare. The contributions of both majority churches and minority religions will be central in meeting these needs, reflecting the experiences recounted in these chapters. They should be read with this in mind.

Notes

[1]   Brexit refers to the outcome of the UK referendum on whether to remain in or leave the European Union (EU), which took place on 23 June 2016. The UK population voted to leave the EU by a narrow margin (51.9% for; 48.1% against).

[2]   The 2017 Dutch and French elections offered more space for optimism. In the second round of the French presidential election the centrist candidate Emmanuel Macron defeated Marine Le Pen of the Front National by a wide margin.

[3]   Molokotos-Liederman (2016) contains interesting material regarding the impact of the Greek crisis on the Orthodox Church of Greece.

[4]   These issues – and thus the work of WaVE as well – should be seen in light of a growing body of material on religious literacy. See www.gold.ac.uk/faithsunit/literacy for more information. See also Dinham and Francis (2015).

[5]   Particularly unsettling at the time of writing were the attacks in Nice (on 14 July 2016), shortly followed by the killing of a Catholic priest in St-Etienne-du-Rouvray, near Rouen.

[6]   We are grateful to Johan Gärde, a member of the Ersta Sköndal research team, for bringing this point to our attention.

[7]   The Impact of Religion programme at Uppsala University gathers together a number of these themes. See www.crs.uu.se/Research/impactofreligion/?languageId=1

[8]   The themed section was entitled 'Social policy and religion in contemporary Britain' and appeared in *Social Policy and Society*, 11(4), October 2012.

[9]   For an up-to-date list of publications, see http://williamtemplefoundation.org.uk/our-work/research

[10]   A number of these are listed in Dinham and Jackson (2012).

References

Beaumont, J. and Cloke, P. (eds) (2012) *Faith-Based Organizations and Exclusion in European Cities*, Bristol: Policy Press.

Davie, G. (2006) 'Religion in Europe in the 21st century: the factors to take into account', *European Journal of Sociology*, 47(2): 271-96.

Davie, G. (2015) *Religion in Britain: A Persistent Paradox*, Oxford: Wiley-Blackwell.

Dinham, A. (2009) *Faiths, Public Policy and Civil Society: Problems, Policies, Controversies*, Basingstoke: Palgrave MacMillan.

Dinham, A. and Francis, M. (eds) (2015) *Religious Literacy in Secular Society: Theories, Policies and Practices of Faith in the Public Realm*, Bristol: Policy Press.

Dinham, A. and Jackson, R. (2012) 'Religion, welfare and education', in L. Woodhead and R. Catto (eds) *Religion and Change in Modern Britain*, London: Routledge, pp 272-94.

Dinham, A., Furbey, R. and Lowndes, V. (eds) (2009) *Faith in the Public Realm: Controversies, Policies and Practices*, Bristol: Policy Press.

Ekstrand, T. (2011) 'Thinking theologically about welfare and religion', in A. Bäckström, G. Davie, N. with Edgardh and P. Pettersson (eds) *Welfare and Religion in 21st Century Europe: Volume 2. Gendered, Religious and Social Change*, Farnham: Ashgate, pp 107-50.

Harris, M. (1998) *Organizing God's Work. Challenges for Churches and Synagogues*, Basingstoke: Palgrave Macmillan.

Jawad, R. (2012) *Religion and Faith-Based Welfare: From Wellbeing to Ways of Being*, Bristol: Policy Press.

Molokotos-Liederman, L. (2016) 'The impact of the crisis on the Orthodox Church of Greece: a moment of challenge and opportunity, *Religion, State and Society*, 44(1): 32-50.

Prochaska, F. (2006) *Christianity and Social Services in Modern Britain. The Disinherited Spirit*, Oxford: Oxford University Press.

Ryan, B. (2016) *Catholic Social Thought and Catholic Charities in Britain Today: Need and Opportunity*, London: Theos.

Spencer, N. (ed) (2014) *The Welfare Collection*, London: Theos.

Appendix: the WaVE team

In total, the following 34 researchers were included in the WaVE project. Below, the senior scholars are named first with their respective institutional affiliations at the time of the project, followed by the junior researchers. The project was coordinated by the Faculty of Theology, Uppsala University.

Project direction

Anders Bäckström, Faculty of Theology, Uppsala University

Grace Davie, Department of Sociology and Philosophy, University of Exeter

Effie Fokas, Faculty of Theology, Uppsala University

Per Petterson, Service Research Centre, Karlstad University; Faculty of Theology, Uppsala University

Ninna Edgardh, Faculty of Theology, Uppsala University

Northern Europe
Sweden

Anders Bäckström, Faculty of Theology, Uppsala University

Ninna Edgardh, Researcher for the Swedish case study

Per Pettersson, Researcher for the Swedish case study

Norway

Pål Repstad, Institute of Religion, Philosophy and History, Agder University

Olav Helge Angell, Researcher for the Norwegian case study

Finland

Eila Helander, Faculty of Theology, University of Helsinki

Anne Birgitta Pessi, Researcher for the Finnish case study

Henrietta Grönlund, Assistant Researcher

Elina Juntunen, Assistant Researcher

Western and southern Europe

England

Douglas Davies, Department of Theology and Religion, Durham University

Martha Middlemiss Lé Mon, Researcher for the English case study

Germany, Reutlingen

Heinz Schmidt, Diakoniewissenschaftliches Institut, Heidelberg University

Annette Leis-Peters, Researcher for the German case study of Reutlingen

Anika Albert, Researcher for the German case study of Reutlingen

Germany, Schweinfurt

Hans-Georg Ziebertz, Institute of Practical Theology, University of Würzburg

Ilona Biendarra, Researcher for the German case study of Schweinfurt

France

Danièle Hervieu-Léger, École des Hautes Études en Sciences Sociales, Paris

Corinne Valasik, Researcher for the French case study

Italy

Chantal Saint-Blancat, Department of Sociology, University of Padua

Annalisa Frisina, Researcher for the Italian case study

Valentina Longo, Researcher for the Italian case study

Adriano Cancellieri, Researcher for the Italian case study

Greece

Nikos Kokosalakis, Centre for Social Policy, Panteion University

Effie Fokas, Researcher for the Greek case study

Eastern Europe

Latvia

Zaneta Ozolina, Department of Political Science, University of Latvia

Raimonds Graudins, Researcher for the Latvian case study

Poland

Irene Borowik, Institute for the Scientific Study of Religion, Jagellonian University

Agnieszka Dyczewska, Research for the Polish case study

Eliza Litak, Researcher for the Polish case study

Croatia

Siniša Zrinščak, Faculty of Law, Department of Social Work, University of Zagreb

Marija Geiger, Researcher for the Croatian case study

Tamara Puhovski, Researcher for the Croatian case study

Romania

Martin Hauser, UNESCO Chair on the Study of Intercultural and Interreligious Exchanges, Fribourg University/University of Bucharest

Nicoleta Zagura, Researcher for the Romanian case study

Index